CANADIAN MENNONITE BRETHREN: 1910 - 2010

# LEADERS WHO
# SHAPED US

CANADIAN MENNONITE BRETHREN: 1910 - 2010

# LEADERS WHO SHAPED US

Harold Jantz, Editor

Goessel, Kansas
KINDRED
PRODUCTIONS
Winnipeg , Manitoba

Published simultaneously by Kindred Productions, Winnipeg, Manitoba R3M 3Z6 and Kindred Productions, Goessel, Kansas 67053.

Cover and Book Design: Makus Design
Printed by The Christian Press

**Library and Archives Canada Cataloguing in Publication**


Jantz, Harold, 1937-
Canadian Mennonite Brethren, 1910-2010 : leaders who shaped us / Harold Jantz, editor.


ISBN 978-1-894791-23-6


1. Canadian Conference of Mennonite Brethren Churches--Biography.
2. Mennonites--Canada--Biography. 3. Christian leadership--Mennonites.
I. Title: Leaders who shaped us.


BX8141.C35 2010          289.7092'271          C2010-900405-1

Photo Credits
Most of the photographs in this book were provided from the rich photo files at the Centre for Mennonite Brethren Studies, Winnipeg, Manitoba. Other photos for John F. Harms came from the Center for Mennonite Brethren Studies, Hillsboro, KS; for Henry S. Voth, from Julianna Enns, Winnipeg; for C.N. and Helen (Harms) Hiebert, from Peter Kroeker of Winnipeg; for Heinrich A. Neufeld, from Joyce Schimpky of St. Catharines, ON; for A.A. Kroeker, from the brothers Don Kroeker and Peter Kroeker, both of Winnipeg; for Marie Wiebe, from Lois Wedel of Winnipeg; for Katy Penner, from Anne Tymos of Winnipeg; for David Poon, from family sources and David Leung of Vancouver; for Katie Funk Wiebe, from family sources; and for Walter Unger, from family sources.

Visit our website at www.kindredproductions.com
Printed in Canada

*Dedicated*
*to the men and women, our "saints,"*
*who showed us the way.*

# Contents

# Preface

# GETTING TO KNOW OURSELVES BETTER

For Mennonite Brethren, the year 2010 marks two important milestones. Most importantly, it is 150 years since this movement within the larger Anabaptist family had its beginning in southern Russia.

For Canadian Mennonite Brethren, another date matters. A.D. 2010 marks the 100th anniversary of the formation of a conference of Mennonite Brethren churches in Canada. That milestone provided the occasion for this volume's collection of biographies.

Only 25 biographies have been included in this book. They could have been many more, but the ones that were selected contributed a great deal to the DNA of our fellowship of Mennonite churches.

Mennonite Brethren, of course, had a beginning in Canada earlier than 1910. Over a quarter of a century earlier, in fact. A Minnesota Mennonite Brethren evangelist, Heinrich H. Voth, together with his Kansas partner, David Dyck, had come up to Manitoba to sow the seeds of renewal among the conservative Mennonites colonies in the province. They started out using family and friendship contacts. By 1888 they had a small church emerging a few miles north of Winkler.

By 1905 the church in Winkler under the leadership of David Dyck had grown to several hundred members. But the growth was even faster in Saskatchewan. Congregations were springing up in a number of places north of Saskatoon as well as in southern Saskatchewan. The first decade of the 20th century saw large numbers of immigrants flowing into the Northwest Territories (soon to be called Saskatchewan), among them many Mennonite Brethren from both the United States and Russia, besides those who moved in from Manitoba. That explains the rapid emergence of Mennonite Brethren churches there.

During that first decade Mennonite Brethren leaders in America began asking whether a better way of grouping themselves might help them both in strengthening their sense of unity and in assisting their growth. The outcome was a decision to begin to meet in three district conferences, a Southern, a Central and a Northern District. A few years later a Pacific District was added. Three of these districts were in the U.S., because that's where most of the churches were found. Canada—specifically Saskatch-ewan—formed the Northern District.

At the very beginning the Winkler church wasn't quite sure where to belong. At first it joined the Central District, along with churches in the Dakotas, Minnesota, Nebraska, Michigan and Montana. All the districts met together in what became known as a General Conference once in three years and separately in the intervening years. It was in 1910 that the districts had their first separate meetings. In 1913 Manitoba joined Saskatchewan in the Northern District. The new configuration gave the churches breathing room to grow.

One gets an idea of the attraction that the conferences had when one reads some of the introductions to the annual reports. Large tents had to be erected to hold the crowds. People flowed in from every direction. One of the early Northern District yearbooks even noted a family who rode in by oxcart. Because the conventions usually took place in late June, the descriptions of the weather and spirit were almost rhapsodic in their expressions of happiness about gathering. The 1911 conference at Broth-erfield near Waldheim, Sask., drew a thousand people. That's more than we normally bring together today. The spirit of joy as the "brothers and sisters" of the churches worshipped and engaged with one another in the work of the kingdom was very strong.

## TRAITS THAT STAND OUT

When we read the stories of some of the people who influenced Menno-nite Brethren life in Canada so profoundly during this conference's cen-tury, a number of traits stand out.

Mennonite Brethren in Canada grew out of a sense of mission. It's all over the conventions right from the beginning, and it's obvious from the decisions made about appointing *Reiseprediger* (circuit preachers) who would build up the churches, supporting missionaries to India, strengthening the mission outreach in Winnipeg and somewhat lat-er sending many scores of young people into summer vacation Bible schools.

Anyone reading the stories of the early and later leaders can't help but be impressed by their confidence in the gospel. They didn't seem to be intimidated by their relatively small numbers. They might have been new-comers on this continent, but they weren't afraid to head out into their world. For the most part, all of these people were a hardy group, quite will-ing to face the rigors of nurturing the life of the churches and the gospel in what was at times quite hostile ground. They believed their message that Christ saves and wants all to come to him.

Though later leaders had much different situations to deal with, early leaders were often very poor. Their families suffered because of their poverty. Their stories must be read against such a backdrop. Some leaders will have made their families sacrifice too much. It bred resentments that later attempts to redeem seem to have been too great to overcome.

The early story of Mennonite Brethren in Canada prior to the coming of the 1920s immigrants—especially in Saskatchewan—highlights the entrance into the church of a substantial number of people—almost all German-speaking—who didn't carry traditional Mennonite names. The first Mennonite Brethren church in Saskatchewan began in the Carl Gloeckler home, for example. There were Engels, Biffarts, Ollenbergers, Zimmermanns, Seibels, Hodels, Horches, Hinzes, Speisers, Wirsches and Labuns and still others who were part of those early churches. These were people out of German Lutheran or German Catholic backgrounds, who were converted and had joined in Russia, Manitoba or the Dakotas. Many of them moved into Saskatchewan to help form churches there.

There has often been a strong entrepreneurial strain among the leaders in Mennonite Brethren circles. They didn't wait for the conference to approve their vision for a ministry or institution. This was true for both the Herbert and Winkler Bible schools and for the Western Children's Mission and for many other projects like camps and radio ministries over the years. Often the conference later embraced these as its own, but not always. Mennonite Brethren churches of the past have produced an unusually large number of entrepreneurial leaders, people who in many cases had to look farther afield to put their vision and energy to good use.

Despite the willingness to strike out on their own that characterized many of the people in this book, most of them also displayed a great desire to work together. That's an interesting paradox that a close examination of the history will likely bear out. These people clearly enjoyed the work of the conference, in some cases perhaps too much. Even tension and controversy did not dampen that desire. At times it was common to conclude a conference with requests for forgiveness for language that was too heated. Others had to find their forgiveness at home from families who felt neglected.

No one reading the stories of the people found in this book will come away with the impression that they had it all together, never failed, always did good, always were faithful to their God. They didn't and weren't. Yet God used them and the church was blessed and built by them. They gave their gifts generously to the kingdom of God in the world and we are all their beneficiaries. The church is always made up of sinning, imperfect people. Yet if they have a passion for Christ and the church, as all of the ones in this book did or still do, they can become the means through whom the kingdom of God is extended.

## MANY MORE LEADERS

One of the burdens of a book like this is the awareness that the choices of whose stories get in is in some ways quite arbitrary.

As already mentioned, Mennonite Brethren as a movement have had a strong tradition of lay leadership. While there were those that the church ordained as ministers and elders, the belief that all, in a real sense, are ministers has been a strong motif for Mennonite Brethren. That is a reason why so many leaders emerged out of our ranks. So this book could have had many more such people in it. Think of the Klassen brothers, Henry F. and Cornelius F., the former an editor and the latter a key leader in the immigration movement of the '40s, the Block brothers, Art and Henry, or the DeFehr brothers, Art and Frank, or the Fast brothers, Neil and Bill, all successful in business and all institution builders in the church, and you have some idea of what is meant. The educators Dr. Peter Bargen and Dr. Abe Konrad, the businessmen Henry Redekop and David Redekop, the MP Jake Epp, the advocate for MCC and conference trust funds C.J. Rempel, or someone like Peter Loewen, the Abbotsford cabinet maker who started the Disciplemaking International program, and many others too might be named.

But another entire group of people could be named, people who were also very much involved in the growth of the Mennonite Brethren church in Canada during the past century.

One could name Ernest Dyck, the father of the Quebec churches, who turned his attention to a Canadian French community after starting out as a missionary in Congo. Or think of William Bestvater, the leading light of the Herbert Bible School, strong exponent of dispensationalist teaching and inspiration to many of his students, or of Johann Warkentin, the longtime, enlightened leader of the Winkler church, or the patriarch of the Dalmeny Church, Jacob Lepp, a man of great wisdom and energy. Think of other educators like Jake Epp of Bethany; A.J. Schierling of Coaldale and LaGlace; Rueben Baerg of Bethany, MBBC and the Biblical Seminary; Jacob F. Redekop of the Herbert and Abbotsford Bible schools; or David Neumann, Rudy Bartel, Isaac Dyck, Peter Peters, Hugo Friesen, and others of their band who did so much for the high schools in Mennonite Brethren circles.

Or there are church leaders such as Johann Harder of Yarrow, a spiritual leader of great authority and giftedness; Henry Brucks, a church statesman and conciliator who nurtured struggling churches wherever he encountered them; William Falk, another great-hearted Winnipeg city missionary; Herb Brandt and Jake H. Quiring, both pastors, teachers and moderators of great wisdom; James Nikkel, church planter and pastor, to whom the northern Manitoba circle of churches owe special thanks; Jake Balzer, a B.C. church planter who provided strong support to every effort to grow churches; or Randy Friesen, whose gifts at inspiring young people has done much to create an expansive spirit of missions among Mennonite Brethren.

Besides the people whose biographies appear in this book, missionary pioneers like Helena Warkentin, the first to go to India from Canada, or Henry and Anna Bartsch or Hermann and Tina Lenzmann, who went to Congo, could have been included. Others such as the evangelists and pastors, Rudy Boschman and Henry H. Epp, could also have found their way into this book.

Such a list does not begin to address the women who clearly brought a great deal to our churches, women like Anna Bestvater Redekopp of Herbert, always visible wherever she was present at a convention or other church gathering; Holda Fast Redekopp of Abbotsford, whose gift of music raised the level of singing wherever she came; Joyce Schimpky of St. Catharines, a teacher and Camp Crossroads director and promoter of all manner of Christian education causes; Lorina Marsch, our first woman editor (of the *Mennonitische Rundschau*); or Lorraine Dyck of Langley, the first Mennonite Brethren woman leader to chair the Board of Faith and Life.

Lists such as these merely beg the question, who else might be included? Many more are worthy of equal attention. God provides the church with the people it needs for its health, growth and nurture.

This collection of biographies was undertaken so we might celebrate a milestone, but also so we might get a better sense of what's in our bones: who were the people who played a large role in what we are today—for good or ill—as a church? We want many to read the stories of the twenty-five and know ourselves [themselves] better.

*Harold Jantz*
*October 28, 2009*

David Dyck

# FATHER AND BUILDER
# OF THE CHURCH

*By Harold Jantz*

Few people exemplified the spirit of the young Mennonite Brethren movement better than David Dyck. During his years as leader among Canadian Mennonite Brethren no one deserved the title "father of the church" more than he. He had been there with Heinrich Voth in 1884 when the first visits to Manitoba had taken place to test the openness to an MB witness of new birth and renewal. Shepherd and pastor in no fewer than seven places, he kept on responding to opportunities to witness to his Saviour wherever they arose—and for him they never seemed to cease. In Canada, he became best known as the early leader of the Winkler Church and the first moderator of the Northern District (later the Canadian Conference), which he was for 10 years. But more than anything he was a tireless itinerant minister at conference request. He certainly slept in hundreds of beds during a long life of ministry.

### CAN WE TALK WITH GOD?

Dyck was born in Nieder Chortitza, in the Old Colony in southern Russia, on January 25, 1846. The winds of spiritual renewal awaft in the Mennonite colonies touched David early. He heard about the conversion of others, including some cousins, when he was a young teenager. His own village

---

*The Writer*
Harold Jantz started out close to the North Saskatchewan valley area where David Dyck spent many of his years. Most of Harold's working years were devoted to editorial activity within the Canadian Mennonite Brethren Conference, serving as *MB Herald* editor. Later he founded *ChristianWeek*, a national evangelical periodical of news and commentary.

teacher was the father of another early influential Mennonite Brethren, Johann Wieler. Years later, Dyck wrote how he had pondered whether there were people who spoke with God and whether he could himself speak with God. One profound encounter with the Saviour happened at the age of 16 when he lay alone on the grass one evening, gazing at the stars. He felt a wonderful peace, but the problem of continuing sin was not resolved. He doesn't seem to have spoken with anyone who might have helped him in his search.

On September 17, 1867 he was married to Helena Rempel of Rosenthal, a marriage that lasted over 65 years and brought 15 children into the world, nine sons and six daughters. Three children died in infancy. The young couple lived with her parents for a year and a half and David worked in their mill. They then returned to nearby Nieder Chortitza. It took an outbreak of cholera among Russian villagers with whom David did business as a miller to bring him to a place of genuine trust in Christ. For nine years, he says, he had been stalemated by the question of the sin he saw in himself after he thought he had committed himself to the Saviour. Now studying Romans 7 he came to see that he could trust God to save him even though he still struggled with sin. It was the turning point for him. The following year, in 1873, both David and Helena were baptized by Cornelius Unger and joined the young Mennonite Brethren movement. He became active almost immediately in the church, engaging in colportage work.

A few years later, in the summer of 1876, the Dycks joined the movement to America, arriving in New York aboard the Anchovia that July 19 to begin a new life. Only a few Mennonite families were on that ship, but they included the Bernard Pauls family, who became partners in the work of the church for years to come. David was 30, his wife 28 and their three children, all under 10, but they were ready to face the challenges of their new life.

### STARTED OUT IN KANSAS
Like many fellow Russian Mennonite Brethren immigrants they started out in Kansas. After a winter in Marion County, they moved a hundred miles east to Woodson County, where land was cheaper, and there started a church. About 20 families moved with them, built a schoolhouse, and in 1878 Dyck and Pauls were elected as ministers. At Woodson, Pauls, who was Dyck's senior by 13 years, was the presiding minister and Dyck his assistant. David writes that the church prospered, all but one of the adult children of the families were converted. In 1881 Elder Abraham Schellenberg visited the Woodson church and ordained Dyck as minister.

Though he was in America only a few years, David wanted training for church work. He decided in 1883 to go to the German Baptist Seminary in Rochester, N.Y., but after only six weeks he was called back home when his eldest daughter was bitten by a rabid dog. Happily she survived; his studies however never were resumed. He seems to have taken the experience as a sign that his first duty was to his family. Years later Helena wrote that even if he was denied formal studies, he "always read a lot."

Dyck's family was growing but the Woodson settlement wasn't doing very well and in 1884 the Dycks accepted an invitation to come to the Goessel area where a group of ten families out of the Alexanderwohl Mennonite settlement had formed a Mennonite Brethren group under the leadership of Cornelius P. Wedel and Abraham Schellenberg. The gifted evangelist missionary Peter Wedel came from that family as did Cornelius H. Wedel, who became the first president of Bethel College in Newton, Kansas. Dyck was asked to take charge of the Lehigh group. A church was built the same year. Dyck was ordained an elder by Abraham Schellenberg in 1884. It was during this time that Dyck also made his first visit to Canada.

Bernard Pauls followed Dyck to Lehigh a year later. He was the first person assigned by Mennonite Brethren in America to collect and publish reports about the work done by the churches in what became known as the *Zionsbote* (Zion's Herald). The *Zionsbote* played a very large role in giving cohesion to the conference.

 The Lehigh church had the distinction of being the first Mennonite Brethren church in North America to be located in a town. Significantly, it was also during Dyck's time in Winkler that the Mennonite Brethren church was moved into town, and when he moved to Waldheim, Sask., late in life, he also helped start the church in town there. As historian P.M. Friesen notes in his account of the Lehigh church, despite the doubts many Mennonites had about such a move, these people believed Christians are called to be a light "in the world" with emphasis on the "in." Today we would think it strange if we questioned whether it was right to move the church into a mixed community—some conservative Mennonites still do—but in the 1880s it was a big issue.

For Dyck as church leader, the years in Lehigh were his happiest, he wrote at the end of his life. The spirit in the church was good, there were conversions and growth. The communion between members was spiritually stimulating. The church had gifted resources. As a practical necessity, however, Dyck always had to think about land for his children. In 1888 he had already taken a look at lower California but decided it was too far from other Mennonites.

So it was in 1892 that Dyck followed a group who had already made a move to eastern Colorado where new land was opening up. The group became the Kirk Mennonite Brethren Church and Dyck its leader. Again they built a meeting place and experienced vigorous growth, notably after an evangelistic visit by Peter Wedel. But poor crops, especially in 1894, put a lot of pressure on the church and the Dycks too. Their time in Kirk lasted only three years.

## FINALLY TO CANADA

In 1895 he accepted the urgent request of the conference to come to Manitoba to give leadership to the Winkler church and the growing Canadian Mennonite Brethren church community. Dyck must have reviewed the travel options, the belongings they wanted to take with them, the size of the family and their resources and decided overland travel was the best choice, though he sent son John ahead by train with some of their belongings. We have no indication that the church offered to help with the costs. It's clear that neither David nor Helena seem to have lacked courage. They loaded nine of their children and other belongings onto wagons and drove to Winkler, arriving there on July 11, 1895, after a "difficult and yet successful journey," a church reporter wrote. They had been on the way for two months.

By this time Dyck was no stranger to Canada. He had numerous connections to the Mennonites in southern Manitoba. Helena's own parents, the Rempels, a number of her siblings and many old acquaintances lived there. These included the man who would become the heart of the Manitoba Mennonite Brethren after Dyck later moved on to Saskatchewan, a teacher in Hoffnungsfeld near Winkler. His name was Johann Warkentin and he too had started out in Nieder Chortitza in southern Russia, David Dyck's original home.

David Dyck's earlier visit to Manitoba with Heinrich Voth of Minnesota drew on Dyck's contacts. In 1884 the two came to "the West Reserve" to survey the spiritual hunger there. They found, as they said, "devout and seeking souls." Some of Heinrich Voth's most effective evangelism when he returned following the initial visit happened at Hoffnungsfeld, near Winkler, Johann Warkentin's community.

When the Dycks arrived in Winkler, the church was still out at Burwalde, a few miles north of town. Membership stood at 84. Three years later, in 1898, it was moved into town. In preparation for the all-Mennonite Brethren conference which would take place in Winkler that year, a new much roomier building was erected. When the Dycks moved on to Saskatchewan in 1906, the membership of the church stood at 225.

The years in Winkler were important to Dyck's ministry in several ways. He brought gifted people into the work of the church. A few months after coming he ordained Johann Warkentin to the ministry. When Dyck left, Warkentin would begin a very fruitful 25-year ministry as leader in Winkler. Ordaining Warkentin freed Dyck to begin a number of years of highly active itinerant work. He had often been asked before, but probably because of his family's needs and local responsibilities, he declined. But now he agreed. He traveled widely in southern Manitoba, Saskatchewan, into the Dakotas, and elsewhere. His reports appeared frequently in the conference paper, the *Zionsbote*, beginning with the first report in the April 15, 1896 issue.

## RIGORS OF TRAVEL

One gets the impression of a person who gladly accepted the rigors of difficult travel, strange beds and inconveniences to share the gospel among people he truly loved. His reports are filled with expressions of affection. On a trip to the Rosthern area he comments that as he stepped from the train, "I spotted several familiar faces as soon as I disembarked, ones I had come to love...." When he sees little children peering through train windows to see if they recognize a familiar face, he says, "How the human heart longs for reunion with those one grieved to leave." And as he celebrated communion with the brothers and sisters before leaving, he expressed the hope that they could fulfill the Apostle's wish, "Make every effort to keep the unity of the Spirit through the bond of peace."

He could enjoy himself with people in a variety of ways. He describes how he went down to the North Saskatchewan to join others fishing and witnessed the capture of two sturgeon, one 33 pounds and the other 17 pounds. When the weather turned bad as they were fishing, he went to the Peter Hoeppners where they enjoyed a good fish fry together. The large sturgeon returned with him to Winkler, he wrote.

During that trip, which began June 20 and ended July 5, 1898, with 12 days in the Rosthern area, he conducted nine services and made at least 15 home visits and appears to have slept in four different beds. He made a point of visiting the bishop of the Rosenorter Mennonite Church, Peter Regier, as well.

In a report that describes the beginning of Dyck's itinerant witness after arriving in Winkler, he reviews the work he did between mid-November, 1895 and the end of February, 1896. During that time he made extended visits to Plum Coulee, the Blumstein-Hoffnungsfeld area close to Winkler, an area in North Dakota, Plum Coulee again, then Winkler during Christmas and the prayer week, then Morden and places south of it, and finally places in the East Reserve, east of the Red River.

It wouldn't be unusual for a reporter to say that Dyck had visited at every home, if there was an emerging Mennonite Brethren church somewhere. That's what happened when Dyck came for a month to Burwalde in the fall of 1894. The anonymous writer added, "We too had the joy of receiving him into our hut and sheltering him for the night. Such times remain in the heart: how wonderful, to have lived far apart and never to have known one another before, and yet knit so deeply together, that we can love and understand one another from the heart." That seems to have been the effect Dyck had on many. Again and again he is described as "the dear brother Dyck."

He in turn repeatedly would say how he came away from meetings or visits strengthened in the faith after being met with much "friendliness and support." He freely commended those whose work preceded his.

Much of his travelling had to be done during harsh winter months, since summers also had to be given to farming. That meant travel in snowstorms, on roads that virtually disappeared at times, in very cold weather and often late at night. Meetings would sometimes be scheduled for times of good moonlight, so travelers could find their way home at night. Dyck's hardy constitution seems to have handled the strains of all these conditions remarkably well.

One gets an idea of the nature of many of his meetings from his reports written for the *Zionsbote*. They usually involved conversation around the spiritual experiences or testimonies of people, singing, a presentation or teaching from the Bible and a time of prayer. Because much of the evangelistic activity was done among other Mennonites—and often opposed by leaders in the community—the only place where gatherings could usually be held was within homes. Yet these laid a sturdy foundation for Mennonite Brethren churches that grew up around Winkler and in central and southern Saskatchewan.

He was present on June 8, 1899 when the first Mennonite Brethren church in Saskatchewan was organized in the Carl Gloeckler home out in the countryside between Rosthern and Laird. He came twice more in the following year to help the church organize for ministry and choose its leaders. That first group called themselves the Ebenfeld Mennonite Brethren Church (later Laird).

## CONFERENCE LEADER

In addition, Dyck was active in the leadership of the conference. From 1903 to 1906 he was a member of the first constitutionally structured Mennonite Brethren Board of Foreign Missions. He was part of the group that began the work that led to the formation of three district conferences—

Southern (Kansas, Oklahoma, Texas), Central (North and South Dakota, Minnesota, Nebraska and, at the very start, Manitoba) and Northern (Saskatchewan)—that opened the way to vigorous expansion of the churches. When the reorganization process was completed in 1909, Dyck began his decade-long stint as Northern District (Canadian conference) moderator. His imprint was all over the young conference.

In 1906 Dyck had been in Winkler 11 years when the family moved to Borden, Saskatchewan. His family's need for land encouraged the move. He was 60 years old. The Borden area had land that had been held in reserve for the Doukhobors and was now available for free homesteads. Dyck didn't become the leader of the Borden church, but he clearly was a strong encouragement to its leader, David R. Klaassen. As in so many places where Dyck came, he soon prodded the young group to build a church. The two-acre plot on which the Borden church and cemetery were located was donated by Dyck. The church had the attractive name Hoffnungsfeld (Field of Hope), perhaps recalling the school district in Manitoba where the doors first opened for Mennonite Brethren.

The Dycks only stayed in Borden for four years. In 1910, when Dyck was 64, they bought a farm four miles west of Waldheim and joined the Brotherfield Church. The years at Brotherfield again were years of great activity for Dyck, his itinerant ministry and conference work often taking him away.

In a real sense Dyck must be seen as the father of the young Mennonite Brethren conference in Canada. He was there at the very beginning, when the first individual contacts were made. During the first decade as a Canadian conference, from 1910 to 1920, he was elected moderator year after year, and during the second decade he was usually the person asked to preach the first sermon, lead the *Vorberatung* (pre-conference planning meeting), preside at the communion service, or be the one to greet the guests. In 1926 at the ripe old age of 80, when the new immigrants coming to Alberta began forming churches, Dyck was asked to travel there to see about bringing them into the conference. In the year of his death, the conference numbered over five thousand members with a community probably closer to eight or nine thousand. What changes and growth he had been a part of!

Dyck's preaching was not narrow. Sometimes he expounded texts, treated personalities of the Bible, talked on the family, argued for a high view of the church, preached evangelistically (did that often), spoke on prophecy, or argued the truth claims of Jesus. A listing of themes and texts suggests a preacher who spoke easily from both Old and New Testament texts, clearly preached for conversion, emphasized a trinitarian gospel with a strong focus on the work of Christ, and believed strongly in a committed and disciplined church separated from the world. One of his last statements to the conference was an "earnest" warning about practicing biblical discipline and submitting to the Word of God and the fellowship of believers.

When Dyck moved to Brotherfield, he assumed the leadership of the group there, with assistance from several others who had served both as lay and ordained ministers. The church began a growth surge that led to a decision to greatly expand the building in 1911. A conference at Brotherfield that year drew an attendance of a thousand. At that time Brotherfield was also the central church for a cluster of six churches north of Saskatoon.

There is an account of a 50th wedding celebration for the Dycks in 1917. Every seat in the church was filled and friends came from considerable distance. Among the guests were the Rosenorter Mennonite elder David Toews of Rosthern, William Bestvater of Winnipeg and Jacob Lepp of Dalmeny. David and Helena are described as the "dear old brother and sister."

## ONE LAST CHURCH START

But their ministry was not yet at an end. The following year, they decided to move into nearby Waldheim and help a group who wanted to start a church there. On October 14, 1918, Dyck called a meeting of people interested in such a move and soon thereafter a group began meeting in town. By 1920 they had built their own meeting place, with Dyck as leader. They began with 65 members in 1918 with an active Sunday school program, choir, women's group and monthly youth meeting and by 1924 they had a hundred members. Again, Dyck's leadership appears to have given the group great impetus in attracting people to them and building them into a lively spiritual fellowship.

The greatest shadow on Dyck's ministry may well have been his attitude to the needs of his spiritual kin in Russia. He appears never to have brought it into the annual conferences. Indeed, in July, 1921, Dyck was the spokesperson for a group who met in the Rosthern area, who voiced opposition to support for Mennonite brothers trying to flee Russia in the wake of the revolution. The following year, his area also opposed support for a delegation to Ottawa—proposed by Heinrich Neufeld of Herbert, a fellow Mennonite Brethren—to negotiate for opportunities to bring immigrants to Canada. He clearly cannot have sensed the desperate struggle many brothers and sisters in Russia were enduring. When the first immigrants came in 1923, the Mennonite Brethren were at first conspicuous for their absence from the lists of those who welcomed the newcomers into their homes.

David Dyck lived out his last years in Waldheim and there he died on January 6, 1933, at the ripe age of 87. He left a good legacy, despite his shortsightedness toward his Russian brothers and sisters. He was not afraid to confront, but he also sought to reconcile. At the end of a conference, he might typically ask for forgiveness where he had offended. His tireless church building—both of the living body and the meeting places to house them—was a testimony to his conviction that people could come to new life in Christ and become lively, witnessing communities of believers. Through his organizational leadership, he deserves a good deal of credit for setting Mennonite Brethren in Canada onto a path of sturdy and healthy growth.

In a remarkable coincidence, he died in the same half year as Heinrich Neufeld of Herbert (as well as Jacob W. Thiessen of southern Saskatchewan), and all three were honoured in a special memorial service in 1933. Speaking for the conference, John P. Wiebe of Herbert said Dyck (and the others) were "teachers" of the church. The memory of one like him should lead the church to bow in reverence to God. Such leaders should be remembered with gratitude and their service recognized for what it was: from God.

And, urged Wiebe, the churches should also remember their families with support and prayer. The memory of leaders like Dyck should give hope to the church because now they were seeing the glory they had once served in weakness. The person who wrote up that event noted that a time of deep silence followed before a number of "brethren" followed with their own tributes and prayers.

SOURCES:
This chapter has drawn on a brief autobiographical account written by David Dyck in 1933 and his sermon notebooks 1 and 2. Other works consulted were A.H. Unruh's *Die Geschichte der Mennoniten-Bruedergemeinde* (Hillsboro: 1955); J.A. Toews, *A History of the Mennonite Brethren Church* (Fresno: 1975); A.J. Klassen, ed., *The Church in Mission* (Fresno: 1967); Frank H. Epp, *Mennonite Exodus* (Altona: 1962); William Neufeld, *From Faith to Faith* (Winnipeg: 1989); William J. Ratzlaff et al, *Waldhim Remembers the Past* (Waldheim: 1981); G.W. Peters, *The Growth of Foreign Missions in the Mennonite Brethren Church* (Hillsboro: 1952); John H. Lohrenz, *The Mennonite Brethren Church* (Hillsboro: 1950); Clarence Hiebert, *Brothers in Deed to Brothers in Need*, (Newton: self-published, 1974); P.M.

Friesen, *Alt-Evangelische Mennonitische Bruderschaft in Russland*, (Halbstadt: Raduga, 1911); J. F. Harms, *Geschichte der Mennoniten Bruedergemeinde 1860-1924* (Hillsboro: 1924); and issues of the *Zionsbote* (Hillsboro) and the *Mennonitische Rundschau* (Scottdale and Winnipeg). A footnoted copy of this chapter is on file with the Centre for MB Studies in Winnipeg.

# John F. Harms

# EDITOR HARMS,
## RESTLESS AND VISIONARY

*By Wally Kroeker*

Onlookers winced as John Harms stepped into the icy pond. It was winter on the plains of Saskatchewan and he had come to perform a baptism. For Mennonite Brethren this meant full immersion, and with no indoor baptistries in those days, his hosts had chopped a hole in the ice.

Frost laced his straggly beard as Harms, waist deep, intoned the traditional words of baptism and immersed each candidate in the frigid water.

Then a fur coat was thrown over him and he hurried to the farmhouse to change clothes and formally welcome the new members into the church with a service of communion.

Later he said it hadn't been all that cold, and might even have been good for his health.

## A MOBILE MINISTRY

It was 1907 in a small community west of Saskatoon, and this was one of three ice-tisms he performed that winter. He'd preach the sermon in the home, then put on some borrowed overalls and proceed to the pond. It was all part of an itinerant ministry that the Mennonite Brethren conference

*The Writer*
Wally Kroeker knows very well the settings in which John F. Harms worked: in 1975 he became the *Christian Leader* editor in Hillsboro in the denominational publishing enterprise Harms once began. Most of Kroeker's life has been involved with journalism, in recent years as editor of *Marketplace*, the publication of Mennonite Economic Development Associates. A bit of trivia: back in 1914 Wally Kroeker's grandparents, A.A. and Lizzie Kroeker, were married by Harms in Hepburn, Sask.

had asked him to carry out among ethnic Russians in Saskatchewan and North Dakota.

For two years Harms ministered to these new immigrants whose many personal and spiritual needs were aggravated by disorder and discord. Traipsing through blowing snow in sub-zero weather with no thought to his own comfort, he faithfully visited their sparse homes, preached, led services, counseled and, of course, baptized. Today there are still ethnic Russians in Saskatchewan and North Dakota whose ancestors he brought to faith.

This mobile ministry suited the restless temperament of John F. Harms, who over the years would hopscotch across North America, picking up on a whim to seek out a new field of service. Shifting geography aside, he put down deep stakes on which the Mennonite Brethren Church could build. Who was this man and should anyone care about him today?

If you've read Mennonite periodicals you can thank this multi-textured man who was known as a pioneer publisher.

If you've attended a Mennonite Brethren school, you are heir to his educational foresight, for his home-based instruction ignited a spark that was fanned into Bible schools and colleges.

If you've been moved by the plight of the hungry and oppressed, you share lineage with one of the earliest Mennonite Brethren to promote help for the needy as central to Christian discipleship.

## A PRECOCIOUS CHILD

John F. Harms (often known simply as "JF") was born in 1855 in Kleefeld, one of many tiny villages in the Molotschna Colony of Russia (present-day Ukraine). A precocious child, he learned to read and write before starting school. He loved books and accumulated an impressive library even as a youngster. He accepted Jesus early, and as a teenager was baptized by his local Mennonite church. While still in school he was invited to be a teacher's assistant, and by 18 was teaching in the nearby village of Lichtfelde.

He also married that year and was thrust into a sequence of tragedies. A daughter died as a toddler and a son died shortly after birth, followed closely by the death of his wife from tuberculosis. He had suffered three deaths in two months and for a time descended into depression.

As was common, he remarried quickly, this time to Margaretha Isaac, and by 1878 was ready to join the growing trek to North America, settling in Mountain Lake, Minnesota.

Harms went into farming, as many immigrants did regardless of aptitude, but within a year moved into town and began teaching. He also tried to start a periodical, which failed. Another publishing opportunity soon presented itself, however, and Harms moved to Elkhart, Indiana, to help the legendary Mennonite publisher John F. Funk launch the *Mennonitische Rundschau* (Mennonite Observer). Harms was appointed its first editor and took to the new task with zeal.

The *Rundschau* began as a bi-weekly newspaper to connect Mennonites in North America and Russia. It caught on quickly and soon graduated to a weekly. It became the most popular German-language Mennonite publication in North America and lasted more than a hundred years.

### A PAPER FOR THE CHURCH

Harms yearned for theological training to accompany his new calling in publishing. From 1882-84 he attended the Evangelical Bible Institute in Naperville, Illinois, continuing to edit the *Rundschau* from a distance.

It was a move with momentous implications for the Mennonite Brethren Church.

Harms had belonged to the "other" Mennonite group, from which the Mennonite Brethren had split in Russia in 1860. At Naperville he became spiritually quickened and found himself attracted to the Mennonite Brethren. Upon completing his studies, Harms decided not to return to Elkhart but instead moved to the hamlet of Canada, Kansas, not far from the town of Hillsboro that was emerging as an MB

*For Harms, Christian faith was a stern undertaking.*

center. He was re-baptized into the new MB congregation nearby, which became the Hillsboro Mennonite Brethren Church.

For the next year he continued to edit the inter-Mennonite *Rundschau* from this tiny community while managing a lumber business as well. When the business was sold he opened a private German school in his home.

Attending the MB conference of 1884 turned out to be a watershed event for the young teacher/editor. His gifts were immediately recognized and he was appointed to a committee to examine how an MB publication might help unite a fledgling denomination scattered over several midwestern states. The committee decided to launch its own newspaper, the *Zionsbote* (Zion's Herald), with Harms as editor.

The new periodical operated without subsidy from the conference. It was up to Harms to cover its costs beyond the 25 cents a year paid by subscribers. In 1887 the conference voted to give him $50 for that year's labor. The next year he got $25, and some years he got only a word of thanks and a pat on the back. To support himself he started a printshop in Hillsboro to produce the periodical and do commercial printing for others.

The *Zionsbote* was right for its time. Initially a four-page quarterly sent to churches in bundles, it expanded to a monthly, and then a weekly.

Along with spiritual exposition it contained world news as well as reports on Mennonite activities, missions and global humanitarian needs. It appealed widely to other German-speaking religious groups who didn't have access to world news in their own language. It also sold well among Mennonites back in Russia, who were eager to hear about their brothers and sisters abroad.

"With the founding of the *Zionsbote*, the die was cast for J.F. Harms," writes his biographer Orlando Harms (a distant relative and mentee). "He was inextricably involved with the Mennonite Brethren, and his involvement was to continue for more than fifty years."

## SPIN-OFFS

The next several years were a flurry of publishing activity, made all the more chaotic by Harms' frequent moves around the country. While continuing to edit the *Zionsbote*, he spun off community papers like the *Hillsboro Anzeiger* (Advertiser), which catered to a widespread German audience of Mennonites, Lutherans, Adventists and Baptists.

As with many newspapers, financial stability was less easily attained than readership, and Harms experimented with various locations where commercial printing revenue could subsidize his beloved *Zionsbote*.

He was soon immersed in the politics of his new land, apparently willing to step out of the traditional "quiet in the land" mold. He became an avid supporter of the Republican Party, drawn by its embrace of protectionist tariffs, patriotism and prohibition, all of which he equated with morality and justice. His papers became increasingly partisan, with little room for dissenting viewpoints.

These interests faded over time (helped, perhaps, by a conference reprimand that he was becoming too political), but from 1887 to 1897 "his controversial newspaper editorship was the most visible—and possibly the most significant—politicizing force among the Kansas Mennonites," according to historian James Juhnke.

The ever-restless Harms found new Mennonite settlements alluring. Returning from a visit to Europe in the winter of 1897-98 he decided to leave Kansas. With his printing equipment in tow, he moved to a farm near Medford in northern Oklahoma's newly-opened Cherokee territory and set up a printshop in a lean-to next to his house. During the day he toiled on the hardscrabble fields while his daughters set type. At night he cranked the hand-fed press, printing two pages at a time because there wasn't enough metal type to do more .

With this privately-owned printshop Harms continued to produce the *Zionsbote* for the conference, but overwork caught up with him and he grew discouraged. The conference stepped in and took over the operation in 1904 to establish the Mennonite Brethren Publishing House, with Harms as editor and manager. Equipment was upgraded and the *Zionsbote* given a crisp new look with clean type and pictures from zinc etchings.

In 1905 the Russian language *Golos* (Voice) was launched to serve Russian brothers and sisters who had settled in Saskatchewan and North Dakota. The monthly publication achieved a circulation of 1,500 and continued for seven years.

During this time Margaretha fell ill and her physician suggested a colder climate, like Canada. In 1906 Harms resigned as editor and manager to head north, prompting the conference to move the publishing house to McPherson, Kansas, and later to more ethnically familiar Hillsboro, where it remained until being sold to private interests in the 1980s.

Though not finished with Kansas, Harms would spend the next dozen years on the Canadian prairies, prospecting new veins of ministry.

## ROAMING THE PRAIRIES

The prairies were booming, and Alberta and Saskatchewan were flexing their muscles as the latest "in" provinces, both having joined Canada's Confederation in 1905. Many Mennonites had migrated there to take up an offer of free land. Harms spent time in both provinces, finally settling on a homestead near the community of Flowing Well in southern

Saskatchewan. It didn't take long for the conference to give him a new assignment as an itinerant minister to recent Russian immigrants in Saskatchewan and North Dakota.

Harms roamed about, conducted services, led music, visited homes and offered pastoral counselling to people carrying heavy loads of spiritual and social baggage. Some had left unsavoury lifestyles back in Russia and were ready for a fresh start. Others had been divorced in the old country and remarried in Canada without informing their new spouses about their past. Many were so busy carving out a new life they had little appetite for spiritual nurture. "They used their children as work machines, the parents became materialistic and the children godless," Harms noted in his diary.

Harms walked long distances between farms, up to 12 miles at a time. He'd stay in homes and make do with whatever the hosts had available.

Some didn't have extra beds, and the lodging of last resort would be to sleep in the main bed with the man of the house while the wife slept on the floor. "Once three men slept crosswise on one bed with chairs at the side for their feet," Orlando Harms recounts. In some homes the bedding hadn't been changed for months, and children didn't change clothes at night, nor even clean the manure from their shoes.

For two years Harms carried out this mobile ministry, and led many to faith. But it was an unsettled time on the prairies and he'd sometimes return to an area and find that converts had drifted away or defected to other groups.

Despite lacking any evidence of agricultural skill, Harms still fancied himself a farmer. At one point he filed a homestead claim in Saskatchewan but naively checked it out in winter when it was thick with snow. As the snow melted, the land beneath was revealed to be nothing more than marsh and rocks, unsuitable for crops. "Why did this have to happen to me?" he lamented in his diary. "I don't know, but I am beginning to believe that I am unable to assess anything temporal and will have to bury my hopes for a more prosperous earthly life." He ended up finding a different homestead near the town of Herbert.

## NO NOVICE AT EDUCATION

It was there that Harms undertook his most lasting Canadian contribution—planting  and watering the seeds that would grow into the Mennonite Brethren Bible school movement.

When it came to education, Harms was no novice. Back in the hamlet of Canada, Kansas, while struggling to make ends meet, he had started a small private school in his home, teaching German and Bible. The con-

*In the early 1940s, Harms could often be spotted on the streets of Hillsboro.*

ference absorbed his enthusiasm, and two years later formed an association to adopt the school. It was relocated to the town of Lehigh, on the other side of Hillsboro, with Harms continuing as instructor. Historians say this modest effort was the first Mennonite Brethren school in North America, thus making Harms not only a pioneer publisher but also a pioneer educator.

As an editor he had persistently advocated higher education and had fashioned the *Zionsbote* into a respected medium of instruction. He also prepared and published many Bible studies for youth and adapted them for Sunday school use.

In Saskatchewan, Bible courses he taught in his farm home morphed into a "migrant Bible school" that travelled to various churches during the winter months. His vision led to the formation of the Herbert Bible School in 1913, with him as the first principal and teacher. It was the first such school for Mennonite Brethren in Canada and the second for any group in western Canada.

The Herbert school ran during farming's off-season, starting after fall harvest and concluding before spring seeding. The first student body consisted of five girls and nine boys who came from surrounding farms for a live-in experience. As reported by Margaret Epp in her book *Proclaim Jubilee!,* the boys slept on tables in the meagre first building, and the girls slept in the drafty attic, where they sometimes awoke to find snow had blown onto their blankets overnight. Harms, meanwhile, bunked in a tiny "cell" about six feet square. Even this spartan enterprise could strain some budgets and Harms made secret interest-free loans to some students so they could return the following winter.

Though stern and sometimes gruff, Principal Harms was known fondly as "the man with the beard." He taught Bible, world history, German literature, grammar (both German and English), nature study and archaeology. He also taught English courses in the community.

After five years the Herbert Bible School closed when Harms moved back to the U.S., but reopened under new leadership in 1921 and enjoyed many years of vigor. By the time it closed for good in 1957 and its program amalgamated with Bethany Bible Institute in Hepburn, Saskatchewan, it had trained more than a thousand students, many of whom became preachers, teachers, missionaries and church workers. Harms' vision for formal Bible training had been thoroughly entrenched in the MB Conference.

### MORE WANDERING AHEAD

For Harms there was still more wandering and publishing ahead.

In 1918, as the First World War was ending, he moved his family to Seattle on the United States west coast. This placed him closer to Russia, to which his wife hoped to return for a family visit. Harms used the time to assemble relief shipments (140 chests of clothing) for the needy brothers and sisters whose lives had been ravaged by the Bolshevik Revolution in 1917.

A trip to the former homeland was not to be, however, as Margaretha was diagnosed with cancer. Hoping warmer weather might help, Harms moved the family to Reedley, California. But his wife continued to decline and expressed the wish to spend her last days in Hillsboro. So, once again they moved, and shortly after reaching Kansas, Margaretha passed away. Harms, now 66, remarried half a year later.

Back in familiar Hillsboro, Harms began the final chapter of his publishing ministry, resuming work with the MB Publishing House that had grown out of his earlier efforts. By now the *Zionsbote* was being edited by the pugnacious A.L. Schellenberg. From 1922-34 Harms served as assistant editor of the periodical he had started, worked with the *Hillsboro Vorwaerts* (another product of the Publishing House) and stepped in as interim editor of the *Zionsbote* when Schellenberg quit suddenly.

## A HEART FOR THE SUFFERING

During his last stint at the MBPH Harms defined yet another facet of ministry—relief for the needy.

Concern for the hungry and suffering, especially the Mennonites in Russia who were thrust into poverty and even starvation in the aftermath of the Bolshevik Revolution, had long been close to his heart and was regularly reflected in his writings.

He threw himself into mobilizing response to the Russian famine, the tragedy that led to the creation of the Mennonite Central Committee in the early 1920s. He worked closely with J.G. Ewert, the legendary invalid editor who, despite being bedridden, was ground zero of a momentous outpouring of generosity among American Mennonites. When Ewert died, Harms carried on the work himself, arranging substantial shipments of money and relief.

According to Orlando Harms, the bulk of his energy during this final chapter was spent dispatching relief. His view of tangible social action as central to Christian discipleship was likely bolstered by his admiration for Walter Rauschenbusch, a popular Baptist preacher of the time who is regarded as the father of the social gospel movement. Orlando Harms observes that JF's sermons displayed a forward-looking integration of evangelism, discipline and the ethical mandate of the gospel to society. "Continuing in Christ is not only remaining in fellowship with him, it is also serving him," he quotes the elder Harms as saying in one sermon. "It is not only having a right position toward God but also toward man. It is not only looking toward Jesus, but also having open eyes, quick feet and willing hands toward the needs of our fellowman."

## A STERN UNDERTAKING

J.F. Harms was an imposing figure, both spiritually and physically. Over six feet tall, he was overweight for much of his working life, though in later years he appeared gaunt in photographs.

By most accounts, he was not personally engaging, nor always pleasant. To him, Christian faith was a stern undertaking. People who knew him said he seldom laughed, and never used levity in his sermons. A woman who worked for him as a young girl in Hillsboro and continued to help out with German proofreading at the MBPH into the 1970s, said he could be impatient and had quite a temper, though he could also be kind.

He was inclined to be dogmatic about "worldly pleasures," which by his broad sweep included making noise at ball games. When his eldest son Peter, 13, died while swimming on a Sunday, Harms took it as a divine rebuke for breaking the Sabbath.

He yearned for a world not only without strife and racial hatred but also without tobacco, movies, beauty salons or short skirts—all heathenish pursuits for which a perfect church had no room.

In later years he became eccentric. He acquired a small mill to grind grains to eat and sell as a health food. Porridge seasoned with onions became his staple diet.

Harms' earnest ministry came at a cost to his family, who often felt neglected. When at home, his mind was elsewhere. His final years were haunted by remorse for his parental deficiencies. Only one of his five children showed up at his funeral.

### AN INDELIBLE MARK

Yet like an artisan's skilled fingers on supple clay, J.F. Harms shaped the Mennonite Brethren Church with single-minded devotion.

He left an indelible mark on publishing and is often described as a founder, father or dean of MB publishing.

He was an innovator in education, and was socially progressive despite his personal conservatism. As early as 1890 he urged the conference to work among blacks in the south, though nothing was done for decades. He helped set up the first mission station among the Comanche Indians of Oklahoma, and outpaced fellow Mennonite Brethren in trying to push beyond German and provide resources in English. Orlando Harms calls him "a trailblazer in English...ahead of his time."

His last pastor, J.W. Vogt, described Harms as a visionary who entrenched education, publications and missions—"the prime factors in unifying Mennonite Brethren over the years"—in the DNA of the church.

J.F. Harms died January 7, 1945 at the age of 89 and was buried in the Hillsboro MB Church cemetery.

His gravestone, like the man himself, is austere and plain, a modest slab of white marble. All it says is "John F. Harms 1855-1945." No mention is made of his mammoth contributions.

It could have said more. At the very least, "Editor Harms."

## SOURCES

The major source for this chapter was the book written by Orlando Harms, *Pioneer Publisher: The Life and Times of J.F. Harms* (Hillsboro and Winnipeg: 1984). Other sources were *A History of the Mennonite Brethren Church* by J.A. Toews (Fresno: 1975); *A People of Two Kingdoms: The Political Acculturation of the Kansas Mennonites* by James C. Juhnke (Newton: 1975); and *Proclaim Jubilee! A History of Bethany Bible Institute* by Margaret Epp (Hepburn: 1976).

# Henry S. Voth

# A LEADER WHO KEPT THE TRUST OF MANY

*By Harold Jantz*

Who was Henry S. Voth and why did he come to play such a prominent role among early Canadian Mennonite Brethren? For nearly
twenty years from 1921 on—even after the passage of a resolution calling for a rotation of leaders—year after year he was elected moderator of
the Canadian conference.

Here was a farmer minister who preached tirelessly—just under five
thousand times by his own account—baptized over six hundred people;
saw many more come to saving faith through his preaching; travelled by
buggy and bike in the early years and then by train and car, all over western Canada and the United States; and took part in countless committee,
board and conference meetings.

At the end of five decades of ministry in 1953, his wife described
the driving passion of his life. She wrote that Henry S. Voth had recognized a gift for evangelism within himself early in life. "This burning
desire to save souls kept on growing in strength, so that in his later
years, throughout the conference and here in Manitoba within the sur-

---

### The Writer

Learning to know the story of his own faith family has energized Harold Jantz
throughout the years of his public work. Beginning as a high school teacher and
then during many years as editor, first of the *Mennonite Brethren Herald* and then
of *ChristianWeek*, the stories of others in the church have been some of his greatest
sources of inspiration. Henry S. Voth is one of these, both in his strengths and his
weaknesses.

rounding communities, many testified that they found the way of salvation through his clear proclamation of the Word."

In the southern Manitoba community of Winkler in the early 1900s, the Voth name resonated widely. If one person could be named as the pioneering evangelist and church planter for the fledgling Mennonite Brethren community in the late 19th century, it would have been Heinrich H. Voth (the father of Henry S.), an immigrant to America in 1876 from the Russian Mennonite colony of Molotschna.

## BEGINNINGS

Back in Russia, father Heinrich H. Voth had experienced a profound conversion as a village teacher. That led to a revival in his community and a year after arriving in Bingham Lake, Minnesota, he joined the Mennonite Brethren. A hard-working, intense Christian, he quickly became involved in the church's work, first in Sunday school, then in a preaching ministry and by 1885 he was ordained an *Aeltester* [bishop: a role no longer in practice among Mennonite Brethren]. It was through his itinerant evangelistic ministry in southern Manitoba—along with another early Mennonite Brethren leader, David Dyck—that the first couples to be converted and baptized were brought into the infant Canadian Mennonite Brethren community. It was the mid-1880s.

The elder Voth was an evangelist farmer with his home base in Minnesota. He carried on a wide-ranging itinerant ministry common to that era. His eldest son, also named Heinrich (Henry S.), would eventually make southern Manitoba his home, and in 1908 the younger Voth was ordained to the ministry by the Winkler Mennonite Brethren Church with his father present to lay hands on him. He married Susie, the daughter of the Winkler Church's leader, Johann Warkentin. H.S. Voth's father-in-law, a former teacher and farmer, was known as a "progressive" and generous-spirited man. He could hold views not widely shared without antagonizing others. The younger Voth clearly benefitted from the esteem with which Warkentin was held in his community. Yet it was the example of his own father upon which he most modeled his practice.

## FATHER HIS MODEL

There he had seen a man with a passionate sense of calling. His father could be gone for weeks and even months at a time—evangelizing, travelling around the country conducting church meetings, doing visits in homes, always attempting to persuade people to faith—while his family worked at home in an effort to secure their livelihood on the farm. When

*The church patriarch, Heinrich H. Voth, with his six sons, Henry, John (early missionary to India), Jake, Peter, Isaac and Abe.*

he was home he might still spend days in his room, secluded from his family, at times not even emerging for meals.

The children saw the burden their father carried and embraced it too, though not without a struggle. Son John H. Voth became one of the early Mennonite Brethren missionaries to India. Son Henry S. Voth was recommended for a similar assignment in 1906, but he had already accepted invitations to engage in home missions, so he did not follow the call to a foreign country.

Henry had been led to faith at the age of 13 through the influence of his parents and Sunday school teachers. However, it seems to have been the preaching of two very talented young missionary candidates, Peter Wedel and H.E. Enns, that really stirred him to an all-out commitment and led to his baptism in 1895. From that point on, from the age of 17, he became a "forceful, active worker in the church's youth group, in the choir and in personal witness," his wife wrote later, though he was not spared intense spiritual struggles as well.

Henry S. appears to have been a keen student, a gifted evangelist with a strong stage presence, a natural leader. According to one account, "by the end of 1901, he had already been noticed as a hard-working colporteur, having recorded 26 sermons in North Dakota, Manitoba and Kansas in that year. His father [also] sent him, rather than an older man, on a delicate church mission to North Dakota." He was only 23. Colporteurs were people who traveled about selling Bibles and books and speaking wherever the opportunity arose.

Yet despite his early involvement in public ministry, he apparently struggled with stage fright almost his entire life and on one early memorable occasion, he apparently ran out of something to say and walked straight off the stage, three feet down. It took him several months to get over the experience. Even much later in life, the entries in his preaching diaries often ended with "O, God help! O, Lord, have mercy!"

### MOSTLY SELF-TAUGHT

Henry S. Voth's education included a good deal of self-study and some formal education. He started out in his own father's classroom as well as that of another [possibly two] other German Mennonite teachers, but also received formal education in the Mountain Lake, Minnesota schools. By 1901 he had gained a certificate to teach in the public schools in Langdon, North Dakota. He followed this with a term in 1902 at the Dunker Brethren school, McPherson College, in Kansas, where Mennonite Brethren offered the German department program. The rest of his education he acquired on his own. His brother once described him as "equipped with a weak education but possessing strong courage and a hardy constitution." One could add, plenty of natural talent too.

Henry S. Voth was in his early twenties when he began a public ministry. He clearly felt a calling. It was at a time when U.S. and Canadian Mennonite Brethren churches all met at one annual meeting that an invitation was extended to him. At that meeting in Cottonwood County, Minnesota, in October 1901, Henry was asked to use his vacation time to itinerate for a quarter year in the northern states and Manitoba and the Northwest Territories. He took the assignment and found his ministry strongly affirmed.

In the following year, the conference in Washita County, Oklahoma, asked Henry to take a six-month appointment at $30 a month. He would work in North and South Dakota, Nebraska and Minnesota. A year later, in 1903, the annual conference in Nebraska asked Henry to accept a full year's assignment for $350 plus traveling expenses. Though his territory was mainly the northern states and Canada, he would also visit Oklahoma, Kansas and Colorado that year.

At the 1903 conference, Henry was still single and came as a delegate from Minnesota. The following year he was listed as a delegate from

*Susie and Henry Voth shared a clear vision.*

Winkler and came along with his father-in-law, Johann Warkentin. That same year, on August 28, 1904, he married the young Susie Warkentin. She was also an active worker in the Winkler church. (While he was teaching in Langdon County, North Dakota, and Henry was courting Susie, he would sometimes make the 77-mile trip to Winkler by bicycle on weekends.) For the next several years, Henry was always identified as a delegate from Manitoba.

### GREAT PREACHING ACTIVITY

The years from 1903 to 1908, all years when Henry was still in his twenties, were years of great preaching activity. He travelled constantly and in one of those years he preached 218 sermons. Many settlers were moving into Saskatchewan—which became a province in 1905—and Henry spent a good deal of time there. In 1905 he conducted services in the Laird-Ebenfeld area and as many as a hundred individuals were converted.

He began to take on conference roles too: in 1906, for example, Henry was asked to audit the financial report for the conference.

In 1908 Henry moved his family to Dallas, Oregon, to take responsibility for several small churches in Dallas and the city of Portland. He also accepted a role as evangelist for Oregon and the west that continued until 1915. He began with a one-year salary of $550. It was a time in his life when his health was good and his vigorous constitution stood him in good stead. While giving leadership locally and carrying on a travelling ministry, he also ran a 23-acre plum orchard and felled trees in the forest to supplement his income. Years later he would say that the Oregon years were the happiest of his life in ministry.

In 1909 the conference made the decision to reorganize the growing Mennonite Brethren church community into districts—Southern, Central and Northern—and a few years later the Pacific District was added. The Canadian churches became the Northern District, though for the first several years Manitoba was grouped with the Central District before becoming linked to the Saskatchewan churches in the Northern District. His father's old friend and colleague in the first ministry in southern Manitoba, David Dyck, became the first moderator.

Young Henry had a growing presence at conferences. At the second Central District conference held in Winkler in 1911, Henry gave one of the messages and was elected assistant secretary of the conference. At the first official Pacific District conference held in 1912 in Reedley, Henry came as a visitor and preached several sermons. Oregon, where Henry was then living, still belonged to the Central District and so the Pacific District asked the Central District whether they could secure Henry for two and a half months as evangelist. The following year Oregon was welcomed into the Pacific District and Henry was elected chairman of the conference.

### UNDER PRESSURE

These were years of intense activity and much outside pressure. In 1915 Henry moved his family back to Winkler, where they stayed for the winter of 1916 before moving back to his parents' farm in Minnesota. That's where they remained for the next several years. These became some of his most difficult years, probably as a result of a combination of overwork and tensions generated by other circumstances. There appears to have been a period during the war years when he suffered what may have been an emotional breakdown. By that time the family already included four children.

In 1916 America was on the cusp of entering the First World War. While Henry did some preaching in Canada, most of it was done in the U.S. That year he preached 275 times, though only 36 of those in Canada. Then his preaching dropped off sharply to a low of 38 appointments in 1920. The pressures of the war seem to have weighed heavily on him. In 1917 two of his brothers, Isaac and Abe, fled to Canada to evade the draft. On one occasion, friends in Nebraska heard about a plan of some American "patriots" to catch Henry at a train station, possibly to tar and feather him. The brethren took him to another station and he escaped without harm.

In 1918 Henry's aging parents decided to leave their Minnesota home for a new Mennonite Brethren settlement in Vanderhoof, B.C. There, mere months later, the aging family and church patriarch died. Before his death, on a visit back to Minnesota, the elder Voth had been interrogated by authorities [he called them secret police] about his sons Isaac and Abe.

Henry and Susie had been left alone on the Minnesota farm after the departure of Henry's brothers and parents, and in 1919 the couple decided to sell and move to Canada as well. Such a move meant finding a new means of support. They made Winkler their home and with the help of Susie's father, Johann Warkentin, they were able to buy a half section of farmland at Roland, north of Winkler.

Some years later, in 1931, when Warkentin's wife died, Henry and Susie moved their family onto Warkentin's farm near Winkler. That year Warkentin also stepped down from the leadership of the Winkler Church and Henry was asked to assume the role of leading minister for the church. It was a position he was to hold for the next 20 years.

From 1919 onward Henry and his family lived in Canada. It became the setting for most of his passion and energy, though his vision always extended beyond national borders. In the following nearly 35 years, he played a central role in the church at Winkler, the growing Canadian Mennonite Brethren community, and several key boards of the church. He was involved virtually till the day he died.

## CENTRAL ROLES

A quick summary gives an idea of how widely his leadership ranged. Beginning in 1921 and ending in 1946 he served as Canadian Conference moderator at least 19 times and took the role of vice-moderator of the General Conference (all the North American MB churches) at least a half dozen times during those same years. When the Canadian Conference adopted a structure that included a Board of Reference and Counsel in the mid-1940s, he became a member there too until 1951.

He was a member of the General Conference Board of Foreign Missions continuously from 1927 to 1953, serving either as vice-president or secretary, and a member of the General Conference Board of Education, responsible for Tabor College in Kansas, for the years 1930-36. Those were years when the overseas missions team rose to 140. His interest in city missions was reflected in the role he played for the conference mission in Minneapolis, whose board he chaired for a decade and a half starting in 1921. He was also repeatedly elected to the Board of Reference and Counsel of the General Conference during the 1930s and 1940s.

## ALL UNPAID WORK

It must be understood that all of this was unpaid work, as was his leadership in the church at Winkler. He might receive an allowance as an itinerant evangelist, and have help to cover travelling expenses, but the burden of the costs to support his family had to come out of his farm. This put enormous pressure on his family and was perhaps one of the factors that created the alienation with two of his sons that was never quite bridged.

Henry S. Voth faced a number of major challenges during his years in public ministry. One was the question of sheer survival at a time when church leaders rooted in farming communities were expected to find a way to support themselves. Some managed reasonably well, but for others it was an endless struggle. If Henry had not had his father-in-law's support, he could barely have managed. As it was, the family still struggled, since he had to be away so much of the time and, as leader of the Winkler church, others in greater need might come to the family and ask for help from them. It meant giving away chickens so others could eat or picking up the bill for someone's sack of flour. He could hardly refuse to give help.

Once, when he was about to leave on a preaching trip, Susie saw that his suit pants had worn out on the seat and so she sewed patches on them. Apparently they were quite obvious because, when he returned, the people of the church had supplied him with a brand new suit. Henry was still driving a 1917 Ford received from his father twenty years later. For Henry the concerns about finances followed him his entire life and once he even wrote about it in something he called the *Advantages and Disadvantages of being a Farmer Preacher*. It was hard on Susie too, though she fully supported him in his ministry. She may have escaped from some of the pressures of their life by a great amount of reading. Housework often appeared to take second place to her wide reading.

Another large challenge for H.S. Voth had to do with the coming of the Russian Mennonites. Beginning in 1923, waves of Mennonite refugees from the turmoil in Russia began arriving in western Canada. Large numbers came to Saskatchewan and Manitoba. Many of these were people who had benefitted from a better education in their homeland than the Mennonites who had come earlier and pioneered the west.

In Henry's own community, a Bible school begun in 1926 was a transplant of a Mennonite Brethren school begun in the Crimea in 1918. Abraham H. Unruh, John G. Wiens and Gerhard Reimer had all taught in the school in Russia and then picked up the reins again in Canada. The Peniel (Winkler) Bible School quickly flourished. These teachers were theologically astute men with rich experience. For Voth they were not a little intimidating and the people there felt he never really supported their project. It was other Winkler men such as J.A. Kroeker and A.A. Kroeker who stood behind the Bible school, while Henry threw his support behind Tabor College.

Beyond the local community, Mennonite Brethren churches grew rapidly in numbers and membership because of the influx of the immigrants. From 1923 to 1930, over twenty thousand Mennonite immigrants came to Canada, a significant number of them Mennonite Brethren. Henry's own church received 37 such families in those years.

### STRUGGLES AND VISION

When the immigrant flow began in 1923, there were 19 churches and 1774 members within the Mennonite Brethren churches in Canada; a decade later there were 54 churches and 4700 members and a church community probably close to twice that size. During eight of those 10 years he was conference moderator. Again and again he continued to be chosen to assume that role even though, by the early 1940s, the leaders of Russian background were probably in the majority and included many very able people.

H.S. Voth could continue to lead because no one could doubt his love for the church and his vision for its growth and well-being. His wife and partner, Susie, who possessed a clear vision herself, described him thus: "He had acute judgment, kept steadfastly to his path and possessed a clear vision in all his dealings. He knew what was right and to the best of his ability acted for it.

"The conference has scarcely had another person…who worked for its well-being with such heart and hand. His greatest interests had to do with missions and the well-being of our youth….He was willing to expend the last ounce of his energy for the building of God's kingdom." On the day he died he still wrote two letters to other church leaders. Both of them, Jacob Lepp, a fellow leader from Dalmeny, Sask., and P.R. Lange, the president of Tabor College, participated in his funeral.

His successor in Winkler, George D. Pries, described Voth as "peerless in giving direction and balance to the conference. He was a great inspirational leader, gentle but firm, and his guidelines were given respectful attention."

Another of the great challenges Voth faced had to do with reconciling his public and his private life. In part that had to do with the struggle with finances. But in part it also had to do with the extent to which his own children could follow his teaching. He was a strict father and did not hesitate to use discipline. If he was travelling to churches near by, he liked to take the children with him, even if they were reluctant to come along. The older boys discovered that if they slept in and lingered at the chores, they could to be left behind. The oldest son remembers how one Sunday their father got up early and did the chores by himself so they couldn't escape coming along.

Henry was deeply pained that some in his family might not follow him. At the graduation from high school of one of his children he gave an address on the Christian family and confessed that his family should not be considered a model. Yet even then he kept his children's respect. John wrote about an experience of travelling with his father and how moved he was by his father's preaching "art" and his ability to move his listeners. One of his daughters recalls how they resented his appeal for understanding when he was gone from home for long weeks during the winter months. Later, however, she said, "we came to appreciate what he was doing for others and took pride in his work. We were indeed privileged to be Dad's children."

Henry also never pressured his children into a conversion. He had such strong convictions about his children's freedom to choose, that he refused to put any pressure on them and two did not (to the parents' knowledge). It grieved Henry and Susie greatly and they will have spent many hours in prayer about it, but it did not change their loving approach.

A further challenge that H.S. Voth faced dealt with balance. He had grown up in a household deeply influenced by the pietist-evangelical awakening in the Mennonite colonies in Russia and the evangelicalism of the American frontier. His greatest desire was to see people come to salvation. His preaching from the outset called listeners to make a choice for Christ. He used familiar texts like Luke 23 ("Today you will be with me in paradise") or Matthew 11 ("Come unto me all you who labor...") or Genesis 19 (The salvation of Lot as by fire) to bring home his message.

While he was always most comfortable working in the German language—almost all his preaching was German—he could easily absorb information from the English. He used illustrations and anecdotes easily.

He tried to balance the interests of evangelism and education. Both had his strong support. He balanced foreign missions and home missions. While foreign missions had a very high profile within the conference during his years on the Board, he gave strong support to the MB city mission in Minneapolis and became personally involved in one of the early mission churches west of Morden, Manitoba. He took a leading role in conceptualizing what became known as the Canada Inland Mission in the early 1940s. He tried to balance witness and service. When MCC became heavily engaged in helping in the aftermath of World War II, Henry wrote to B.B. Janz in Coaldale that Mennonite Brethren should not stand idly by.

*Voth and his fellow ministers with Winkler Church young people baptized in 1945.*

They should rally to the cause. He added, however, "Above all, we should never neglect evangelism. That would heal, help and save."

When Henry died on October 25, 1953, he was 75 years old and homesick for heaven. At his funeral, the many friends who surrounded the family and casket were led by church leaders who typified his life and ministry: G.D. Pries, the local church leader, Abraham Unruh, the Bible school principal and prominent Russian Mennonite theologian, P.R. Lange, the Tabor College president, and Jacob Lepp, the Dalmeny Church patriarch and old friend. Besides musicians and choirs, a number of others spoke prayers and read obituaries in German and English. It marked the passage of a great leader and churchman. The words of Jacob Lepp probably captured the feelings of many best in a text taken from Deut. 33:3: "How he loved his people."

SOURCES

Among the sources drawn on for this chapter were Peter Penner's article, "Guardian of the Way: The Farmer Preacher, Henry S. Voth," *Mennonite Life*, September, 1982; Dennis Voth, "H.S. Voth, A Preliminary Sketch," paper written for a MB Biblical Seminary course in 1981; *Recollections of My Father*, by John H. Voth; "A Daughter Remembers," by Sara Klippenstein (published in the *Christian Leader*, Jan. 1, 1954); several articles from the *Zionsbote* (Nov. 11, 18 and 25, 1953); an item from *Konferenz-Jugendblatt*, June, 1946; "God gave much Grace" by William Schroeder in *Heritage Postings*, Dec. 13, 2001; and various documents and letters from the Henry S. Voth fonds at the Centre for Mennonite Brethren Studies, Winnipeg. Also consulted were Canadian and General Conference yearbooks for the period of Voth's conference leadership.

# Anna J. Thiessen

# THE WOMAN WHO CARED FOR "HER GIRLS"

*By Ingrid Koss*

A nna Thiessen saw Winnipeg, aptly named for the Cree words *win nipee* that mean "muddy waters," as a place of spiritual murkiness. "But praise God," exclaimed the woman who committed her life to bringing light into the heart of the city, "there are always people who want to be cleansed from sin."

Anna J. Thiessen entered the world on January 26, 1892 in Wassieljewka, Russia, the eldest of 13 children born to Jacob and Helena (Siemens) Thiessen. One of Anna's earliest memories was of her mother helping her fold her hands and close her eyes to pray. *"Lieber Heiland, mach mich fromm…"* Beloved Saviour, make me good….

She learned about Jesus from her parents, but Anna's life's dream began one Sunday when the teacher spoke of the need for missionaries in India. Anna decided then and there that she would go tell the Indian children about Jesus' love for them. Mother said otherwise. "It is too hot in India and you are not strong enough." When Mother rested with the younger children, Anna sat in the noontime sun without covering her head. "It was terribly hot," she recounted later, "but I never got sick." Flushed with success, Anna knew she had what it took to be a missionary.

---

*The Writer*

Ingrid Koss is a writer and playwright who lives in Winnipeg with her husband Rick and a menagerie of adult children, grandchildren and four-legged friends. Ingrid is a part-time student at Canadian Mennonite University. The more she studies theology, the more she appreciates the real people who boldly live it out. These are stories she loves to tell.

The Thiessens immigrated to southern Manitoba with five small girls in 1903. Anna had attended school in Russia but in Canada, more often than not, Mother depended on her help at home. When the family moved to the small Mennonite community of Herbert, Saskatchewan in 1906, fourteen-year-old Anna took up her "… duty, as the oldest daughter, to help Father cultivate the land, fight the prairie fire… the mosquitoes and the stones. It was a hard beginning for settlers." Hard indeed. By this time, Anna had watched three of her siblings die.

The Herbert Bible School opened in 1913 "to train young people for Sunday school work, evangelism, and the teaching of German." Anna eagerly attended and studied under John F. Harms. The same young woman who had dreamed of becoming a missionary to India suddenly felt unworthy of such a calling. Not wanting to put herself forward, she prayed to the Lord, "If you want me to serve Thee in a special way, let somebody ask me to come and help them."

## EYES ON WINNIPEG

Meanwhile, the Mennonites who had arrived in southern Manitoba in the 1870s and set themselves up in segregated farming settlements to avoid worldly evils began casting missional eyes towards Winnipeg. William and Helena Bestvater were hired in 1913 to lead the Mennonite Brethren Winnipeg city mission. William visited the Herbert Bible School and met all the students, including the "unworthy" Anna. In 1915, he invited her to join the City Mission for a six-month term. Anna thought, "India? Winnipeg?" With its population of nearly 150,000 people, she decided Winnipeg probably had as many heathens as any foreign country. She accepted the short-term call and stayed for more than 60 years.

Anna was 23 years old when she arrived in Winnipeg. Those who knew her in later years would hardly recognize the determined no-nonsense woman in her own self-description of that day. "It was a cold December morning when I arrived, timid and hesitant." Timidity notwithstanding, Anna plunged into the work that included visitation, Sunday worship services, midweek prayer meetings, Bible school classes, choir practice, a monthly women's association, handing out used clothing and household items, and—Anna's particular responsibilities—a children's Sunday school and Saturday German school, a girls' sewing class, and the Young People's association. In their spare time, Anna and the Bestvaters corresponded for those who could not read or visited German speakers who came in to Winnipeg's hospitals from rural areas.

The missionaries passed out tracts in seven languages as they went door to door among the city's poor immigrant neighborhoods. They prayed and

*The basement North End Chapel where Anna and her assistant (ca. 1920) gathered bright young girls.*

sang with householders, played with children so mothers could work un-hindered, and invited adults to church and children to Sunday school.

### NEVER INDIFFERENT

One elderly woman was concerned about her salvation and asked Anna to visit her soon. Before she could go, Anna heard the woman had died. "I reproached myself deeply for my indifference for a long time, but I know the Lord forgives when we come to him in penitence." But no one else thought of Anna as "indifferent." More typical was a husband's report that his wife, before she died, often spoke of Anna and the other missionaries as "… angels who came and sang for her."

Sometimes the missionaries were welcomed wholeheartedly; other times not. Once, when they tried to visit a woman they had previously be-friended, they were threatened with an axe by a young man splitting wood in a backyard. "Don't try to get in or I will use my axe," he said. Anna was not personally hurt by rejection, but commented, "People who don't want to know anything about Jesus—that hurts." She prayed for the woman and her axe-wielding son.

The missionaries ministered to people of all nationalities and denominations but held their worship services in German. This caused them to be regarded with suspicion at times, especially during the tumultuous years of the Great War of 1914-18 when German was the language of the enemy. Anna's early years in Winnipeg were tumultuous in other ways as well: thousands of Winnipeggers died of an influenza epidemic in 1918. Anna herself had the flu on November 11, 1918, the day the Great War ended. In 1919, the Winnipeg General Strike crippled the city for six weeks.

## ALWAYS IN FLUX

Illness in the city, war in Europe, floods and crop failures in the country meant a congregation always in flux as people moved further west to greener pastures. When the Northern District Conference (later, the Canadian Conference) faced a deficit in 1922, the board decided they could no longer support "their sisters in the City Mission." The many women attending the conference protested their dismissal and asked to be allowed to demonstrate, by a show of hands, their willingness to personally support this work. The show of hands was substantial, a silent shout of protest in a male-dominated setting. The Conference yearbook of 1923 shows that the women put their money where their hands were. Seventy-one individuals and women's groups—significantly listed by their own names, not their husbands'—donated a total of $391.03 for Anna's support. By daring to follow God's leading into the uncharted heart of the city, Anna unintentionally inspired other women of her conference also to follow God's leading into uncharted and daring territory—that of seeking God's will directly instead of through their husbands.

In June 1923, Anna went to the Bible Institute of Los Angeles (BIOLA). There, at the "Free Training School for Christian Workers in the Delightful Climate of Southern California," Anna studied to improve her Bible knowledge and her English. Anna gradually spoke and wrote more in English, but German remained her first language. "Na, excuse me for thinking German and the next minute English," she wrote to her siblings many years later.

## TWO RENTED ROOMS

When Anna returned to Winnipeg in 1925, Cornelius and Tina (Harms) Hiebert were leading the City Mission. Anna rented two rooms upstairs at 608 Mountain Avenue instead of staying with the Hieberts, whose generous hospitality kept their home bursting at the seams. Little did she know that this decision would literally open the door to her next ministry, the one with which she would become synonymous.

In 1925, European immigrants arrived in Canada by the hundreds every day, many passing through Winnipeg. Among them were Mennonites who arrived with little more than horrific memories of a war-torn homeland and a considerable travel debt owed to the Canadian Pacific Railway (CPR). Anna and Tina Hiebert regularly went to the Immigration Hall to serve buns with syrup and coffee while Cornelius Hiebert offered comfort from the Bible.

Coinciding with this newest wave of immigrants was a severe shortage of domestic servants for wealthy Canadians. Women and girls as young as 13 or 14 were aggressively sought out by prospective employers looking for cheap immigrant labour. Some of the girls had lost their families through separation or illness or murder and were all alone in their new country. Others arrived with families who were loath to let go of them in this new land where they didn't know the language or the customs. Would their daughters be safe? Who would care for them in this strange and threatening city? The mission workers took note of the girls who stayed in Winnipeg as domestics—where they lived and worked—and invited them to church.

The Mary Martha Home began with an innocuous event that only became significant in retrospect. One day in October—it was a Thursday, Anna remembered—two girls arrived at her doorstep, alone and afraid in the city. "I never thought of starting a home, but they pushed me. What could you do? They cried. They didn't have no place to go. They didn't know the language. They didn't have nothing," Anna reminisced. She had little more than prayer and two small rooms to offer them. "Still, I could not send them away into the darkness but tried to comfort and help them as best I could."

Anna welcomed them that afternoon and invited them back on their next day off. One girl told another, who told another, and soon it was a regular Thursday afternoon event. Within a few months, sixty girls were visiting Anna on a regular basis. She rented two more rooms and the girls crowded in. "Not a corner was left unused, even the stairway was put to use." And still the girls came. They came because they discovered the innate kindness and generous love that lay beneath Anna's frugal efficiency. They came because they saw in her the surrogate mother, the protector, the confidante, counsellor and confessor they were so desperate for. And they came because, as it turned out, Anna did have what it took to be a missionary.

In May, 1927, the City Mission rented the entire house at 608 Mountain. Without really planning it, a *Maedchenheim*—a home for girls—had been established with the legendary *Schwester* (Sister) Anna as its matron. *Schwester* Anna and her girls named their *Maedchenheim* the Mary Martha Home after the two sisters of Lazarus in John's Gospel: Martha prepared and served the meal while Mary listened at the feet of Jesus. Explained Anna, "Mary represents worship and Martha, service. Both must be found in a home. Martha service only would make work a burden, but with the spirit of Mary, it receives vision."

While most of the girls visited only on Sundays and Thursdays, there were always a few who lived at the Home between domestic jobs, while taking courses, when recuperating from illness or as they prepared to go out on foreign mission assignments. They paid as they were able, the MB conference contributed $20 a month, and the rest of the money for rent and upkeep came through donations.

Anna was as prudent a guardian of the finances as she was of the girls. Even so, one evening there was not enough money to pay the rent. Anna did what came naturally: she prayed to the Lord. She felt the Holy Spirit prompting her to go to the Hieberts because sometimes the mail for the Home was delivered there. "I went there," Anna explained. "Sister Hiebert and I talked for a while. She did not mention any mail and I hesitated to ask or to let her see how anxious I was." Anna started to leave. Then Sister Hiebert called out, "Anna, here is some mail for you. I almost forgot to tell you." Anna hurried home with the letters. Sure enough, there was enough money to pay the rent.

When the house at 608 Mountain became too small, Anna and the Mary Martha Home went on the move: to 413 Boyd Avenue in 1928, to 398 Mountain Avenue a year later, and finally to 437 Mountain in 1931. Always the homes were rented, and always there was the threat they could be sold at any time, especially once Anna and her girls made them more desirable.

One day Anna told a man delivering vegetables of her dream to buy the house so they would not have to move again. The man handed Anna a quarter and said, "This is the beginning of your building fund." Anna was tempted to laugh at the tiny amount. Instead, she mused, "Little is much when God is in it." A home committee was established and the building fund grew. Each donation, as small as 12¢ or as grand as $200, was recorded in Anna's meticulous writing. One woman donated a sewing machine. With a down payment of $750 and a mortgage for the rest, the home committee bought the house at 437 Mountain for $3,500 in 1931 and that's where they stayed.

*The Mary Martha Home at 437 Mountain Aveue; a haven for Anna Thiessen's "girls."*

At first, Anna accompanied the girls to the employment agency to find a job. This was too time-consuming so Anna placed ads in the paper under the name of the Mary Martha Home. When employers called, they invariably asked if they were speaking to Mary or Martha. To clear up the confusion, Anna told the Bible story that had inspired the name. Always the missionary, Anna chose to hear each doorbell or telephone ring as an opportunity to witness. "Awaken my heart and show your love, for whoever is coming or calling is being sent by the Lord."

### LIKE A MOTHER BEAR

The Mary Martha girls established a reputation as efficient and trustworthy workers and Anna began to flex her muscles as a labour boss. She lobbied the Winnipeg City Council for a universal day off for all of the city's domestic workers. Rather than letting employers choose, Thursday—the day the two girls first came to her—became the half day off for all domestic workers. Anna met with prospective employers and decided which girl

---

*"Martha's diligence is deeply impressed in my mind,*
*And Mary's heart, devout and pure.*
*Lord, let me be both Martha and Mary;*
*Let only this become my goal:*
*That I may choose first what is needful,*
*Service in the Kingdom with my full heart and soul."*

Author unknown, translated from German by Ida Toews, from The City Mission in Winnipeg by Anna Thiessen.

---

was suitable for them. She laid down the law: each girl was to have a suitable place to sleep (not in the basement) and be given adequate food (including meat). Girls were to be provided with a packed lunch on their Thursdays off. They were also to have Sundays off. Employers who did not comply or who treated a girl poorly went onto Anna's blacklist and never got a Mary Martha girl again.

At the same time, Anna and the other Home workers trained the girls and accompanied them to their first day of work. They kept close tabs on the girls and visited any who did not show up at the Home or at church for a period of time. Were they sick? Were they being mistreated? Were they straying from the Lord's way?

In the 1920s and '30s, most of the girls were paying off their own or their family's travel debt (*Reiseschuld)* of $200 per person. Many of them were sending money home. It was a strange state of affairs that many Mennonite families were being supported by their daughters in the city instead of by their fathers and sons on the family farm. For Mennonites who valued separation from the world as a godly virtue, having daughters living in the city in and amongst the worldly evils was frightening indeed. It was a relief that someone was watching over their daughters.

The girls themselves eagerly anticipated their days off when upwards of 200 young women crowded into the Home. They sang around a piano or guitar, did fancy needlework to sell, and socialized with friends. Others sought private counsel from *Schwester* Anna or the other mission workers regarding hurts from their past or struggles in their workplace. Anna listened to all who came to her. She prayed with them and used her considerable influence to improve their circumstances. She befriended each girl, believed each girl and protected each one like a mother bear. She was particularly protective of their eternal salvation.

Every Thursday included a time when coffee was served and the girls ate their packed lunches, as well as a time of Bible reading and prayer. Under the banner of the Tabitha *Verein*, a society named for another virtuous New Testament woman who demonstrated the twin virtues of service and worship, the girls of the Home enjoyed a regular Thursday evening service

*A severe-looking Anna Thiessen surrounded by her young Mary Martha Home charges in 1932.*

where they heard the word of God and joined together in prayer. The life of a domestic was usually difficult and through the Tabitha *Verein*, the girls were challenged to make a first-time or a deeper commitment to the Lord. Following their motto, the girls organized into teams to visit the sick, plan and lead the worship service, do handwork to sell for the Home and introduce newcomers to the Home and the city.

### ONCE WEALTHY, NOW SERVING

Many of the girls came from wealthier and happier times in Russia where their own families had employed Russian servants. Now, with the tables turned, Anna encouraged them to think of their domestic service not as a reversal in fortune but as an opportunity to build God's kingdom. "It is surely not a matter of chance that the Lord sent our Christian girls into the big cities to serve in the homes of those we would not reach otherwise. Some of these homes did not wish to have repentance and holiness preached to them…. And then our sisters entered homes of the wealthy, the influential, and the professional people of our country as servants. Their quiet, Christian diligence presented the message of the Cross as powerfully as a sermon."

Marriage was a major topic of interest when hundreds of young women gathered to socialize. Those with boyfriends often met them "under the clock at Eaton's" because Anna had a firm rule of "no men in the Home"; only ministers could visit the girls. This caused one of the girls who frequented the Mary Martha Home in the 1930s to complain, "Where the girls ever managed to get husbands, I don't know." With a heavy workload and only a close-knit community of women with which to socialize, many of the girls found few social opportunities to meet men. From Anna's point of view, it seemed that many of the girls, and especially her co-workers, seemed always to be leaving the work and getting married. The numerous wedding photos in Anna's personal effects suggest this was true. The married girls returned to visit, proudly introducing their husbands and each new baby to the woman who had given them a start in the city and a place to belong.

In an era when Mennonite women rarely, if ever, spoke in front of men in formal settings, Anna reported to the delegates of the Northern District MB Conference every summer. She is remembered as a meek and peace-loving woman, yet she was quite capable of speaking her mind when the need arose. In 1937 she lectured the parents at the conference who sent their daughters to the city before they were mature enough to withstand the temptations of city life.

Some of the girls reminisced in later years that *Schwester* Anna was somewhat stern, that "things might have gone better with a little more humour." One woman remembered when a new girl arrived at the Home and sang a German love song in the hall: *Du, du liegst mir im Herzen.* (You, you, lie in my heart…) "That was out of the question, as far as Anna was concerned. No Christian girl should sing a song like that! The girl was aggravated and chose to sing it even more."

How was this problem resolved? Doubtless, Anna would have prayed about it and taken it to the group of women from Winnipeg's MB congregations who regularly prayed with her, and then she would have spoken to the girl.

Gradually the needs of the girls changed. They paid off their travel debts and became more independent. They took on day work in sewing factories or trained as teachers and nurses. They became comfortable with the language and customs of their new country. In a rare reversal of roles, Anna's girls—not their husbands and fathers—confidently led the wave of rural Mennonites who moved into the city. As the urban Mennonite community grew, new girls who arrived in Winnipeg were more likely to have relatives and friends to look out for them in the city. There were murmurings that the Home had outlived its usefulness.

Still, one young woman who came to Winnipeg to train as a lab technician in the 1950s was so homesick that she was ready to quit until she and

*At Anna Thiessen's funeral many of her "girls" gathered one more time.*

her sister discovered "The Home." It was not just a place to rent, it was like being with family, getting to know women of all ages, laughing and eating and praying together. And always there were stories, fascinating stories from days gone by. Though many things had changed drastically over the years, *Schwester* Anna's peaceful presence at the Home still provided a necessary sense of safety and belonging.

## CLOSING THE HOME

The MB Conference didn't see it that way. Even with a new wave of immigrants pouring into Winnipeg after WWII, the male-dominated Conference decided the Home had run its course. In 1959, the Mary Martha Home closed and Anna moved into an apartment with Tina Friesen, a longtime friend and co-worker.

In December 1961, Anna wrote in one of many letters to her siblings, "The Mary Martha Home is gone, but not the girls and they help that I don't get lonely." As Anna had faithfully ministered to her girls over a lifetime, the "girls," many of whom were now in their 50s and 60s, remained faithful to her.

A group of them celebrated her 70th birthday with a dinner party. In case "the girls" had not yet got the all-important message of salvation, Anna typed Bible verses onto their serviettes so they could read them while they ate. Anna may have reached the far side of her prescribed three score and ten years, but she was not about to give up on her life's work. "These years are all years of grace and I like to live accordingly…," she reflected. "I feel like when I was 16 years old, but … I am not looking forward to life, but look forward to graduate from faith to sight."

In fact, Anna enjoyed another 15 years of grace. She became her family's correspondent, historian and spiritual guardian. Her journals show a careful record of visits paid to and received from her girls, co-workers and ministers. She listed those who had gone to be with the Lord, "the glory graduates," she liked to call them.

Anna herself graduated to glory on April 1, 1977. More than a hundred of her girls gathered at her funeral in the Elmwood Mennonite Brethren Church to pay tribute to a remarkable woman who always befriended them, always believed in them, always protected them, and spent her life in the tireless pursuit of their salvation.

SOURCES

Information for this biography was drawn from "Autobiographical Sketches from our Diaries," by William and Helena Bestvater; an item by Abe Dueck on the Herbert Bible School on the *Global Anabaptist Mennonite Encyclopedia Online (GAMEO)*; Marlene Epp's essay "The Mennonite Girls' Homes of Winnipeg: A Home Away From Home," in the *Journal of Mennonite Studies;* Frieda Esau's interviews with Maria Warkentin, Kathie Loewen and Mitzie Peters on file at the Centre for MB Studies; A. Grenke's interview of Anna Thiessen in the Manitoba Museum; G.D. Huebert's item on "Mary-Martha Home (Winnipeg, Manitoba)" in *GAMEO;* Harold Jantz's item, "Mother of Many—Anna Thiessen," in *The Mennonite Brethren Herald;* translations of sections of *Yearbooks of the Northern District Conference, 1916-23*; Neoma Jantz's biography, "Sister to Many: Anna Thiessen (1892-1977)," in *Women Among the Brethren;* Frieda Esau Klippenstein's "Doing What We Could: Mennonite Domestic Servants in Winnipeg, 1920's to 1950's," in the *Journal of Mennonite Studies;* Peter Penner's *No Longer at Arms Length*; Ken Reddig's "A Call and a Dream" DVD, produced for the Centennial Committee of the Mennonite Brethren Church of Manitoba, and his "Anna J. Thiessen – City Missionary," in *Profiles of Mennonite Faith;* a 1937 *Saturday Evening Post* article, "Some Busy Women"; Anna Thiessen's own *The City Mission in Winnipeg,* translated by Ida Toews; Anna Thiessen's personal correspondence; and Marguerite Wieler's "The Mary Martha Home, Winnipeg, Manitoba: Its Origin and Developments." A footnoted copy of this chapter is on file at the Centre for Mennonite Brethren Studies in Winnipeg.

# Cornelius N. Hiebert

# A PREACHER OF THE PEOPLE

*By Menno Martens*

The story of Cornelius N. Hiebert is one of an unassuming but gifted country boy who grew up to have a profound influence upon hundreds of lives, many within Canada. He became a pioneer Mennonite Brethren evangelist, dedicated to God, working with a keen sense of God's blessing, direction and leadership. Most people knew him simply by his initials, CN, a common naming practice in the early decades of the church.

Born into poverty in 1881, raised in Minnesota, handicapped by a farm accident, frail and without the advantage of education, CN at age 23 spoke to the Lord in a cornfield and uttered a few simple but heartfelt words. "Lord," he said, "I am willing to do whatever you want me to do. If I cannot get enough education to become a preacher, I am willing to be a Bible colporteur and go house to house to speak with people about the salvation of their souls."

It seems the Lord took him at his word and gave Hiebert a ministry that extended beyond what he could have imagined, taking him to many states in the United States, to many parts of Canada, and also to Europe and South America. A later church leader, David Ewert, once said of

*The Writer*

Menno Martens is a retired teacher and comprehensive high school principal living in Swift Current, Sask. He has played an active role in his home church, the Bridgeway Community (MB) congregation, has served as Canadian Conference secretary and also was a member of boards both provincially and nationally. Most recently he represented the Board of Faith and Life on the executive board of the Canadian Conference.

him, "Perhaps no servant of the church was so widely known and so greatly loved in our entire brotherhood as C.N. Hiebert."

And why was that? The simple answer appears to be that Hiebert was truly faithful to what Jesus described as the first and greatest commandment: to love God and love people. Moreover, he possessed a uniquely colourful, warm and attractive personality.

CN's parents, Nikolai and Marie Hiebert, came to Minnesota from Russia in 1876. Nikolai made a living as a blacksmith, a farmer and small-scale flour miller whose skills, good as they were, hardly provided even the basic necessities for the family of 10 children. Years later when CN had his own family, he would regale his children with stories of poverty from his childhood. And what a masterful story-teller he was! His listeners were accustomed to respond both with laughter and tears. At Christmas gatherings his children cried when he told them of one Christmas when his only treat was a *Zwieback* (double bun).

But poverty was not the only problem of CN's childhood. While hauling water in icy conditions he slipped and broke his right arm. It was never set properly, stiffened up completely and got to be of little use. For the rest of his life he did all his writing on a clipboard held on his lap because he couldn't lift his arm to reach a desk or table.

At the age of 14, CN accepted Christ as his Saviour. Nine more years came and went. School for him ended at grade seven. Working at home and for neighbours to help support the family became his life. Deep within, however, he nursed a desire to do more in service to God. With some trepidation he approached his father with a request for help. Would his father, he asked, let him use a horse and buggy in winter to do some Bible colportage work? And would his father be willing to buy some Bibles to help him get started? The answer was yes.

## ON THE ROAD FOR GOD

From small beginnings as a colporteur in his own community in the first decade of the 1900s, CN's radius of operations expanded to Minnesota, South Dakota, Nebraska, Kansas, Oklahoma and Colorado.

CN never owned a car. He travelled by horse and buggy, train or on foot. He found accommodations with godly people who extended hospitality to him. Sometimes they asked him to preach. Although no pulpit pounder, he put a great deal of emotion into his delivery and typically brought his sermons to a climax with his illustrations. Wherever he went, he spoke to people about their salvation. As for monetary profits from his Bible selling business, they were never great. CN probably gave away more Bibles than he sold.

Once he went for 14 days with total sales of no more than 25 cents, of which his profit was five cents. During that time, he was asked to preach at a local church. Before the service ended, a gentleman in the pews rose and said, "I believe we ought to support brother Hiebert. He came to our home and spoke to us about our salvation. And he prayed with my sons and gave them tracts. I move that we have a collection for him." The proceeds that evening were $50. Once more, God had supplied CN's needs.

In 1908, CN married Tina Harms, a young nurse whom he had met in his travels to Oklahoma. The following year a daughter was born, the first of a family of seven children: Esther, Albert, Erwin, Martha, Ruth, Naomi and Clarence.

One of CN's favorite Bible passages was Genesis 12 where Abraham was asked by God to go to the land that God would show him. Like Abraham, CN was on the move most of his life. His daughter Esther

*CN from childhood to old age.*

counted 24 moves made by the family. Clarence, the youngest son, counted 17 moves. One never knew when CN would say, "God is calling—we will move." Once when asked her address, Esther answered, "A suitcase."

## INVITED TO CANADA

At a convention of the Mennonite Brethren churches of North America in 1909, just before the creation of the Northern District, CN was invited to go to Saskatchewan to do colportage work among the newly arrived Mennonite immigrants. The deal was that the Rosthern community would furnish CN with horse and buggy transportation and would pay him an annual salary of $250, the assumption being that he could additionally make a profit of $250 selling books and thus have an income of $500 per annum. For the next six years CN resided for short periods in the Saskatchewan communities of Langham, Hepburn, Dalmeny, Waldheim and Herbert. It was the Dalmeny church in Saskatchewan that ordained CN as a minister in 1913.

The very first yearbook of the newly-formed Northern District in 1910 notes that CN was recognized as *Reiseprediger* (circuit preacher) for the Rosthern district and given a half-year assignment there. It also reports that the remuneration was increased from $30 to $40 a month and that the churches were happy with his ministry.

In 1915 the family was back in Minnesota for a year. In 1916 they moved to Oklahoma. Colportage work occupied him in both those and the neighbouring states. In 1917, they were back to Saskatchewan, where the terrible Spanish flu epidemic was raging. Sometimes CN was called upon to speak at funerals morning and afternoon. At one afternoon service three people from one family lay in the caskets.

In 1919 CN moved his family to California, so he could become a student at the Bible Institute of Los Angeles for two winters and continue evangelistic work in California, Oregon and Idaho in the summer. The family in the meantime lived and worked in the San Joaquin Valley, harvesting peaches and grapes. An indefatigable worker himself, he regarded indolence as one of the worst faults anyone could have and saw to it that his children learned to be productive citizens. He liked to joke about laziness, his favorite line being about someone who asked, "Why does everyone think I am lazy when no one has ever seen me work?"

## CITY MISSIONARY

Move after move followed, the next major one being to Winnipeg in 1925 to take up "City Mission" work there. Between 1923 and 1930 more than 20,000 Mennonite refugees arrived in Canada, a significant number of whom settled in Winnipeg. It was there that the Mennonite Brethren had their only urban church in Canada, a place called the North End MB Mission. The work had been started by Mennonite Brethren from Winkler and led first by William Bestvater and then by Erdmann A. Nickel. In 1925 the small Mennonite Brethren conference grew from 1774 members to 2080 members, a 17% increase in one year. Many of these were immigrants CN welcomed, along with newcomers of other backgrounds and Mennonite groups.

When the Hieberts came they identified their role as that of visiting families in homes and hospitals, preaching and distributing clothes, listening empathetically to the stories of pillage, murder and rape which the immigrants told, and even supplying food as needed. The oft-repeated process of welcoming refugees became a routine. CN might meet a typical group of up to hundreds of immigrants in the immigration hall, have a bit of hymn singing with them, preach a short sermon and offer a prayer. Then he and his helpers would serve them all a little lunch of coffee, buns and syrup, items that they had bought. Thereafter things became more difficult. The clothing depot for the newcomers was set up in the Hiebert basement. Moreover, the Hieberts took it upon themselves to feed and house needy people who came to their door. Since most refugees spoke no English, they required assistance at every stage: getting short-term and long-term accommodations, jobs, food and transportation. Everything.

Getting food for all of them was actually the first order of business. CN had his own partial solution to that problem. In the coldest part of winter he would persuade someone to take him a distance of about 150 kilometers north to a lake, where he would buy hundreds of pounds of frozen fish at half a cent per pound. Back in Winnipeg, he would bury the fish in the deep snow in the backyard and supply his own family, guests and other needy people from this stockpile.

Meanwhile, the Conference secured a large house to accommodate the many single women looking for work as domestics for wealthy families in Winnipeg and placed a caring house mother, Anna Thiessen, in charge.

The burden was not CN's alone but also his family's. Guests in the Hiebert home who came and stayed or who just came for some hours had to be shown hospitality. When laundry piled up, the children were assigned to the hand-operated washing machine and other duties. But for Mrs. Hiebert it was sometimes almost too much. She wrote her teacher-daughter Esther—married to Ben Horch—in 1929, "I can hardly manage alone. We had a lot of company again—18 for night and 25 for Sunday dinner."

Unfortunately, Hiebert's frugality and ingenuity were not enough: there had to be cash. The Canadian Conference recognized this need and dispatched CN to the United States to collect money, clothing, bedding and whatever else could be useful back in Winnipeg. In his report at the conference in 1926, CN related that in addition to his work in Winnipeg, he had preached 113 times and made 206 home visits elsewhere. Folks welcomed him everywhere.

He was away from home as much as three months at a time. That circumstance brought Heinrich S. and Anna Rempel into the Winnipeg scene as assistants in the City Mission. CN and H.S. Rempel had a fine working and personal relationship. The church in Winnipeg prospered and grew. In a single year, 1926, the membership of the North End chapel nearly doubled.

That rapid growth of the Winnipeg church membership led to a new problem. The basement building used by the City Mission was too small. CN, who had assumed the position of pastor in 1926, was called upon in 1929 to travel for the purpose of canvassing for money to enable the congregation to erect a new building. By the summer of 1930 the new building was completed. In his time in Winnipeg, from 1925 to 1938, CN officiated at 57 weddings and baptized 253 persons. From those humble beginnings in a basement, the Winnipeg Mennonite Brethren community has grown until—in 2008—it numbered over four thousand in 18 congregations. CN's legacy was to embrace the city.

### A NEW MINISTRY OF HEALING

During the years 1936-38, C.N. Hiebert divided his time between Hillsboro, Kansas, and Winnipeg, Manitoba. From his base in Winnipeg, CN did evangelistic work in the U.S. Southern Conference. The break with Winnipeg was finally made in October of 1941 and Hillsboro became home. There, in August of 1942, the Hieberts moved into the first house they actually owned. Unfortunately, CN's wife Tina died only three days later. Her sudden death left CN grief-stricken, the loss exacerbated by the automobile accident experienced by daughter Esther and her husband Ben Horch while coming to the funeral from California. Both survived but Esther, a violinist, had her arm amputated. All grief aside, CN was left facing the task of single-handedly raising those in the family still at home.

The following year CN married Tina's sister, Helen Harms, a Saskatchewan schoolteacher. They settled down in Hillsboro and together carried on the work to which CN felt called. Life was normal. Although there were preaching assignments in different parts of the U.S. and Canada, the pace was no longer as hectic as before.

*C.N. and his teacher wife and partner, Helen (Harms) Hiebert*

All of that changed when in 1948 CN was called upon to minister to the many Mennonite refugees who had fled from Russia and migrated to Paraguay. He was 67, an age when most people retired from active duties. (He was close to 70 by the time this assignment ended.) From Asuncion, Paraguay, CN and his wife undertook the journey to the Chaco in a smallish boat that plied the Paraguay River. On board were 134 Mennonite newcomers and others from Europe. En route CN preached and wife Helen told stories to the children. The day came when all had to disembark and sit all night in a large unfurnished building. Many had already become ill. The next day all were loaded on a cattle train for the last leg of the journey, a distance of only 150 kilometers but requiring 17 hours of travel! They were in what was called "the green hell" and in the centre of it lay the Mennonite colonies.

Although no one would describe the Chaco colonies of 1950 as a holiday destination for the elderly, the Hieberts made themselves at home there and went to work. Hiebert writes that each day they "walked or drove with oxen from village to village and from house to house preaching, comforting and helping along financially with the help we received from friends in the U.S. and Canada. We visited every village in the colonies of Fernheim, Neuland, Friesland, Volendam and Menno Colony. We also visited the refugee settlements in Brazil, Uruguay and Argentina."

CN, who had never been very strong physically, experienced the trauma of having to undergo a hernia operation while in Paraguay. The hospital where this took place had an earthen floor, no running water and no electricity after 10 p.m. During the surgery the power went off and the operation was prolonged to the point that the local anesthetic wore off. While one nurse held a flashlight and another chased away flies, the surgery proceeded. The doctor suggested that to take his mind off the pain CN should preach them a sermon. Whether he did or not is not said. His post-surgery conditions, however, were described. The water was contaminated, meat was in short supply, vegetables were wormy and the hospital was greatly overcrowded. Typically, instead of complaining, CN spoke of the reasons to be thankful in a place where so many Mennonite patients, unlike himself, also had the stress of having to cope with the loss of loved ones in war-torn lands far away.

Not content with all that was entailed in visiting so many hurting refugees and hearing of their bitter wartime experiences, the Hieberts felt led to visit the missionaries in Colombia. This visit required them to travel by river boat to several different stations. That went well enough, but the trip by horseback did not. When the horses used on the tour had to jump a small mountain stream, CN fell off and fractured his hand. How this injury was treated cannot be discovered from his writings. Instead, what he talks about subsequently is the visit to a home where people were "hungry for the Word of God." Something of a record keeper, CN noted that on the South American trip he and Helen visited 1,573 homes and held "many meetings." Back home on North American soil at last, CN made it his task to travel to the MB churches in Canada and the U.S., giving reports of their experiences in the southern hemisphere.

## A NEW GENERATION OF REFUGEES

In 1952, Hiebert received yet another call to minister abroad. Again there were refugees who needed help and comfort, this time in Germany. At that time thousands of refugees—some of them Mennonites—were escaping to the west from the East Zone of Germany. In Neuwied, Germany, the Hieberts rented a room and began conducting services for the refugees, first in private homes and then in a rented hall. Also, many refugees were sent to the Hieberts for a night's lodging and breakfast the next morning. Of course, guests had to sleep on the floor. To visit all the people in this growing congregation, CN went on foot, something he had done all his life, in his words "walking, walking, walking until our shoes gave out." Before long, the church had a Sunday school, choir, prayer meetings and worship services. Eventually, the Hieberts even organized a

Sunday school teachers' training class. It drew girls, but no boys; the girls were dedicated students and became effective church workers.

A huge refugee camp was located in Linz, Austria. The Hieberts travelled there by train and saw for themselves "31 camps of barracks, housing thousands of homeless, helpless, hopeless, breadless, Christless refugees." The response of the Hieberts was the same here as everywhere else they went. They made visitations, distributed necessities, held meetings and distributed tracts.

At Neustadt, Germany, the Hieberts became involved in ministry at an MCC-operated institution for people traumatized by the horrors of war. Children were brought there, 50 at a time, to recover. After three months they were dismissed and another 50 were brought in. Another institution was dedicated to helping old and young mentally disturbed people. Many teenagers had suffered mental breakdowns as a result of war, and many older people had become emotionally and mentally disturbed by the rigors of their flight to some place of safety. The never-complaining Hieberts saw these places as open doors, just what they had asked the Lord for.

The two-year assignment came to a close in 1954, but the work was not fully done until the Hieberts had reported to the churches of their experiences in Europe.

The sale of the Hiebert home in Hillsboro, Kansas, 1955, was followed by the purchase of a place in Reedley, California. There they lived until the time of CN's death in 1975, two months short of his 94th birthday. Helen Hiebert died in Reedley in 1983.

The death of C.N. Hiebert brought tributes from far and wide. He had many friends for he had made it his practice to get acquainted with everyone he met. Many knew him as the kindly shepherd who had brought them into the fold of God. Maybe the best tribute came from a former refugee, who said, "As a little girl I felt this man was more like Jesus than anyone else I knew."

The final destiny of C.N. Hiebert is described well in Daniel 12: 3: "Those who are wise shall shine as the brightness of the sky, and those who lead many to righteousness, like the stars forever and ever." On his grave marker are these four words: "Chosen to bear fruit."

## SOURCES

Material for this chapter was drawn from *Mennonites in Winnipeg* by Leo Driedger; Esther Horch's biography, *C.N. Hiebert was my Father* and its review by David Ewert; Peter Letkemann's *The Ben Horch Story;* John A. Toews's *A History of the Mennonite Brethren Church;* A.H. Unruh's *Die Geschichte der Mennoniten-Bruedergemeinde;* a biographical sketch of CN from his memorial service bulletin; Alma Beier's *Hiebert Family Record;* two items by Clarence Hiebert on his father; an unpublished autobiography by C.N. Hiebert, *My Life's Story;* and an essay by Victor Wall on "Mennonites and Politics in Paraguay," published in the bulletin of the California Mennonite Historical Society.

# Heinrich A. Neufeld

# WHO WOULD SPEAK FOR THE RUSSIAN MENNONITES?

### By Harold Jantz

Not all Mennonites in Canada and the United States were moved by news of the tragic plight of Mennonites filtering out of Russia in 1919-20. An itinerant minister from southern Saskatchewan, Heinrich A. Neufeld, was, however. So affected, he felt driven to do something about it. Why? A providential coincidence played a critical role for Neufeld.

Neufeld's active years cover a relatively small segment of the life of the Mennonite Brethren church in Canada—they began in 1912 and ended in 1933. He came as an immigrant to Canada in 1912 and found a home in Herbert, Saskatchewan, where he almost immediately became leader of the church. When he died, the account reads like that of a national leader given a state funeral. Again, why?

To find the answer it is necessary to remember that his years overlap entirely with the most tumultuous years for Mennonites in Russia, who endured the most terrible experiences in their history and then desperately sought a country of refuge. In that story Neufeld played a uniquely important role.

---

*The Writer*

Harold Jantz has loved the stories of the Mennonite Brethren from his youth and enjoyed the opportunity to tell many of them during a two-decade tenure as editor of the *Mennonite Brethren Herald*. Later he enjoyed a similar opportunity with *ChristianWeek*, an evangelical newspaper that serves Christians of many denominations across Canada.

## GREW UP WITH LITTLE

Heinrich Neufeld had a difficult childhood and youth, much of it characterized by a struggle with poverty. He was born in 1865—not long after the Mennonite Brethren movement had its beginning—in the village of Kronsweide in the Mennonite Old Colony. Heinrich's father had worked as a miller on a Mennonite estate. Unfortunately, the estate owner died, the Neufelds bought a farm in a nearby colony and then Heinrich's father too died. Heinrich was only 11. Because his mother was too poor to support them, Heinrich and his older siblings were farmed out to various well-to-do landowners, not all of whom treated them well.

Heinrich doesn't appear to have had much education. It certainly didn't go beyond the sixth level offered in most Mennonite villages, for at the age of 14 he was apprenticed to a carpenter and coach-maker. He was a keen learner, however. It was during this time that he and his older brother Hermann began attending church, went through catechism classes and were baptized. Later, Hermann would say the experience had been laced with tradition and made little impact on their lives. Their story suggests that both hungered for a deeper encounter with God.

For Heinrich, the apprenticeship was followed by a time of work in a Mennonite-owned foundry and then several years in the obligatory forestry service required of military-age Mennonite youth. Since the forestry camp happened to be located on the edge of the Sagradowka Mennonite colony, he often stayed with friends in the colony and there he met the woman who became his first wife, Anna Martens. They married in 1891. He grew very close to the Martens family and followed them in a move to the Don River area, where they tried a milling and farming venture. It failed, however, and the young Neufeld family eventually returned to the Sagradowka colony and finally to the village of Muensterberg. He appears to have done diligent and good work, yet seldom did it really pay off materially.

## YOUNG PREACHER

During those years as a young married man, Heinrich became increasingly active as a preacher. He had been baptized in the Mennonite tradition in his mid-teens, but at the age of 18 he experienced a life-transforming conversion and was baptized by the early Mennonite Brethren leader Aron Lepp and received into the young MB movement. He preached his first sermon before turning nineteen. He had a gift for preaching and was ordained to the ministry while still in his twenties. Already in Russia he commenced the wide-ranging travelling ministry that was to characterize the rest of his life. (Interestingly, he was not alone. His brother Hermann had a very similar experience and began a very fruitful ministry in Russia

*Heinrich and Aganetha Neufeld with their growing family (ca 1915).*

that led the Mennonite Brethren to ordain him as an *Aeltester* [bishop]. An account of his life is told in *Hermann and Katharina: Their Story*.)

Four decades after he first heard it, Heinrich's brother-in-law could still vividly recall a sermon Heinrich preached taken from Ezekiel 47. The text pictures a stream issuing out from the temple of God that broadens and deepens as it flows. Some people only step into it up to their ankles, when we were meant to bathe and swim and find cleansing for our sins in it. Heinrich immersed himself in a pietistic reading of the Scriptures and developed a vivid, forceful and inviting way of preaching. He wanted his hearers to encounter God. He prepared well and had little difficulty keeping the attention of listeners.

In addition to his gift at preaching, he sang well and enjoyed music, especially the new songs coming into the life of the church in those years. He was the village choir conductor in Altonau in the Sagradowka colony and became both a choir conductor and preacher in the first church he came to in America. His choirs noted the careful attention he paid to the song texts.

Neufeld's personal life, however, was often touched by tragedy. In 1901, a decade after he married, his wife of only 29 years died. She left him with four young children. Three had already died in infancy. Some time later he married a young widow, Aganetha Dyck, who became the mother to another seven children.

## OFF TO AMERICA

Heinrich's first wife's kin, the Martens family, decided in 1905 to make the move to America and wanted Heinrich and his family to accompany them, but he didn't have the money to pay for it. In 1909 Hutterites loaned them the money and that September Heinrich and his family arrived in Carpenter, South Dakota, to begin a new life for themselves on this continent. His brother-in-law wrote that virtually from the "first days" Heinrich served the Mennonite Brethren church in Carpenter as "preacher and conductor." He also launched into an attempt at farming, with his young family helping. He was healthy, strong and ambitious and made a valiant effort—and may have taken some unnecessary risks, according to his brother-in-law. Whatever the case, despite his efforts, his first attempt failed.

Such setbacks notwithstanding, Heinrich's vision for ministry did not flag. He didn't spend a great amount of emotional energy on his losses and wherever he had the opportunity, he engaged in a travelling ministry. In 1912, Heinrich and Aganetha decided to make another move and that May, they settled onto a farm near Herbert in southern Saskatchewan. It became their permanent home. Heinrich immediately took up a leading role in the Herbert church and soon became one of the key *Reiseprediger* [itinerant ministers] of the young Canadian Mennonite Brethren movement. In those years the Saskatchewan churches were organized into two circuits, one centred around Herbert and the other around Rosthern.

Itinerant ministers in the early 1900s needed a healthy constitution and Heinrich possessed it. Travel took place on primitive roads and could be done by buggy, train (for longer distances), even by foot, and meetings might be held in homes, churches or schoolhouses. The preacher had to adapt to many different beds, always in the homes of people of the church. Much of the early work happened in Mennonite settings and certainly among German-speaking people if they were not Mennonite. Aganetha commented that "his heart beat very warmly for all our Mennonite people."

Others might have seen Heinrich as an evangelist, but he would say that he was not a "revivalist preacher," rather someone who saw himself called to "strengthen and admonish believers" in their faith. He did such ministry very well. On the farm, however, he always remained poor and the income from his travelling ministry never allowed the family to really prosper. The poverty of the Neufelds caused tensions for Heinrich within his own family and at times with others too.

## TERRIBLE EVENTS IN RUSSIA

While Heinrich had a widening sphere of influence through his preaching ministry, if there had not been a World War, the Bolshevik revolution, civil war and devastation in Russia, his significance for Canadian Mennonites might have remained a relatively minor one. As it was, he became a key figure in the effort to

*Heinrich loved his family, but his resources to provide adequately were always stretched.*

help thousands of Mennonites in the early years of the Soviet Union to flee that place of suffering. His role lay especially in the support he gave at particularly critical junctures to Bishop David Toews of the Canadian Mennonite Board of Colonization, when the whole enterprise could have collapsed and no effective mechanism could have emerged to assist the huge movement of people. As it was, eventually over 20 thousand Mennonites arrived in Canada between 1923 and 1930. It transformed the Canadian Mennonite communities and the Mennonite Brethren as a church.

As the terrible months of civil war were ending in 1920 and the Bolsheviks were gradually gaining control of the Mennonite areas of southern Russia, the problem faced by them was that no country offered easy access for those who were desperate to leave. Both Canada and the United States had effectively closed their doors to Mennonites as well as to Hutterites and Doukhobours. A very small quota allowed a few in, but for most the opposition to military duty had sealed the borders. The Canadian government had an additional reason to be unhappy with Mennonites because its most conservative groups had agitated strongly for German schools taught by their own teachers. The conflict boiled over into sharp confrontations and by the beginning of the 1920s a strong likelihood existed that thousands might want to leave for a more hospitable homeland elsewhere.

In some ways an even greater problem existed for Canadian and U.S. Mennonites themselves when the disaster in Russia began to become apparent in 1919 and 1920. How could people half a world away be helped? The flow of correspondence and news that had existed prior to World War 1 between people on both sides of the Atlantic had virtually ceased after the revolution, civil war and the Red seizure of power in late 1919 and early 1920. Few in America knew of the thousands of deaths, destruction of property and the rape and pillage that had occurred there.

Even when reports began appearing in publications like the *Mennonitische Rundschau* [the newspaper of all Mennonites of Russian background], the *Zionsbote* [the church-wide Mennonite Brethren paper], *Der Christliche Bundesbote* [General Conference Mennonite Church paper], *Vorwaerts* [MB-edited German-language paper for a general audience] and other papers, some found it difficult to identify with the suffering. Curiously, the earliest and strongest responses appear to have come from within Swiss Mennonite circles in the U.S., with additional support from General Conference Mennonite and Mennonite Brethren leaders in the U.S., but very little from Canadian Mennonite Brethren. The Swiss Mennonites had a relief program in place for war sufferers immediately after the war ended. A local initiative from California also saw some aid going to far-eastern Russia beginning in 1919.

Then, in the summer of 1920, a delegation of four from Russia and Germany arrived in the U.S. to relay news of the terrible events of the previous several years. Large crowds heard their accounts. In response the groundwork was laid for the formation of a "Mennonite central committee" in the U.S. The intention was to coordinate the response from all Mennonite groups and find ways both to channel material aid into Russia as well as assist those who wanted to leave. Even though no one knew it in 1920, it wouldn't be the United States that would be receiving almost all the Russian refugees, however; it would be Canada.

Several reasons help explain why—among Mennonite Brethren—Heinrich Neufeld felt so deeply about the tragedy that befell Russian

Mennonites. One clearly linked to his own fairly recent arrival from Russia. Memories of the Russian homeland were still fresh in his mind. Another was far more personal. His last home before leaving for America was Muensterberg in the Sagradowka colony. Among all the hundreds of Mennonite villages in Russia, not a single one suffered the horrors that Muensterberg did. On one terrible weekend, November 29 to December 1, 1919, 99 men, women and children were shot or hacked to death in that single village. In one barbaric case, a mother and her six children were first murdered and then decapitated, and the heads lined up on a circle of chairs for the father to find when he returned home. Neufeld will have known virtually all the families who suffered the tragedy of those events.

It is little wonder then that it was Neufeld who chaired the Regina meeting on October 18, 1920, attended by 14 Canadian Mennonite leaders including the future head of the Canadian Mennonite Board of Colonization, Bishop David Toews, that saw the formation of the first "Mennonite central committee" for Canada. A later news report on the meeting stated that after the "situation of our people in Russia had been portrayed as much as was known by various brethren," the group agreed that it "was absolutely necessary that Canadian Mennonites form a 'central committee' so they might help our people in Russia in appropriate ways." The meeting decided on a five-person committee. Also decided at that meeting—moved by Neufeld—was that they should seek a connection with the American "central committee."

A brief appeal issued by that first committee and published in the Nov. 24, 1920 *Rundschau* called on Mennonites to "put all our energies into helping, so that Matt. 25:35 and 36 may one day apply to us too." Any money or clothing collected was to be sent to C.K. Unruh in Hepburn. A longer appeal sent out over Neufeld's signature asked people to put themselves into the position of fellow believers in Russia, "how we would be looking out longingly for help and crying out to God for rescue from the distress that is beyond description and telling—how men and boys have been murdered in the most bestial fashion and wives and young women and children violated in the most shameful manner." Neufeld *understood* what was happening.

Neufeld and the church community in southern Saskatchewan already had a clear idea of the conditions in Russia because three members of the travelling Russian Mennonite delegation began their Canadian visits in Herbert. After a brief stay there, two went on to Rosthern, where they were met by Gerhard Ens, a former Mennonite (he had converted to the Swedenborgian teaching, a theosophist belief). Ens too was anxious to find a way of helping the people in Russia, but unfortunately chose to present the guests mainly to academics and non-Mennonite community leaders in Saskatoon and Rosthern. David Toews himself was away at a church convention in Pennsylvania at the time. The visit of the delegates did little to build support for the needy in Russia and probably garnered a fair amount of distrust because of Ens's choices for their exposure.

## BOARD OF COLONIZATION

The story of the events transpiring in Russia and the gradual coalescing of resources in Canada is a complicated one that can't be told here. Several strands are clear, however, and within them the eventual head of the Board of Colonization, Bishop Toews, stands out. In the summer of 1920, he had already called a meeting in the Mennonite church at Eigenheim, near Rosthern, which then issued an appeal to all Mennonites to remember the desperate plight of the people in Russia. Another meeting in the Hepburn MB church voted to send a delegation to meet the Saskatchewan premier to see if a way could be found to help Mennonite refugees into the province.

During 1920 and 1921 much of the energy among Mennonite Brethren in aid of the suffering in Russia happened on the American side of the border. For example in 1921 the churches of the Southern District Conference of the Mennonite Brethren decided to collect $2000 a month for Russian relief. When the Mennonite Central Committee was formally organized in 1920, P.C. Hiebert, a member of the Tabor College faculty, the MB school in Kansas, was chosen to be the chair. At a MB General Conference in Reedley, California in late fall of 1921, delegates voted to ask all church members to set aside $1 a month for Russia. They also said that when it became clear how immigration could occur, the conference wanted to be ready.

In Canada, however, the Mennonite Brethren Northern District Conference had virtually sidelined the issue. Nothing was said about Russia at the 1920 convention in Morse, Sask., until Erdmann Nickel of Laird referred to "our poor suffering brethren in Europe virtually succumbing under the heat of tribulation." Formally, the first time that the urgent needs in Russia got onto the agenda was under Submitted Questions, right at the end of the convention. Heinrich Neufeld then reported about the terrible things happening in Russia and P.J. Friesen and C.K. Unruh of Hepburn reported on the meeting with the Saskatchewan premier. The convention named all three to a committee with the Conference of Mennonites to do what was possible for their spiritual kin in Russia. In the months that followed, the pleas for help from Russia kept piling up and papers carried scores of letters and lengthy reports detailed the harrowing stories of what was transpiring there.

The following summer, in 1921, a plan was developed to send a delegation to Ottawa to appeal to the Canadian government to lift the Order-in-Council that kept the door closed to Mennonites from Russia. It came about at a meeting at Heinrich Neufeld's home in June, 1921 and included both David Toews and A.A. Friesen, one of the three Mennonites in the 1920 delegation from Russia. They argued the time had come to appeal directly to the government. The subject was debated at both the Mennonite Brethren and Conference of Mennonites conventions. In Winkler, MB delegates again only took up the Russian concerns under Submitted Questions. Would they support sending a delegation to Ottawa? The division among those present was quite apparent: the vote split 15 to 13 in favour of sending two Mennonite Brethren with the delegation. Even then the Rosthern area delegates told the conference they wanted to consult with their churches at home about the issue. It was decided to postpone a final decision until they had reported back.

A week later the Rosthern area Mennonite Brethren met and then telegraphed their decision to the Conference of Mennonites meeting in their convention in Herbert. It read: "Joint meeting on July 5th Rosthern District decided not to support the decision of the Manitoba Conference in any of the following questions: advance of money, guarantee morally or financially for emigrants from Constantinople nor delegation to Ottawa. David Dyck, Chairman." Despite the rebuff, the Conference of Mennonites in Herbert voted 52 to 2 in favour of the Ottawa venture. In the end the Herbert area MB churches decided to include Heinrich Neufeld in the five-member delegation without conference support.

The group travelled to Ottawa in mid-July and met with Deputy Prime Minister Sir George Foster and laid the Mennonite concerns before him. He expressed sympathy for their intervention and in later correspondence the Minister of Immigration, J.A. Calder, suggested a lifting of the restrictions might be possible. The delegates had the wisdom to meet with Mackenzie King, leader of the opposition, however, and laid the same concerns before him. An election was looming. King promised to rescind the Order-in-Council if he was elected. That December 1921 an election resulted in a Liberal—if still a minority—victory, King became prime minister, and in June 1922, the barrier against Mennonites entering Canada from Russia was removed.

After their July visit to Ottawa, the delegates had gone on to Montreal to meet with heads of the Canadian Pacific Railway and now they knew they had to lay the groundwork for the movement of large numbers of people.

In the spring of 1922 a Board of Colonization was created and David Toews became its formal head. (Toews was admirably suited for the role—a man of resolute character and passionate about the well-being of his Mennonite people. He had an intriguing history. When he was a child his parents followed the charismatic millennialist Claas Epp into Russian central Asia. Later they left the movement and came to America. Young Toews received a good education here and became a teacher and minister of the Conference of Mennonites. He was moderator of the Conference of Mennonites 26 times between 1914 and 1940. If ever a man had steel in his backbone, Toews did.) Heinrich Neufeld and another Mennonite Brethren from Herbert, Cornelius J. Andreas, formed the executive of the new board with Toews.

The biggest issue facing Toews at this stage was finding a way to secure the funding for a transportation contract with the CPR. The CPR itself was very supportive—especially a Colonel J.S. Dennis, the man negotiating with the Mennonites—but no one really knew how contracts involving hundreds of thousands of dollars (merely for the first boatloads), half of it to be paid within three months and the rest after six months, could be financed. Toews asked his own conference at their July, 1922 conference in Winkler whether he had their support to sign a contract. He literally put the question to them three times and each time was met with silence. Finally, in what was probably sheer desperation, he told the conference that his own Rosthern Mennonite church community would stand behind his signature. In fact, leaders in his church wrote to the CPR to say they opposed a contract and would not accept any of its obligations.

## A MOMENTOUS CONTRACT

Despite the opposition, Toews signed a contract and in his memoirs later, he noted two people who had encouraged him—Heinrich Neufeld and Gerhard Ens. For Neufeld, the signing was made especially painful because MB leaders in Hepburn called a meeting on August 12, 1922 to muster community support against the contract. It resulted in a letter sent two days later to the CPR that stated, "we refuse to be parties to the contract between the Mennonite Church of Canada and the Canadian Pacific Railway" and "we do not take any part in any contract signed by... Rev. David Toews." The letter contained the names of six Mennonite Brethren, one Brudertaler and two Krimmer Mennonite churches. Later, in correspondence with David Toews, Neufeld called the actions of the brethren in Hepburn "ungodly bad" and declared he would not take responsibility for their "sins."

A tragic confluence of events occurred around the Hepburn meeting of churches. A day after the meeting, on August 13, four young people of the Hepburn Mennonite Brethren Church drowned in the North Saskatchewan. It sent a huge shock through the entire Mennonite community of the region and on August 15 three thousand people—according to a reporter in the *Zionsbote*—attended a funeral for the youths.

It may have provided an object lesson for the region. When a tragedy happened close to home, everyone felt it keenly: it was "shattering news." A Hepburn writer began his report with, "Is there a sorrow like our sorrow?" Somehow, when far greater sorrow happened to people half a world away—even if they were spiritual kin—it did not feel the same. This is the insight Neufeld seemed to possess and some others—including some Mennonite Brethren leaders—appeared to have lacked.

Despite continuing controversy, the Board of Colonization kept on making arrangements to begin moving refugees out of Russia in 1922, though it wasn't until June 22, 1923 that a first contingent of some 750 people left the Mennonite community of Chortitza. On July 21, 450 of them arrived in Rosthern (this writer's parents among them) and about 160 in Herbert. They were the first of 2759 to come that year and of 20,201 that arrived by the end of 1930. Once the newcomers began coming, much of the earlier criticism and opposition began to dissipate.

## KEPT UP ITINERANT MINISTRY

In the following years, Heinrich Neufeld continued the itinerant ministry that had been such a large part of his life prior to the coming of the first of the immigrants of the 1920s. His community remained one of the major destinations for the new arrivals. News of their coming would usually be telegraphed to his home and then a network of people notified the Mennonite community of the numbers who needed hosting.

His relationship to the head of the Board of Colonization, however, appears to have included a good deal of tension. At times it involved delays in having his board-related travel costs paid, at times disagreements about the care given to the immigrants, at times the tendency both had to be too easily offended. Neufeld even sent in letters of resignation that seem simply to have been ignored.

Yet his passion for the needs of the suffering in Russia never diminished. Just weeks before his death in 1933, he helped bring about a meeting in Herbert that issued an appeal to "all Christian churches in all Canada…to remember the persecuted brothers in the faith in Russia." It encouraged church groups to tell the government they wanted it to protest Russia's treatment of its people at the League of Nations. It noted the information that had come through David Toews and urged church leaders to keep on telling the story of Russia's suffering people and to pray for them.

Neufeld was injured in a car accident on a return trip from a preaching assignment in Medicine Hat in the fall of 1932 and some time later was found to have cancer. It turned out to be incurable. His death came on May 13, 1933, quite at peace; his last words were, "Finally, finally, amen, amen." A writer for the Herbert Church wrote the word spread quickly that Saturday, "Brother H.A. Neufeld has died."

The community prepared for the funeral as though it were a state event. To accommodate the expected crowd, a large tent was erected next to the Herbert Church. The town flag was flown at half mast and businesses closed during the hours of the funeral. An intimate service in the Neufeld home preceded the public memorial. After the hearse with the body slowly made its way to the church, six of Neufeld's preaching brethren carried the casket into the tent where it remained open throughout the service. An assembly of fifteen hundred mourners from far and near filled the tent.

The service included many speakers and singers, some using English but most German—Mennonite Brethren and Conference of Mennonites fellow ministers, the pastor of the Lutheran church in Herbert, and others of his own family. His nephew, Hermann Neufeld, the editor of the *Mennonitische Rundschau*, reviewed Neufeld's life and ministry and no fewer than 11 fellow ministers participated in the service from its beginning to the prayers at the end. In almost every case a biblical text formed the setting for words of comfort. Interspersed throughout were songs by a choir and quartet and the congregation.

One of the speakers, Franz Martens, expressed what seemed to be a common theme: Heinrich Neufeld, he said, had become by grace the person for which God had made him. Led along a difficult, tumultuous, often conflicted life journey, God made him into an instrument with a profound knowledge of God and his Word and great dedication to his calling. Others spoke of his sacrificial service to his family, church and community, his example, and his love for his people. Despite a great sense of loss, the hope of the resurrection remained a pervasive theme.

When the service ended, the coffin was closed and the procession to the cemetery began. It was led by a car filled only with flowers, then the hearse with four young men standing on the running boards, then two lines of cars and, finally, many following after who simply walked the distance to the grave site. The whole time bells could be heard pealing their lament. Once at the cemetery, the coffin was opened one last time, a choir sang again, two of Neufeld's colleagues prayed and this man who invested himself so intensely in the spiritual and physical wellbeing of others, was committed to the earth.

One who was there commented later the thought occurred to him, "he died a poor man, but was buried a man of wealth." His wealth could not have been taken to a bank, but it could have been found in the thousands whose lives he helped save, both spiritually and physically.

SOURCES
Consulted for this chapter were *Some Notes on the Neufeld Family* obtained through grandson Victor Neufeld; materials from the Canadian Mennonite Board of Colonization fonds at the Mennonite Heritage Centre, Winnipeg; *Zionsbote* and *Mennonitische Rundschau* articles; J.G. Rempel and A.A. Friesen files, both at the Mennonite Heritage Centre; *Mennonite Exodus* by Frank Epp; *Lost Fatherland* and *With Courage to Spare* by John B. Toews; Northern District Conference yearbooks; *Hermann and Katharina, Their Story*, by Abram Neufeld; and *David Toews Was Here* by Helmut Harder.

## Abraham H. Unruh

# PRINCE OF PREACHERS, SERVANT OF THE WORD

*By Dan Unrau*

A stir went through our little congregation that a great, possibly the greatest, preacher of our denomination was coming. The anticipation lasted some weeks and the day finally came. We young boys scurried up the centre and only aisle of the small country church perched on the edge of small town Boissevain, Manitoba.

But two rows from the front we encountered a table blocking the entrance to our own pew, the front one at the head of the men's side of the sanctuary. We had to settle for a couple of rows back with the risk we would be sharing space with the grumpy old men who regularly pulled our ears or poked our backs when we giggled or wiggled, or turned the pages of the hymn books with too much enthusiasm during any service.

And then he entered. The honoured guest. He was a large man, and he walked with difficulty. It was easy to tell, too, as he shuffled up the aisle with the almost equally famous, but our own senior minister, D.D. Derksen, that he had difficulty seeing. His big Bible had already been placed on the table in the aisle, behind which a chair had been placed, and next to the

<hr>

*The Writer*

Dan Unrau is the pastor of the Fraserview Church of Richmond, B.C., and has pastored churches in Manitoba and British Columbia. He is married to Lois; they have three children and became grandparents for the first time in 2009. Story-telling and writing are avocations of Dan's. He authored two books in the late '90s, *Rogues, Rascals and Rare Gems* and *Saints, Sinners and Angels,* and reports he has almost completed a first novel. Dan has travelled extensively, has a special interest in Israel and Judaism, and still misses the high school classroom that he was called out of to pastor 25 years ago.

Bible lay a large hand-ready magnifying glass. It was a rare sight that this famous preacher, unlike any we had ever seen or heard before, would be sitting to preach. We boys actually paid attention for a time. To a sermon in a language we youngsters no longer wanted to know, in a church service—to be honest—we largely felt captive in. Interestingly, though, while I have no memory of his sermon, I never forgot the gravity and the novelty of having A.H. Unruh preach in our church.

To that point he was the most famous man I had ever seen; in my eyes he was holy, and a man to be revered. Little did I know how significant he was, and would become, in the history of the Mennonite Brethren people, both in its waning days in Russia and its rebirth in Canada in the first half of the 1900s. How interesting, too, in looking back, that in our faith-immigrant-community context our understanding of who might be a significant and a noteworthy person came within the context of the church and its mission, not from politics, Hollywood nor hockey rinks. Some would say that it was a good era with healthy and worthy heroes and values as compared to today.

## EARLY LOSS AND TRAGEDY

Abraham H. Unruh, born in 1878, had roots and early family beginnings not at all unlike almost anyone else in the Russian Mennonite community of that era. Grandfather and grandmother had left Prussia in 1816, settled in Volhynia before moving with other groupings of Mennonites to the Molotschna colony in the Ukraine. A subsequent move of his family took them to the village of Temir-Bulat in the Crimea. Abraham was the third youngest of ten born to Heinrich and Elizabeth (Wall) Unruh. Father Heinrich struggled as a farmer and didn't help his economic situation by becoming the unpaid bishop in the Mennonite Church in the region of their domicile.

Heinrich showed a unique creativity and spiritual vitality in crafting his own sermons rather than depending on the recycled published sermons that were the usual fare in Mennonite Sunday morning services. It could be said that the dynamic, creative, theological genes of Heinrich passed down to his son, Abraham.

Unfortunately, Heinrich's robust faith did not apply to his body, and at age thirty-eight he died, leaving Abraham fatherless at five. His mother Elizabeth, already well familiar with poverty with her husband alive, now had ten children to feed without a husband. Her eldest was only fifteen years old. She had no choice but to foster out her children. As a result, Abraham was sent to live with his uncle Cornelius Unruh in the Molotschna. The little Abraham was treated well by his kind teacher uncle, as if he were one of his own sons, but unfortunately his aunt was less than amiable and reportedly treated him cruelly and unjustly.

*Unruh with his colleagues at the Winkler Bible School in 1941: rear, Abram and Katie Redekopp, Henry and Anna Redekopp, George and Lena Pries, Lizzie Kroeker; Front, J.G. and Helena Wiens, Abraham and Tina Unruh, and Abram Kroeker.*

The precocious but traumatized little boy, without a father and far away from his mother and siblings, grew up in teacher Unruh's home with the clear and unquestioned expectation that he, too, would one day be a teacher. While the familial story of Abraham's growing up is a difficult one, he was blessed to have had significant ministers and gifted educators in his life such as Isaac Ediger, Johann Braeul and Johann Janzen, men known for their strengths and powerful influence. Being bright, Abraham sped through both elementary and secondary school, and passed his secondary examinations by age 15, two years ahead of his classmates. This early graduation found him ready to enter teacher's college in Halbstadt, Molotschna at a very young age.

But his essence was not only the intellectual; Abraham became deeply impacted by teacher Ediger's personal conversion story, and this sense of his teacher's spirituality stayed powerfully with Abraham as he matured and studied. Living in a dormitory setting at teacher's college already at fifteen, Unruh enthusiastically enjoyed the rowdiness of youth in such a setting, but was spared the potentially dangerous consequences of fool-hardiness by the positive, ethical and biblical influence that had already impressed itself in his life. Abraham was not only being prepared by his teachers and God for academic influence over his students, but he was being groomed to uphold high moral standards and serve as a positive role model in his community. Teachers in Mennonite communities were held in high regard and Abraham did not shy away from the anticipated expectations despite his easy humour and love of life.

Still moving through his studies at an accelerated rate, he graduated from teacher's college in two years, and with considerable effort received his Russian teacher's credentials and obtained his first position at an elementary school in the Crimea, all by age 17. He began his teaching career with some trepidation; well aware of his own relative youthfulness and well aware that the villagers were very mindful of how young he was for a man in his position. This first school of Abraham's teaching career was not far from Spat, a fairly large community of Mennonites. There, living with an aunt, a sister of his mother, both grounded and eased him into his new life. What a delight it was when his mother, whom he had not seen for twelve years, came to live with him. She probably wanted to compensate emotionally and redeem the care for him she was not able to give when he was a child and had to go live elsewhere.

## TURNING AROUND

As Abraham adjusted to life as a teacher, and now finally living with his mother, he entered a term of deep spiritual turmoil. He came under the conviction that he needed and wanted to commit his life to Christ. Adding to teacher Ediger's earlier spiritual influence, the witness of itinerant minister evangelist Jacob W. Reimer broke through to Abraham and he yielded his life to Christ, was baptized in the Salgir River near Spat and joined the Mennonite Brethren Church. Unlike so many spiritual crises and commitments that might be made wrapped in the fear of hell and the consequences of sin, Unruh's conversion was centred on the positive—such as the words of the hymn "*Jesus, thy blood and righteousness, my beauty are, my glorious dress.*" They touched him deeply.

Unruh's positive conversion and natural sense of humour would serve him well in influencing following generations of students in the way of Christ and the cross. Unruh developed his teaching skills through experience and constant summer upgrading, and unlike many teachers of his time, he sought to befriend his students rather than approach them as a distant seer and stern disciplinarian. His students liked him and were reported to be well-behaved and studious.

Abraham was attracted to a soloist in the church choir at a church conference one day, and when he was twenty-two, he and this young woman, Katharina Toews, were married. They could not possibly have guessed that this marriage would last sixty years and end with his death in a country half-way around the globe. It was well known in the Unruh inner circle that this adept preacher and teacher was no match for his "Tina" in her practical skills around the home. One story of their domestic life recounts how Abraham would hold the ladder for Tina while she would fix whatever was broken that required the climbing of that ladder. It is reported she once said that "her Abraham wasn't very helpful around the house."

## LAST DIFFICULT YEARS IN RUSSIA

In his career as a teacher Unruh moved through various Mennonite positions and even taught at a Russian trade school for a time. He often said that he learned much from his Russian colleagues in this situation, but in it he also learned how to live his faith in a difficult and dangerous world. Family life for the Unruh's was difficult in those early years. Their firstborn, Elisabeth, died at two years of age, and some years later a four-year-old son also died. Living in trying times through deaths and accidents wasn't uncommon in Russian family and community life in that era, and Abraham and Tina held to their faith for comfort.

When he was 37, Unruh began alternative service with the medical corps while Russia and Germany went to war. His education seems to have earned him an office position in Odessa on the Black Sea as his alternative service. After the Revolution broke out in 1917 and the war with Germany ended, Abraham returned to his family in Barwenkowo. His home town was no longer what it had been, however: anti-German feeling was now *de rigeur* for Russians, and the community was also caught in the conflict between the "Reds" and the "Whites" of Russia. Safety at this time became an issue for the Unruh family. Their house was ransacked once when they had to flee for a time.

An interesting story came out of that ransacking. An envelope of money with their saved tithe money had somehow been overlooked and left in the debris by the bandits. It was still given to the Lord despite the Unruh's own need and the church leaders' hesitance to accept it.

About this time Abraham received an invitation to become the principal of the *Zentralschule* (secondary school) in Karassan, the site of the oldest Mennonite settlement in the Crimea. Immediately upon arrival at Karassan, Unruh was asked to preach in the Mennonite Church, greatly strengthening the pull toward the preaching ministry, which in turn led to his invitation to join the staff of a newly established Mennonite Brethren Bible school at Tschongraw in the Crimea. Tina and Abraham and their six children moved to Tschongraw in 1920, and though this school was not allowed to exist for long, it brought a decisive turn into his life.

While teaching Bible school he continued to preach at various churches, among Mennonites as well as among Russians. During the first years of the Soviet regime, declarations of religious freedom gave many such opportunities. (Earlier, when there was still a Tsarist government, Abraham earned himself a jail sentence and barely escaped being exiled to Siberia for preaching to Russians.)

### STARTING OVER IN CANADA

Life, however, became increasingly difficult for the dynamic Tschongraw school, supported only by the donations of students and their communities from all over the Mennonite commonwealth in Russia. Then, in 1924, the Communist government closed the school. With the closure Unruh and his colleagues knew that there was no hope for freedom in Russia and they began to plan to leave. A former Tschongraw student already in the United States helped the Unruhs buy tickets to come to Canada. Emigration from Russia was still legal at this time and the Unruhs decided to move to Winkler, Manitoba, already praying that there might be an opportunity to open a Bible school in this large community with its Mennonites from earlier decades of immigration.

Once in Winkler, Abraham quickly cut through the prevalent bad feelings between the new Russian immigrants and the already established Mennonites with his easy manner, quick humour and evident teaching gifts. By the end of the fall of 1925 Unruh's fledgling teaching ministry had enrolled thirteen students in what would become the Winkler Bible School. Two of Unruh's teaching colleagues from Tschongraw, Gerhard Reimer and Johann Wiens, soon joined him at the school to continue the service of education to the people of the Mennonite church, much as they had done in the Crimean school before its closure.

The Winkler Bible School functioned as a private school for all the years that Unruh guided it. He had persuaded a small group of investors to back the school. In a short while they had put up a building and assured the teachers' salaries. For the first decade, the enrollment averaged 58 and during the second, it rose to 97. For all the years that Unruh led WBS, he remained the heart of its teaching faculty, with strong support from men like Johann G. Wiens, Gerhard Reimer and A.A. Kroeker. The leading minister of the Winkler Church, H.S. Voth, notably however, never became an enthusiastic supporter.

The Winkler Bible School's reputation under Unruh rested mostly on its ability to prepare preachers and teachers, unlike the Bethany Bible School in Hepburn, which gained a reputation as the school that sent out missionaries.

That wasn't altogether true, of course, because the Africa Mission Society that supported the Heinrich Bartsches and Herman Lenzmanns and several others in Congo in the 1930s had its birth at the Bible School, with teacher Gerhard Reimer acting as its first leader. Unruh himself had two brothers who had been missionaries in India and a son who followed there after studying at Winkler. The school also sent scores of students into vacation Bible schools during Unruh's years.

More importantly, however, Unruh most strongly supported the development of vigorous Sunday schools, and together with A.A. Kroeker, promoted the graded approach to Sunday schools and a common curriculum. The leaders in promotion of strong Sundays schools during the '30s and '40s invariably had a Winkler background.

As in his earlier days in Russia, Abraham's preaching gifts quickly became known and invitations to speak at Bible conferences both in Canada and in the United States began to pour in. In any given year he could be heard in churches as widely scattered as Oklahoma, California, Ontario and Alberta and many in between. He kept a full schedule and his preaching drew students to the fledgling school in Winkler. He remained there as teacher and principal until 1944.

## NATURAL CHOICE FOR MBBC

As the Depression of the 1930s passed and World War II was ending, it became apparent to the Mennonite Brethren community that a "higher" training institute for its churches was needed that could go beyond what the Winkler Bible School provided. In 1944 a new school, the Mennonite Brethren Bible College, came into being in Winnipeg. It was assumed Unruh would be its president. No one else had the teaching stature for its launch that he possessed. Though Abraham and Tina and the children were sad to leave Winkler, they accepted the call and moved with anticipation to Winnipeg. Because of his limited English, Unruh served as president of the College for only a year before relinquishing his position. Now a younger man such as J.B. Toews could take over.

That he continued as an important force and dynamic teacher at the school, however, is still remembered by many who were his eager students. The 1947 issue of the Mennonite Brethren Bible College's yearbook, *The Rainbow*, was dedicated to Dr. A.H. Unruh. Below a stately full-page photo of him, the tribute reads: *Unserm hochgeschätzten und inniggeliebten Lehrer* (Our highly esteemed and dearly beloved teacher.). In the descriptions next to his picture among the faculty of MBBC, later in the yearbook, the write-up notes that Dr. Unruh is a man with a "... strong yet humble personality" and a "pleasing sense of humour." Then it adds, "The expository messages which he delivered during chapel periods always vibrated with original interpretation and contagious enthusiasm."

While Unruh had relinquished the principalship of MBBC because of his difficulty with the English language, he stayed on, teaching Bible in German, until his retirement at 74 years of age. Unruh's teaching and preaching career was remarkable. David Ewert, who worked with A.H. Unruh and remembers him affectionately, writes in the work *Honour Such People* (1997) that "Unruh stood head and shoulders above most of his peers, both figuratively and literally. He was tall and rather corpulent and with his neatly trimmed beard and moustache cut a patriarchal figure....In the matter of dress he was quite fastidious and was rarely seen in public without coat and tie. Unruh was a giant among spiritual men of our Mennonite Brethren history. He had a keen sense of the integration of godliness and being human, and even humour."

Wit came easily to Dr. Unruh, even in relation to Bible teaching. For example, he once said that he had no difficulty believing that Balaam's ass spoke, "I have already heard many asses speak in my lifetime." While his humour is said to have often delayed the movement of what were supposed to be serious meetings, he doesn't seem to have given people the notion that he was flippant nor shallow. Unruh had a good sense of Mennonite social and spiritual politics.

## GIFTED AND TALENTED

Unruh was a self-taught theologian, never attended a seminary, nor ever learned Greek or Hebrew. But he was a life-long learner of everything related to his craft of teaching Anabaptist and biblical faith. Unruh was a kind of spiritual, sermonizing and educational entrepreneur, of a type ahead of his time. Of the German theologians he read, one he seemed to admire over the rest was Adolf Schlatter. He taught that ethics should be stressed over doctrine, and he warned fellow ministers against being legalistic and overly dogmatic in their debates over theological minutiae. He stressed the great truths of the Bible.

Bethel College in Kansas granted Abraham Unruh an honorary Doctor of Divinity degree and in describing this balanced and practical preacher/teacher, said, he presented "lectures that sounded like sermons and sermons that sounded like lectures." He was a man of the Bible, a true churchman.

*The "higher" Bible school in Winnipeg—MBBC. Students in 1946.*

Unruh's lectures and sermons were invariably well-prepared, meticulously organized and carefully written out in longhand. He adhered strictly to careful grammar and read Russian and German literature extensively for rich illustration and communication, and for meaningful application to the daily life of his students and listeners. He wrote with the same care as he spoke: Sunday school lessons for Mennonite Brethren churches, articles for Mennonite journals, and his primary work, *Die Geschichte der Mennoniten Bruedergemeinde* (850 pages in length, *The History of the Mennonite Brethren Church*) all make up what he left his beloved church in print.

The on-line Mennonite encyclopedia, GAMEO, states that Unruh wrote numerous books and pamphlets, among them: *The Mennonite Bible School in Tschongraw*, *An Introduction to Sunday School Teaching*, *Guidelines for Religious Instruction*, *Nicodemus*, *God's Word as our Guide for Church Discipline*, *The Lord's Word to the Church in the End Times*, *The Eternal Son of God*, *The Prophet Isaiah* and his *History of the Mennonite Brethren* (all written in German, of course). He also carried on a great deal of correspondence.

*Die leitende Brüder*

*Unruh in the midst of a company of church leaders in 1948. A caption under the photo states only "The leading brethren."*

## LEADERSHIP, LEADERSHIP, LEADERSHIP

Besides teaching and preaching, Unruh also provided leadership to the Mennonite Brethren Conference, on various boards and as moderator and secretary of the Canadian Conference. For 23 years Unruh was a speaker in the renowned Elmwood MB Church three-day Bible conferences. Abraham H. Unruh retired after sixty years of teaching in 1954, and moved to Chilliwack, at first still preaching, and later, as his eyesight and health ebbed, listening to his beloved Tina as she read to him. The Unruhs lived out their retirement years with their daughter, Lydia, and her two sons.

Not unlike many of his contemporaries, Unruh felt the burden of having made many mistakes in life, but he never forgot the grace of God. On December 26, 1960, Unruh preached his last sermon entitled, "As we beheld his glory." Two weeks later he lapsed into a coma and died at age 82, his last uttered word being "Amen!" at the conclusion of a prayer and the reading of Psalm 23 by a ministering brother.

Children and grandchildren, fifty some ministers, conference leaders, representatives of the Winkler Bible Institute, the Mennonite Brethren Bible Collage, and the Elmwood Church, and former students as pall-bearers, all paid homage to this great man at his funeral as he now lay in his casket clutching his beloved, well-worn Bible. He was laid to rest in the beautiful Little Mountain Cemetery in Chilliwack, facing east, awaiting the resurrection of our Lord and all the saints, a great man of considerable influence to a small people seeking to know and serve God.

I remember this man passionately preaching in my childhood—despite my youth—and his failing eyesight and weakened knees. We dare not forget his deep influence and his profound impact upon his many students and hearers, and more importantly, on us as a Mennonite Brethren people.

SOURCES

I am hugely indebted to David Ewert for much of this piece, from both his writings about A.H. Unruh, and from a morning-long and delightful conversation with David in his home. David was both affectionate and emotional in his memory of Dr. Unruh, a clear testimony to the greatness of brother Unruh. I am also grateful for the conversations I had with Dr. Unruh's grandson, Bob Friesen of Abbotsford; Peter Derksen, D.D.Derksen's son, from Boissevain, Manitoba; Leona Sawatsky, a student of Dr. Unruh's and a number of others who recalled this highly influential man in our denomination in casual conversation. Other sources: *Stalwart for the Truth: The life and legacy of A. H. Unruh* and *Honour Such People,* both by David Ewert and *A Place Called Peniel* by G.D. Pries.

### Abram A. Kroeker

# MR. SUNDAY SCHOOL OR MR. POTATO KING OR...

*By Harold Jantz*

He came to be known as Mr. Sunday School in Mennonite Brethren circles. Elsewhere they called him the Potato King. And for still others he was their Bible school teacher. That merely begins to cite his contributions.

There quite likely never has been a man in Canadian Mennonite Brethren circles who embraced such wide interests and accomplished so much in entirely unrelated fields as Abram Arthur Kroeker of Winkler, or A.A. Kroeker as he was more commonly named.

Businessman, teacher, farmer, musician and singer, writer, preacher, promoter, innovator—A.A. Kroeker was all of these. In the midst of a very busy life, he maintained a simple, happy Christian faith, somehow kept a clear eye and understandable goals, and gave both the church and his community (not to mention his family) much for which they could thank and bless him for generations to come.

His contributions revolve around his part in the birthing of the Winkler Bible School—at one time a key institution in the training of Mennonite Brethren leaders—his efforts at promoting graded Sunday schools, and his leadership in introducing new crops and farming techniques to southern Manitoba. He welcomed change.

---

*The Writer*

Harold Jantz is the editor of this volume of biographies and has been involved in editorial work most of his adult life, for two decades as editor of the *Mennonite Brethren Herald*, and later as the founding editor/publisher of *ChristianWeek*, a national evangelical newspaper. He and Neoma are members of the River East Church of Winnipeg.

AA's story goes back to the very beginnings of the Mennonite Brethren church in Canada. His parents, Abraham and Helena Wiens Kroeker, were baptized and joined the first church at Burwalde, Manitoba, within a half a decade of its beginning in 1888. They had come to Canada in 1876 along with other conservative Old Colony Mennonites and settled on a homestead in Hoffnungsfeld, on the edge of what is now Winkler, Manitoba.

It was a community visited repeatedly by the American Mennonite Brethren evangelist Heinrich Voth beginning in 1884. Abraham and Helena, in their words, "became persuaded about their lost condition and after a long search took Jesus as their Saviour, Lord and Master." To that couple was born Abram Arthur in 1892, one of six of 11 children who lived to adulthood. AA's home appears to have influenced him positively in several ways. For one, it was a very loving home: both parents affected the children very positively. There doesn't appear to have been the harsh discipline common to many Mennonite homes of that day, and AA would later say he couldn't imagine a mother more loving than his.

AA's father also engaged in business as a grain buyer, opening his children to the world of trade. As a nine-year-old Abe started working in his brother-in-law's printshop and took great delight in making the business hum. His mother encouraged an interest in new things and bought a camera for young Abe. He began taking wedding and funeral pictures around the community as a boy of 12 and 13. At the same time, they took an active role in the church and supported the move of the church from its country site into the town of Winkler—onto what had been their homestead—despite the controversy it generated.

At the age of 12 Abe gave his life to Christ. It came early in the new year 1904 after one of the ministers in the Winkler church at the New Year's service, said to him, "Let him (Jesus) have this year." The question haunted him till he made his decision. Later, said Abe, "I knew I was a Christian and I became happy." When he was baptized at the age of 15, he became the youngest member in the church.

## LOSSES AND GAINS

One of the greatest losses of his early life was the death of his father when Abe was 13. In time, his older brother Jacob in some ways took that place. Abe's mother remarried after a period of time and Abe worked on the farm. But he wanted more education, so he attended the Mennonite school in Gretna, completing his grade nine there. Then he continued on at a Normal School in Manitou so he might become a teacher. In 1913, with grade nine under his belt, he received his credentials to teach. The following summer he

*Abram and Elizabeth (Lizzie) Kroeker, partners in a great enterprise.*

married Elizabeth (Lizzie) Nickel of Hepburn and the young couple moved into a teacherage just north of Winkler.

During this period Abe had the opportunity to both teach and continue his education. His teacher was Frederick Philip Grove, a German with a mysterious past, who later came to be known as one of Canada's great prairie writers. Grove was a man with an inquisitive mind and a deep love for nature. A biographer later cited his "eagerness for new methods, new devices, new texts, and new educational theories" [Wally Kroeker quoting Margaret R. Stobie, in *Entrepreneurs in the Faith Community*]. A.A. Kroeker's son Walter thought that Grove's influence on AA may well have emerged in his use of sermon illustrations from nature and perhaps even in his later interest in farming.

Abe enjoyed teaching and might have stayed at it, but after that first year as a married man, his brother Jacob persuaded him and another brother, Peter, to join in a Winkler business together with their brother-in-law, John Dyck. Thus began a 15-year partnership. The Kroeker brothers operated a thriving business and formed an enterprising group. They had keen competitors in several strong Jewish enterprises in Winkler and some of the tactics they employed to capture trade were, to put it mildly, inventive.

During these years, Abe and Lizzie's family was growing and they took active part in the Winkler church, at that time under the leadership of a very fine leading minister, Johann Warkentin. The church had a strong Sunday school—it was the first MB church in the country with a Sunday school—and a great deal of music. Abe's brother Jacob led the choir there for over three decades. Many children and young people were a part of the life of the church.

In 1920 Abe had been married for a half dozen years when his desire for a better grounding in biblical knowledge led him to the Bible Institute of Los Angeles (BIOLA), where the famed Reuben Torrey was president. With his family in tow, he spent two important years there, soaking in the American evangelicalism of the early 20th century as well as its music. His son Walter later wrote, AA "had always been drawn to people who stimulated the mind and imagination, who were not content to remain on well-trodden paths, notably Frederick Philip Grove, Heinrich Ewert, Reuben Torrey and Abraham Unruh." BIOLA did that for him too. AA described them as "very profitable years."

## A BIG TURN AND THEN ANOTHER

In 1925 an event happened that would profoundly affect AA. One day in 1925 a new immigrant from Russia walked into the Kroeker Brothers Store. He was Abraham H. Unruh, a prominent teacher and preacher in Russia and now seeking to re-establish himself in a new homeland. After arriving in Winkler he had taken some part-time work in the local high school and taught a Bible study class at the Bergthaler Church. Now he came to the Kroeker brothers and proposed they join forces to open a private Bible school, patterned after one in which Unruh had taught in the Crimea. The Kroekers and their brother-in-law John Dyck agreed and so was born the Winkler Bible School, or Peniel as it was also known. It started with six students meeting in a single room of a private residence in the fall of 1925. A few months later a second teacher from the Crimea school, Gerhard J. Reimer, joined, and not long after a third, John G. Wiens, also came. By the fall of 1926, the school had its own building. Two years later, the school had 70 students.

That year, 1928, A.A. Kroeker made a momentous decision. He decided to leave the business and move onto a farm. By this time there were six children in the family and with some coming to their teens, even though they had prospered in town, Abe and Lizzie felt their children would benefit from a farm environment. They used their share in the business to buy a 360-acre property six miles out of town and named it Poplar Grove Farm. Then, in 1929, A.A. Kroeker made a second major move: he joined the faculty of the growing Bible school. So Abe became both a farmer and a teacher.

But farming brought unanticipated challenges. Land that was supposedly clean turned out to be full of the pernicious sow thistle. In 1929 too

*AA and his sons Edwin, left, and Walter in front of their innovative corn-drying kiln.*

much rain drowned out the crops. 1930 brought the onslaught of the Depression and a drastic decline in commodity prices. Grasshoppers became a great problem. That's when AA's openness to change and the new began to emerge. As son Walter later put it, "the farm problems required imaginative and innovative solutions." In 1930 he became one of the first to use chemical fertilizers on a Manitoba farm and showed the greatly increased yields that could result. In 1932 at the advice of scientists at the Morden Experimental Station, the university and a representative of the International Harvester Company, he stopped the black summer fallow practices common to much of the prairies in favour of crop rotation, and most importantly, in 1932 he began to grow corn.

With his sons' support and the children pouring their energies into it, he put in 40 acres of corn and took in an excellent crop, though the family spent long hours throughout the summer hoeing and weeding. The corn stalks also trapped precious snow for the following year's wheat crop. They proved corn could grow well on the prairies and opened the region to a succession of row crops. Corn found such demand that the Kroekers went into seed corn and in 1936 introduced the first corn-drying kiln to western Canada. It became "widely copied by others and became the foundation on which a successful industry developed in Manitoba." In 1936 the farm also became a partnership under the name A.A. Kroeker and Sons.

A great setback to the farming—which had gone through a large growth since its beginnings in the late 1920s—occurred in 1942. A heavy frost in August devastated the harvests and Abe and his sons looked for alternatives. That led them to potatoes, which since then have become their major crop. They began to produce potatoes for the fresh market, and expanded to the seed and then the potato chip markets. It led to other crops too—onions, carrots, and other specialty crops—but potatoes have remained the top and made Manitoba a key part of the country's potato production. In 2009 Kroeker Farms Limited had about 6,000 acres in potatoes. These required 18,000 acres in rotation (potatoes one year in three). They therefore made arrangements with neighbouring farmers to trade and rent land to supplement the 13,000 acres they owned. In a recent year, the crop could have supplied every Canadian with a five-pound bag of potatoes. At various times during the early years, the farm also produced large numbers of livestock for the meat market.

In 1955, with AA's encouragement, the farm was converted into a family-owned company, with shares distributed to all nine children, and passed on to their descendants. A mission statement written by son Don for the company in 1970 expressed the values Abe and his children shared. It said, Kroeker Farms exist "To meet people's needs through innovative agriculture in a way that honours God."

## MR. SUNDAY SCHOOL

While A.A. Kroeker was developing his farm with his sons, he was also at work in the church. Change and innovation were at the heart of his efforts there too. Early in the 1930s he became convinced that young people in the

*Students and faculty of the 1930–31 Winkler Bible School. Faculty in the second row (l–r), Gerhard Reimer, A.H. Unruh, J.G. Wiens and A.A. Kroeker. The class contained many future church leaders.*

church needed more from the Sunday schools. One of the traits of Mennonite Brethren from their beginning had been an effort to do more teaching of children within church settings. In Russia most Mennonites left the teaching up to the schools, but Mennonite Brethren usually had additional gatherings on Sundays to nurture children and young people in their faith. The Winkler Church too made this its practice from the beginning.

The Winkler Bible School saw grounding students in the Scriptures as its core task. Many would become teachers in their home churches. So in 1932 A.H. Unruh proposed to his board of directors that the school join the Evangelical Teacher Training Association, which guided and set standards for the preparation of Sunday school teachers. The decision changed aspects of the school's program of studies, but also launched Unruh and Kroeker onto a path that affected the entire Canadian Mennonite Brethren conference.

They set about trying to persuade the churches to embrace the idea of graded Sunday school lessons and a unified teaching curriculum. In 1938

*A Sunday school convention in the '50s at Winnipeg's old South End Church—putting the best resources into improving Sunday schools. Kroeker organized many of these.*

they brought to the conference a recommendation to accept the All Bible Graded Lessons put out by Scripture Press, commending them over Southern Baptist materials. The only problem—they would need to be translated into German. At the following year's convention, a generally positive report nonetheless conveyed some of the criticisms—translations too heavy or too slavishly tied to the English originals, questions for students unclear, unsuitable assignments. The greatest problem, however, was one of language. Many children were already well into the English and while they could understand the German spoken to them by their teachers, they did not have enough to

do assignments in German. They would need instruction in German. Furthermore, too many teachers were poorly equipped to do good teaching.

AA had been elected to head up the Canadian Sunday School Committee in 1938 and he remained in that position until 1956. He poured tremendous energy into promoting the Sunday schools. But after getting a great deal of criticism and resistance, at the 1941 conference the committee was ready to throw in the towel. They were also losing money and too few churches appeared ready to order the German materials. Even so, the delegates voted to continue the German emphasis and asked the committee to keep on working. AA and his team, however, determined to change their tack. Instead of putting the emphasis on their choice of materials, they decided to focus on building unity and offering courses and holding SS teacher conferences aimed at improving the standard of teaching. It seems to have paid off. In the years that followed, Mennonite Brethren Sunday schools reached an extraordinary level of participation. In 1947, for example, a year in which the membership of the Canadian MB churches stood at 8611, the Sunday schools registered 9039 students. Today's stats would tell a very different story.

The letters that flowed between Unruh and Kroeker during their years together in Winkler (usually when Unruh was off on preaching assignments), often had to do with Sunday school matters. Even though they usually dealt with one crisis or another—the opposition from key leaders, looming writer deadlines, worries from their Kansas publisher about low orders, slow church responses to graded lessons—the two fortunately had a good sense of humour. Their letters often poked fun at each other.

## THE BIBLE SCHOOL TEACHER

To backtrack: throughout the 1930s, AA continued to hold his place at the Bible school. At the start he went into town for five days and came home to the farm on weekends during the school term; later the whole family moved into town for the winter and back to the farm for the spring and summer; finally, in 1939, they simply moved into town. "I had the enjoyable part and Lizzie bore the brunt of it," AA related at their golden wedding, but despite the weeklong absences during those first years, when he arrived home she would often greet him with a roast duck, goose or chicken. Lizzie was a strong support. AA also enjoyed having students over to the farm, though sometimes it caused a bit of friction with other teachers who couldn't entertain in the same way.

Both in his Bible school classes and at Sunday school conventions, AA argued a positive philosophy of the child. "I feel the lack of understanding [the child] is one of the basic reasons limiting our endeavours," he said. That understanding meant respecting the child and the choices it was making, accepting it as it was at that moment, allowing it to feel secure because it was loved. Such understanding was necessary, he said, because "teaching is guiding the changes that take place in a person." The contrast he was creating was with an earlier approach in which whoever, in AA's words, could "entertain the largest class was the best teacher." Teaching wasn't treating a child like a container to be "filled," rather it was sharing experiences of value through which changes could take place. The goal was to help the child understand and love God. He encouraged smaller classes.

He also believed in incentives. He encouraged Bible memorizations by offering prizes for those who could recite their verses—everyone received

some award and a few got a special award for outstanding achievement. One
such winner recalled winning a Brownie box camera. A.A. Kroeker's generosity was not limited to the church. When he was given a life membership
in the Vegetable Growers' Association of Manitoba it was reported that for
years he had given all the foundation seed potatoes for all the 4-H potato
clubs of the province, at times as many as a thousand 50-lb bags.

One of the hallmarks of AA was his generosity. It had been inspired by
the story of the American heavy equipment manufacturer R.G. LeTour-
neau, who gave away 90 percent of his profits. AA decided that he could
manage 20 percent of his earnings. As a result, he strongly supported church
and mission causes, and modeled a very generous spirit.

It was during those years also that AA started singing with a quartet that
included his brother Peter, a cousin and a nephew. Invitations came in from
a radius of 75 miles or so and often the quartet would be out Sundays or
even weeknights. Practices sometimes ended with a wiener roast or chicken
dinner for all four families and bonds were created that knit them closely for
their lifetime. AA usually did the preaching. In 1941 he was also ordained to
the ministry by the Winkler Church.

### SUMMER CAMPS

Two areas that connected quite naturally to AA's support for the Sunday
school were vacation Bible schools and camping. Back in the 1920s, some
Mennonite Brethren young people were already involved in the Canadian
Sunday School Mission vacation Bible schools. In the early 1930s, the
Winkler Bible School began sending students into vacation Bible schools
on its own. Out of this effort grew a mission outreach in the mid-thirties at a
place called Lindal, southwest of Morden. A few years later, the school began
renting the CSSM camp at Gimli for a few weeks of camp designed to give
Sunday school and VBS teachers refresher courses.

Through that experience, AA started hunting for a site for a Mennonite
Brethren camp and in 1939 he found one near Arnes on Lake Winnipeg,
north of Gimli, which he bought for $1000 together with a group of friends.
World War II came hard on the heels of the purchase and everyone felt this
was not a time to begin a camp program. A decade elapsed before the first
buildings were erected and a program started. When it did, son Alfred became the first director. The camp became one of the province's finest.

(It is intriguing to recall that a later director, David Loewen, became the
founder of Kingdom Ventures, an entrepreneurial camping program that has
brought Christian camping to the countries of the former Soviet Union and
inspired, literally, a thousand camps (by a 2009 estimate) into existence there
and touched the lives of tens of thousands of young people for Christ. Many

years earlier, David's father, P.D. Loewen of Yarrow, B.C. was a student of the Winkler Bible School and became a leader of Sunday school development in his province.)

## A NEW SCHOOL TO PROMOTE

In 1944, the Winkler Bible School faced a crisis. Years of discussion had led to the creation of a new school for the Canadian Mennonite Brethren Church, the so-called "higher" Bible school, the Mennonite Brethren Bible College in Winnipeg. The most natural leader to launch this school was A.H. Unruh. That fall he moved to Winnipeg to start the new program and in the ensuing restructuring, the Winkler school became a provincial conference institution. More internal shifts occurred that fall, as several teachers resigned, among them A.A. Kroeker. In 1945 the Kroekers moved into Winnipeg along with the children who were still at home. Older ones carried on with the management of the farm.

One of the early tasks AA took on soon after arriving in Winnipeg involved the infant Bible College. Someone was needed who could advocate for it. In 1947 he was asked to visit all the churches of the conference—from Ontario to British Columbia—to explain the school and to invite students. According to his report, out of 83 churches he got to all but eight of them—an amazing achievement. He was a great advocate and came back with reports that the conference was rich in "youth who want to prepare themselves and work for the Lord." Even where he sensed a certain coolness to the College, he felt it was either because of "misinformation" or needed persuasion through the "positive work" of the College faculty.

## SUPPORT FOR CHURCH MUSIC

One item noted in particular in his report concerned the singing in the churches. AA commented on its improvement and how it lifted the spiritual life in the churches. Church music was not a passing interest for him. Apart from his own music-making, he had been a strong promoter of the work of the gifted conductor and musician Ben Horch going back to the 1930s, in conductors' courses, at the Winkler Bible School and later at the MBBC. Horch himself described AA as the friend and mentor who was closer to him than his own father. A great deal of correspondence flowed between the two and AA's help extended even to funding Horch's salary at times and securing a house for him to live in. AA was also one of strongest promoters of Mennonite orchestras in his own community of Winkler and later in Winnipeg, where he chaired the Mennonite Symphony Board for eight years. When Ben Horch was awarded an honourary doctorate for his musical contributions by the University of Winnipeg, he paid special tribute to

*Abe and Elizabeth Kroeker gave a volume of Manitoba conference minutes for 1929-39 to the archivist Herb Giesbrecht in 1976.*

A.A. Kroeker as "the...prophet of musical things as far back as 1935 when he was just a humble farmer." Few people influenced the music in Canadian Mennonite Brethren churches more in their lifetime than did Ben Horch, aided by people like AA.

Still other areas benefited from A.A. Kroeker's contributions. In 1964 he founded the Winkler Home for the Aged and secured the funding for its first seniors' home and later initiated a program to build a six-storey apartment for seniors, the largest such facility at the time in rural Manitoba. He also served as a school trustee and on the Winkler Hospital Board.

### SUMMING UP

Abram and Lizzie Kroeker died less than two weeks apart in 1981. They had lived a rich and full life, but were longing for their prospective home, secure in their faith in Christ.

Grandson Wally Kroeker described his grandfather well in a chapter he wrote about him for *Entrepreneurs in the Faith Community*: "Abe Kroeker had a knack for infusing others with his own excitement. In both agriculture and church work, Abram Kroeker was known as a motivator and entrepreneur, a man of vision not bound to tradition, yet firmly committed to the fundamentals of the faith. He had a unique ability to recognize opportunities, accept challenges, impart his insights and infect those about him with his irrepressible enthusiasm.

"A significant factor in Abe Kroeker's success was that he always had a mission beyond profit....Leading entrepreneurs have promoted the view that profit is to business what breathing is to life; we must breathe in order to live, but breathing itself is not the chief goal of existence.

"Abe Kroeker always had a larger mission in mind. While he tended his business interests with vigilance and energy (he was very reluctant to go into debt, for example), the larger issues in his life were his family, his church and the community. He once wrote, 'We are living in times in which all of us should place our personal entrepreneurial interests in the background. Our rallying cry should be: Our best efforts for the Lord. In that way we will help our neighbour and our country in the best possible way.'"

**SOURCES**
Much of the material for this biography was obtained through the A.A. Kroeker fonds at the Centre for Mennonite Brethren Studies in Winnipeg. Other sources were the *The Ben Horch Story* (Winnipeg: Old Oak Publishing, 2007) by Peter Letkemann; Northern District (Canadian Conference) Yearbooks; *No Longer at Arms Length* (Winnipeg: Kindred Press, 1987) by Peter Penner; *Entrepreneurs in the Faith Community*, edited by Calvin Redekop and Benjamin Redekop (Scottdale: Herald Press, 1996); *A Place Called Peniel*, by G.D. Pries (Winkler: By the Author, 1975); and interviews and materials from A.A. Kroeker's sons, Alfred, Don and Peter Kroeker, and grandson, Wally Kroeker.

# Henry S. Rempel

# HE SPREAD
# A LOT OF LOVE

*By Dorothy Siebert*

S topping in the yard where the sweet pea vines twined around the fence,
he picked a fresh flower, tucked it into his lapel and was on his way.
That Sunday morning, he was preaching the sermon at Salem Mennonite
Brethren Church in Winnipeg.

At the church, Pastor Arno Fast, who had known Henry as a minister
in Saskatchewan, greeted him and smiled to see the customary sweet pea.
Yes, that was Henry–whether visiting patients in the hospital or preaching,
the flower was part of his attire. Even now when Henry was more than 90
years old.

Concerned for his health, Arno cautioned, "Don't exert yourself, brother."
But Henry smiled and preached a powerful sermon with his usual great
passion. His messages inspired the listeners–they were the words of a man
whose life experience was shaped by his eagerness to keep learning, regardless of age.

"A day or two later," recalls Arno Fast, "he suffered a heart attack or
stroke. That may have been his last public sermon."

Henry Rempel was a communicator. He loved to teach and spent much
of his life as a teacher of Scripture. The majority of his working years he

*The Writer*
Dorothy Siebert worked in a church planting team in Colombia for 10 years, assisting in the birth of two congregations alongside other MBMSI team members. She
has been a print editor with the Family Life Network of Winnipeg for 11 years, is
the author of *Whatever It Takes*, the story of Albert and Anna Enns, and has an MA
in Old Testament studies. She and her husband Harold have four grown children.

ministered in the province of Saskatchewan, admired and held in high esteem.

"I have really fond memories of him," said Albertine Speiser, 93, of Saskatoon, a full sixty years after sitting under Henry's ministry. "He used to give Bible studies at my home church in Laird, Saskatchewan. And these were on a whole book, like all of Galatians or Ephesians. He'd stay several days. We didn't have Bible school then and so that was our Bible school.

"He did a whole series, going through the chapters verse by verse, bringing out wonderful truths and a solid foundation. He inspired trust. People came from all over to hear him and liked him very much."

Teaching was in Henry's blood. His father, Heinrich, a teacher in Russia, had been Henry's teacher in the elementary grades. Henry greatly admired his father. Through all the moves and travels of his life, he kept with him a photograph of his father that showed him as a teacher in the village schoolhouse in Russia.

Henry was born on November 27, 1882 in Waldheim, a village of the Molotschna settlement of Mennonites in South Russia. His parents, Heinrich and Margaretha Schlabach Rempel, emigrated to Canada in 1886, settling in Kleefeld, Manitoba with young Henry, three and a half years old.

At age 19 he made the decision to live his life in obedience to Jesus Christ. Three years later he married Maria Hiebert, the daughter of the Mennonite preacher David Hiebert. Though he only reached a height of five feet six inches, Henry carried himself with confidence and is remembered as always neat and well-groomed.

The young couple started out as farmers on a homestead near Watrous, Saskatchewan. Together they had six children: Harry (1904), Margaret (1905), Bernhard (1908), Linda (1911) and Peter (1916) as well as one who died as an infant.

But Henry was not fulfilled in farm work. Often he fondly reflected on his classroom experiences and dreamt of following his father in a life of teaching.

He and Maria soon gave up farming and moved back to Manitoba to the town of Gretna where Henry studied to become a teacher. He taught for ten years, thoroughly enjoying the classroom. He was heard to say those were the happiest and most carefree years of his life.

In 1912, as the father of four children, he became ordained as a minister in the *Kleinegemeinde* (now the Evangelical Mennonite Church). In 1924, when the family moved to Winkler, Manitoba, they changed their membership to the Mennonite Brethren church.

## MEETING NEWCOMERS

Between 1923 and 1930 thousands of Mennonite families were fleeing southern Russia and many arrived in Canada. Winnipeg was a receiving and sorting place for new immigrants. As a settled Canadian, Henry heard of this great influx of forlorn refugees and was moved to serve them in some practical way. He heard that in Winnipeg the Mennonite Brethren workers who were assigned as city missionaries often distributed clothing and blankets to the immigrant families and handed out tracts and Scripture verses in seven languages.

*Anna and H.S. Rempel—willing to accept a life of poverty to help others.*

The only Mennonite Brethren Church in Winnipeg at that time was what they called the North End Chapel, a simple building on the corner of Burrows and Andrews. The chapel was becoming over-filled with new German-speaking immigrants. Henry and Maria Rempel were asked to come and work alongside C.N. Hiebert who was leading the mission work in Winnipeg at the time.

They responded by moving their family from their comfortable rural setting to the city of Winnipeg. Here Henry worked for six years visiting the poor, sick or destitute in their homes, and arranging Sunday school, church meetings and support groups for children and adults. He distributed clothing, blankets and food to new immigrants and helped them in many other ways to adapt to the new country. Sometimes he and a few helpers would hold services right in the Immigration Hall on Higgins Avenue next to the Canadian Pacific Railway Station.

All Henry's work was done travelling by streetcar or on foot. He did not think it unusual to walk for miles to meet the needs of others in their homes or in the hospital. A number of those who attended the North End Chapel to hear him speak would also walk for miles for the Sunday morning service and even return for the evening again.

In 1929 Henry bought a small black leather notebook that fit into the pocket of his suit jacket. In the notebook he started to record the dates and topics of his sermons and talks—one of the organizational aspects carried over from his teaching years. One of the earliest entries, entered under the 'W' tab, gives us his sermon text for that evening: Winnipeg North End, Sept 15/29, 7 pm, Matt 3:13-17.

Home visitation (*Hausbesuche*) to various homes often took the entire day and Henry's feet began to pain him. Yet he would push through to do whatever was needed, visiting new families to tell them about Jesus. His optimistic spirit and friendly, outgoing nature brightened the day for the sick and housebound. On Friday mornings he led prayer meetings at the chapel. His prayers were not lengthy but they were fervent. His co-worker, Anna Thiessen, recalls that through these prayer times "the Lord blessed many...."

The church continued to grow. Baptisms were held in summertime when they could be celebrated on the shoreline of the Assiniboine River in the west part of the city.

It was during these years that Henry suffered his own personal sorrow. In 1930, just one year after moving his family to Winnipeg, his wife Maria died in April at the age of 47. And heaped on that sorrow, a few months later in August, his son Peter, not yet 14 years old, died in a train accident.

Did the overwhelming troubles of the new immigrants engender in him a philosophical view of his own sorrow? Did he flee to the Lord with his tears and pain? We do not know how he handled his sorrow, but it may be during this time that the hymn became his favorite that he quoted in one of his reports. The song ends, "*Und alles was mein Herz begehrt, bei Dir zu finden ist.*" [And all that my heart longs for can be found in you.] Whatever his secret, Henry persevered and continued trudging through Winnipeg streets, visiting others in their distress.

## NEW START IN SASKATOON

Two years later Henry married Anna Neufeld of Winnipeg. Her face was kind and a gentle spirit shone from her eyes. She willingly picked up the duties of the preacher's wife, becoming mother to the children and hostess for immigrants.

After working together a few years, in 1935 they accepted a call to become leaders of the extensive mission work being done by Mennonite Brethren in the province of Saskatchewan. When they moved to the city

MORNING DEVOTION GROUP
1943-44

*During Henry Rempel's time in Saskatoon, they began the first Mennonite Brethren radio broadcast—this was the team in 1943-44. Abe Janzen was the conductor*

of Saskatoon little did they dream they would spend 34 years there. The city, with its population of 42,000 in 1935, was struggling to recover from the Great Depression. Saskatoon's revenues had been sunk into relief for the many unemployed and their destitute families. It was to this city in great need that Henry and Anna responded, willing to adopt a lifestyle of poverty in order to help others.

Saskatoon was the centre of business for dozens of towns and farming communities linked to the city by railway since roads were poor. The Rempels' home became the hub for fellowship, help and information amongst the Mennonite Brethren spread out on farms throughout northern Saskatchewan. From outlying areas people came by rail and road to the city for doctor's appointments and to do business of all kinds.

Albertine Speiser, who was in her twenties at the time recalls that era: "People coming to the city would often stay at the Rempels. It was very pleasant to stay there. Henry was easy to talk to and his wife Anna really supported him wholeheartedly, always keeping people for meals or overnight. People came from all over: Laird, Hepburn, Dalmeny, Waldheim.... Though they brought butter or eggs along from their farms to help out, it must have been hard for the Rempels—they hosted so many."

Prior to the Rempels taking up the work in Saskatoon, all the city mission work across Canada of the Mennonite Brethren was governed by a single committee. But when the Saskatoon mission opened in 1934, and one in Vancouver opened as well, the Canadian Conference shifted responsibility for each city mission project to its respective province. So Henry took up the job in Saskatoon just at a time when the new job description included heavier responsibilities in decision-making and finances.

From 1936-44, Henry was the pastor of the Saskatoon Mennonite Brethren Church (later called Central Mennonite Brethren). Building up a fellowship group in the city was challenging and numbers were small to start with. Yet Henry persevered. He was very punctual and is remembered as "...always on the dot. If it was to start at 7 p.m. and only two or three people were there at 7 o'clock, he started. More people would come later but he always started at 7 o'clock."

To build up a church in Saskatoon meant a lot of walking to make house visitations. Henry would make some 200 visits to homes a year as well as many hospital visits. Though walking was not easy for him because of painful feet, he pushed himself to carry through with his plans. People saw him as always faithful to do whatever he thought God wanted of him.

Once when his former leader, C.N. Hiebert, came on a visit to Saskatoon, he and Henry spent a day visiting homes together. That evening Hiebert dropped in unannounced at his home and found Henry soaking his sore feet. Though Hiebert made a joke about it, Henry felt bashful before the other man more hearty than himself and said, "I didn't want you to see me like this."

After five years of walking the Saskatoon streets, help came along that made the work much easier. He reported to the provincial conference, "The Lord sent us a lovely car!" The delegates responded with a collection to help the Rempels completely pay for the much-needed vehicle.

The financial ledgers were carefully kept by the Rempels and reported to each annual church conference. The following list comprised the complete report of the expenses of the Saskatoon City Mission (*Stadtmission zu Saskatoon*) from May 1941 to June 1942:

Salary for the Rempels – $875.37
For Sister Rempel to run the young women's group – $15.00
For Brother Rempel to give to the poor – $19.20
Postage & paper – $2.56
Taxes on the mission house – $123.55
Travel costs for Brother Rempel – $9.50

*The Rempel family in 1945.*

Each year new members were baptized in the Saskatchewan River and added to the church fellowship. By 1945 Henry's work expanded to include supervising extended mission work in the province. Another pastor took over the local church, which by then had grown to include 70 students in the Sunday school and a church membership of 174.

Even in the city, away from his rural roots, Henry's love for nature and for beauty grew. In describing their good fortune at owning a church building, completely paid for after working just five years in Saskatoon, he used this picture: "The bird has truly found a house and the swallow a nest for her young. To God alone goes the glory!"

During this time Henry was also the speaker on "Morning Devotions" heard at 8:30 on Sunday mornings on the Saskatoon AM radio station, CFQC, the first such radio program among Canadian Mennonite Brethren. Henry taught a lesson from Scripture and a choir of about 20 to 30 women and men gathered in the studio around two grand pianos. They sang on the spot into the mikes that carried the live program directly into the homes of the city and surrounding areas.

Henry reported, "It means not only going to the studio on Sunday mornings and rolling out our program, but it requires a lot of preparation…as a rule we hold two rehearsals each week."

The radio work was supported entirely by freewill offerings with donations coming in from church members as well as from radio listeners. Broadcasting fees totalled $590 for one year. For Henry it was a matter of prayer to wait on the Lord and watch God send the needed funds each month.

## THE GIRLS' HOME

Another vital part of their work was overseeing the *"Maedchenheim"* in Saskatoon, a girls' home for Mennonite young women who came to the city either as new immigrants or from farming families in other parts of the province. The girls' home was a necessity in that era since the daughters of immigrant families needed to find work in the city to help support their families, yet most had no city experience, very little English and often no friends or relatives in Saskatoon.

The house, at 323 - 25th Street, was a square two-story home with a front veranda. For some years, the Rempels lived in rooms at the back of the house. One look at the home and the passerby recognized that here lived people who, in spite of the hard times, loved nature and enjoyed the beauty of plants. Besides being surrounded by bushes, the house was hung thickly with ivy and looked very picturesque with its neatly-crafted white picket fence bordering the yard.

From this house, over the years Henry and Anna supervised hundreds of young women far from their homes and families. Counting those who lived in their employers' homes as maids or nannies, the group of young women numbered up to 70 at any one time. They gathered each Thursday evening and on Sundays when they shared experiences and encouraged each other. They sang in the radio choir and also gave valuable assistance in the church by teaching Sunday school.

One of these young women wrote in a 1941 report that many of the girls that year were not able to go home at Christmastime and so "…the Rempels prepared a very lovely Christmas dinner for us all, going to a lot of trouble to make it just as nice as we would have it at home."

That was also the year the Rempels reported, "Because the harvest was so poor this year, a great number of new girls came to the city. All of them have found work.…We are grateful for the good reputation our girls have." Employers and homeowners found that the girls from Mennonite home could be trusted with their children and with their possessions, so these girls readily found work.

Whether the *Maedchenheim* work was an influence on Henry's perspective or not, he was ahead of his time in his respect for women, going out on a limb to acknowledge the worth of women at a time when many of his Mennonite peers viewed women almost solely as homemakers. In 1937 a missionary woman visiting from overseas presented a report to the group in Saskatoon. Henry so thoroughly admired her report that he declared, "I don't know why they don't let women preach. I know quite a few women who could really beat the men in preaching."

### GROWTH INSIDE AND OUT

As chairman of the missions outreach for northern Saskatchewan, Henry led monthly planning meetings. He organized the colportage work—the distribution of Bibles and literature to isolated farms and villages. For many towns and churches in the province he coordinated summer outreach events as well as itinerant preaching schedules. It was not unusual that during the two months of June and July that Henry would organize meetings of three to seven days each, for three different visiting preachers, in 25 different towns and villages throughout northern Saskatchewan.

For a number of years he was also the chairman of the North Saskatchewan Mennonite Brethren Conference in the years before the north and south districts amalgamated, which happened in 1966. Now the small black notebook in his pocket included the record of other speakers as well as his own engagements. Thousands of entries in tiny European script filled several notebooks. Under the names of the towns in alphabetical order he meticulously recorded who spoke where, when and on what topic.

Henry said his deepest desire was to spread God's love around. In a report to the Saskatchewan Mennonite Brethren Conference, after listing the numbers baptized, the increase in membership and the success of the girls' home, he said, "But the real question we must ask ourselves when looking at these things from a spiritual point of view is [this]: have we ourselves matured inwardly? Amongst all these records is there also a personal inner growth we can record? Can the Holy Spirit say about us as it said about the Thessalonians, 'The love of each one of you towards one another abounds!'"

During the 1950s Henry was named the official hospital chaplain for the Mennonite Brethren churches. He and Anna now lived on 24th St., just a street over from the *Maedchenheim* house. Every day from Monday to Friday he visited hospital patients of any and of no faith. His pay was calculated at $3 a visit. By 1960 the report to the Saskatchewan Conference showed that the number of patients he had visited in hospital "…must run well over the two thousand mark."

"Sometimes I go from bed to bed," he reported, "and speak to them about their soul's salvation.…Sometimes…I have a short devotional with all of them who are in that ward." He read Scripture and conversed with those who had no other family or friends; he approached total strangers to pray for them on their way to surgery. Many people prayed with him and turned their hearts to Jesus. Yet every day the question rose in his mind, "Have I really done all I could to bring these souls to a saving knowledge of Christ and the way of salvation?"

As Henry grew older, he continued to spread love through hospital visits and by visiting sick persons in their homes. Many were blessed by his calming and inspiring visits. He could speak truthfully about the pain and bitterness that beset humans in the face of suffering and death, yet always offering a message of hope.

His inclination to identify himself with the pain of others came through during the annual Canadian Conference of Mennonite Brethren in 1960, in Virgil, Ontario. During a morning session, some delegates had become heated and had spoken bitter words. Henry was called on to say a prayer that would close the session and lead into the noon meal. Everyone's head bowed, waiting. Silence. Then more waiting. But only silence followed; no prayer from Henry.

Later Henry simply said, "I couldn't pray.…" He had been too troubled by the ill will. Harold Jantz, recalling this occasion said, "Not too many people would have had the courage and honesty to do that."

For 34 years Henry worked together with his wife Anna, who it was said, fully supported her husband and worked alongside him in his work as city missionary and church planter in the city of Saskatoon. Henry's leadership helped to shape the identity that the Saskatchewan Mennonite Brethren Conference retains to this day—a group of churches and believers characterized by a deep commitment to care for each other and for others beyond their circle.

## LAST YEARS

After decades in Saskatchewan, the Rempels returned to Manitoba. Even in retirement in Steinbach and later in Winnipeg, he continued visiting in hospitals and seniors' homes. He wrote hundreds of letters to build others up, encouraging them to keep the faith in the face of trials.

On July 6, 1979, after a brief illness, Henry died in Winnipeg at Donwood Manor. In the German-language obituary written by his brother-in-law, William Neufeld, Henry is described as an exemplary husband.

He had lived into his 97th year and was survived by his wife Anna, four children, six grandchildren and 15 great-grandchildren.

His funeral on July 10, 1979 packed out the large North Kildonan Church in Winnipeg. The German-language paper of the Mennonite Brethren, the *Mennonitische Rundschau*, reported that during the fellowship time at the funeral, "From every side people got up to give testimonies about this brother—he was a true God-follower and spread much love all around!"

SOURCES
Information for this chapter was drawn from archives at the Centre for Mennonite Brethren Studies in Winnipeg: yearbooks of the Northern Saskatchewan Mennonite Brethren District Conference; minutes and letters of its Home Missions Committee; reports from the City Mission in Winnipeg; sermons, booklets of annual reports by Henry and Anna Rempel, Henry Rempel's notebooks, and his obituary in the *Mennonitische Rundschau* in 1979; *The City Mission in Winnipeg* by Anna Thiessen, translated by Ida Toews; a copy of the *Carillon News* of Steinbach (1973) and the *Global Anabaptist Mennonite Encyclopedia Online*. Other sources were internet histories for Saskatoon and Winnipeg; and conversations and email exchanges, most notably with Albertine Speiser of Saskatoon, and Arno Fast, Harold Jantz and Edith Neufeld of Winnipeg.

# G. W. Peters

# CREATED A ROAD
# WE ARE STILL UPON

*By Harold Jantz*

Sometimes God surprises us. If George W. Peters hadn't come to the Hepburn community in Saskatchewan to do evangelistic work in 1933, the life of the Canadian Mennonite Brethren Church might have taken a quite different turn, the overseas mission of the church might look much differently today, Fresno Pacific University might be a different place and the MB Biblical Seminary might have developed quite differently.

How could that be? In 1933, Gerhard W. (or simply GW as most came to call him) Peters was a recent immigrant from Russia, still in his mid-twenties. He had come to Hepburn to conduct evangelistic meetings in a nearby country school. He was there, as J.B. Toews put it, "as a freelance evangelist" and Bethany Bible School (now Bethany College) invited the zealous young man to speak in a chapel service.

"There was fire in his bones and his message somehow moved the student body," wrote Toews. Bethany had just lost a key faculty member due to illness. The board was hard pressed to find a replacement. They asked GW to consider filling in for a few weeks. He hadn't planned to be a teacher, nor was he especially attracted to the idea. But he came to

---

*The Writer*
Story and history have always been an interest for Harold Jantz. He had the opportunity to nurture that interest during two decades as *Mennonite Brethren Herald* editor and another decade as the founding editor of *Christian Week*, a Canadian national evangelical periodical of news and comment. He and his wife Neoma are members of River East Mennonite Brethren Church of Winnipeg.

love teaching and his weeks stretched into a decade at Bethany and a lifetime elsewhere. It didn't really end until his death in late 1988. And what an influence he came to have!

In his lifetime, he came to be one of evangelical Christianity's leading missions thinkers. Shortly before his death, a book published in his honor, *Reflection and Projection—Missions at the Threshold of 2001*, carried essays by 22 leading fellow missions leaders. They covered a wide spectrum of backgrounds—Lutheran, Reformed, Pietist, Mennonite, Fundamentalist, and from both sides of the Atlantic—and were edited by Hans Kasdorf of the MB Seminary and Klaus Mueller of the Akademie fuer Weltmission in Germany where Peters spent his last years. What may have distinguished Peters was his strongly biblically rooted and confident Christian faith wedded to an ability to employ the anthropological and social sciences, a legacy of his wide studies.

## A 19-YEAR-OLD IMMIGRANT

When GW arrived in Canada in 1926 with his widowed mother, he was only 19, single and unconverted. For a time even the idea of coming appeared remote, because he was diagnosed with trachoma, an eye disease for which immigrant applicants were routinely rejected.

Years of turmoil and tragedy preceded GW's decision to leave the Soviet Union. He was the youngest of twelve children in the home of a prosperous merchant in the Mennonite village of Orloff, in the Sagradowka colony of southern Russia. His parents, Wilhelm and Anna Peters, were devout people in the tradition of the Mennonite Church of that day. Though the entire family went to church on Sunday, GW never heard his father pray aloud—at the table you bowed and spoke a silent prayer—and the only time he heard his father read a passage of Scripture happened the day three brothers and a brother-in-law were drafted and left for service in the medical corps during World War 1. The elder Peters read Psalm 23 and then all knelt to pray—silently.

GW's father became one of the two hundred people who were murdered in the colony in just one terrible weekend in late 1919. Even more tragically, a sister, Maria (Peters) Martens, together with six children, were hacked to death and burned in their home in neighbouring Muensterberg. Her husband survived but died not long after of typhus. GW witnessed his own father's death.

George came from a very able family, people involved in grain export, farming, teaching and even banking. A keen student, George graduated from what we would consider a high school at the age of 16 and a half, and wanted to study medicine. He was offered but turned down the opportunity to go to medical school because of the abuses of the revolution.

Instead, he told his mother he wanted to emigrate to America. GW was only 17 and she responded she couldn't let him go alone. Then, a disappointment. When he applied for the papers, the trachoma closed the doors to Canada. Undeterred, he travelled to Odessa where he applied for a visa to Mexico instead, an alternate route others had begun using. It took weeks of effort and some bribing, but GW and his mother Anna obtained the necessary documents.

Mexico provided a home for them for a year and some months from early 1925. Then, with the help of relatives, they arrived in Canada. They came first to Borden, Saskatchewan, and then moved to the Mennonite community of Blumenort in the southern part of the province. For George this was a trying period: working at anything to pay down his travel debt, at times for English farmers whose language he struggled to learn.

## MET CHRIST

But during this time he also encountered Christ in a life-transforming fashion. Within him grew a hunger to know the Bible better and that fall, in 1926, he went off to the nearby Herbert Bible School where the highly-regarded William Bestvater was the key teacher. George lapped up all the school could offer and after two terms (the schools normally ran from mid-October to the beginning of April), he transferred to the Winkler Bible School, where Abraham H. Unruh was the dominant teaching influence. (Incidentally, the young woman who later became his wife, Susie Lepp, attended Herbert and Winkler as well, part of the time with him. It would be years before they married.)

Years later, when GW wrote his widely used *A Biblical Theology of Missions*, he cited these two teachers—among others outside the Mennonite fold—as formative influences in his life.

"William Bestvater first made the Bible dear to me," he wrote, "and introduced me to the principle of progressive revelation…and opened my eyes to the glory of the church of Jesus Christ…the total program and plan of God through the ages and [the] future glory and mission of Israel. Abraham Unruh…taught me many deeper truths of the Word and unfolded the concept of *Heilsgeschichte* (salvation history) to me in a remarkable way."

Bestvater was known for his dispensationalist understanding of the Scriptures, Unruh for a broader theological stance that drew both from Anabaptist wells and the best of German biblical scholarship. Bestvater had also already been a city missionary in Winnipeg and much of the early passion for missions absorbed by GW will have come from that source.

Along the way GW also took at semester of study at Prairie Bible Institute in Three Hills, Alberta, and added a term at a school in Moose Jaw. When he came to Bethany in 1933, he was just turning 26, single and intent on evangelism. Much of it he was already doing across northern Alberta and Saskatchewan among immigrants from Russia. One person reported that meetings of his in Swift Current about that time resulted in thirty conversions.

After accepting the assignment at Bethany, he quickly recognized his need for additional studies and for years afterward crammed in as many times of study during holidays and months off as he could. Eventually he studied at or got degrees from Tabor College, the Northern Baptist Theological Seminary in Chicago, St. Andrews College at the University of Saskatchewan and the Kennedy School of Missions at the Hartford Seminary in Connecticut, at that time Protestant America's leading missions study centre. His doctoral thesis for Hartford, published in 1952 as *The Growth of Foreign Missions in the Mennonite Brethren Church*, was completed in 1947 and for the first time offered a thorough insight into our denomination's missions.

When GW accepted the challenge of Bethany, another highly gifted, headstrong young man, J.B. Toews, was just beginning his second year at Bethany. In 1934—a year later—JB became the principal and the two were cast into a relationship in which both had to find ways of working together. Both probably lacked some maturity. Though they became lifelong friends, during the Bethany years they clashed on a number of occasions, Toews viewing Peters as insubordinate. It led to a confrontation in which Toews put an ultimatum to Peters either to agree to subordinate himself to the faculty or cease teaching.

The matter was settled and GW continued teaching. A big help from Toews's point of view was GW's marriage in 1935 to Susie Lepp, daughter of the Dalmeny church leader Jacob Lepp, who provided "a balancing influence to his driving, sometimes impetuous temperament." A few years later Toews stepped down from the principalship and GW replaced him as head of the school!

### BETHANY PRAYER BAND

GW's arrival on the Bethany campus coincided with the beginning of a group who would eventually change the way Canadian Mennonite Brethren related in their witness to people of other ethnic origins. They called themselves the Bethany Prayer Band and at the start the small group of highly committed people—with figures like Peters, Toews and students Jake Epp and Frank Froese in it—made the conversion of un-saved fellow students their main goal. No one could join without an-other student's recommendation. Missions were a central focus. At the end of the first year, 13 students volunteered to do children's outreach with the Canadian Sunday School Mission.

Four years later, in 1937, the summer outreach had grown to the point that a ministry was incorporated under the name the Western Children's Mission. In a short while Peters became its president and Ben Kroeker the executive director. Peters was the movement's spark plug. He scouted the countryside east and especially north of Hepburn in areas recently settled by homesteaders, many of Ukrainian-Russian background, where points of witness could be established. By today's standards workers accepted utterly primitive conditions. A 1944 ac-count described the half-finished log building the Abe Wiebes lived in and used for their work in Pierceland: walls chinked on the outside with mud and lined with paper board on the inside, stovepipes going up the inside straight through the roof, benches made of six-inch wide timber nailed to blocks of wood. They were among homesteaders!

Young people were sent out on allowances of $4 to $5 a month, and if the women and men were driven out to their assignments, the women

*A meeting of the foreign mission board in 1970—G.W. Peters and J.B. Toews side-by-side. Others at the table were Dwight Wiebe, Ernest Schmidt, Rueben Baerg and at the far right, Marion Kliewer.*

were promised a ride back but the men could fend for themselves on the way home. The 1936 annual meeting heard that vacation Bible schools had been held in 30 schools by 34 workers, 735 children had been enrolled, 541 homes visited, 52 services conducted, 180 persons "dealt" with, and 68 professed faith in Christ. The travel stats are interesting: 1800 miles driven in preparatory work, 6200 miles covered taking workers to their assignments, 1680 miles driven by the workers while on assignment, and 2180 miles *walked* while on the field. Total budget for the year: $440.72!

### SETTING A DIRECTION

The emerging mission had several interesting traits. Its early documents describe it as "interdenominational, international, evangelical and evangelistic." It would not allow denominational reluctance to box it in. This was entrepreneurial church outreach. While the head office was in Hepburn, the leadership entirely Mennonite Brethren, and the support almost entirely from Mennonite Brethren circles, it wasn't formally tied to the church. While this created tensions, it also gave the young organization a great deal of freedom. At the conferences of the North Saskatchewan churches, the WCM was given opportunity to report. Minutes invariably indicate that churches were encouraged to support the mission even if, as the 1942 report states, the conference still "lacked the light and clarity" to formally embrace it.

By 1943, Ben Kroeker reported to the North Saskatchewan churches that the mission had projects going in 12 Saskatchewan communities, in 10 of them regular services. Eight couples were at work. In most places there were also Sunday school or youth programs. In addition to the 31 workers who had been involved in the previous eight months, 44 young people were expected to go into VBS programs in the weeks ahead.

At that time, the Western Children's Mission was holding regular promotional conventions, sent out a newsletter called *The Challenger*, carried on a Bible Memory program with children, and sponsored a radio program. And more broadly, it had extended its incorporation to Alberta and British Columbia in 1940-41, to assist those provinces in their early mission outreach. Even more broadly, the WCM had already sent out its first couple overseas, the Abram A. Dycks, to Colombia, and had several women in medical training for an overseas assignment. All this was done in 1943 on a budget of a little over $4700, though it should have been at least several times as much.

GW argued vigorously for stronger conference support—largely because of the financial constraints the WCM was working under—and that year the district accepted it as a conference project.

At this time the church growth movement in Mennonite Brethren circles still had a strong children's focus. It had a considerable distance to go as it evolved through its VBS/Sunday school phase, then the mission and finally its church phases. These early steps, however, set a direction. In a very short time, British Columbia had incorporated its own mission, the West Coast Children's Mission, and by the mid-fifties, had outreach projects going in thirty localities around the province. There would be no turning back. And right up there at the front was G.W. Peters, as plain-speaking and confrontational as he might at times be. When the conference was left with little choice but to accept these projects—they had gained such wide local support—they were formally embraced.

### "BENDING" TO OVERSEAS MISSION

The same happened with overseas missions. GW and Ben Kroeker told the 1943 North Saskatchewan District conference that the WCM's vision was "bending" increasingly to overseas missions. Specifically, Peters was urging work somewhere in Latin America, a direction to which the chair of the U.S. and Canadian Mennonite Brethren mission board, H.W. Lohrenz, was also inclined. There was a great deal of hesitation within the board, however. But because Peters had already gained a reputation for motivating people, he was asked to travel to Colombia to survey the possibilities.

He spent over half a year there, travelled widely, met other mission leaders and evangelical groups, used questionnaires and assessed the situation on the ground. "They gave me an insight into their work, the results, the struggles and difficulties, as well as the ways and means that one must employ here in order to win some," he wrote. He came back advocating for a Mennonite Brethren witness.

Latin American missions—aside from the work done by Mennonite Brethren immigrants in Paraguay—had its beginning in Colombia. At a meeting in Coaldale in 1944, the mission board accepted the work. The first people to enter Colombia were former Bethany students—two Wirsche brothers, Daniel and David, and their wives Elsie and Salome, as well as the Abe Dycks, followed soon after by others such as John and Mary Dyck. These pioneers were highly motivated and gifted people and eventually included others like Jake and Ann Loewen from B.C., Annie Dyck, Herta Voth, Wilmer and Jean Quiring (he was Ja-

cob Lepp's grandson), John and Jan Goertz, and still others. They led
the way into Latin missions, joined in short order by a large number of
American Mennonite Brethren.

### LEAVING CANADA

Quick forward now.

In 1943, GW had ended his work at Bethany and also received a
degree from Tabor College. After returning from Latin America, he
began a year's teaching at Tabor and then went on to Hartford for his
doctoral studies. During his Hartford years, Mennonite Brethren in
California began a Bible school in Fresno, the Pacific Bible Institute
(today Fresno Pacific University), and after completing his ThD, GW
accepted the invitation to become Pacific's principal, though the new
Bible College in Winnipeg had also courted him. He stayed there until 1953 and led the school through years of rapid growth, though his
board often felt his vision far exceeded their capacity.

In 1955 he moved over to the Seminary that Mennonite Brethren
were beginning at Pacific Bible Institute. He became its first academic
dean and helped draw to the Seminary a number of faculty who shared
his vision for mission and the church—and largely his theological perspectives. One of his students was Elmer Martens, later himself the
Seminary's president, who described Peters as one of the two "most
exciting" teachers in all his years of study.

Martens' description explains why Peters had such an effect on his
students. "He [wanted] to persuade and compel us as to his point of
view. The presentation had me fully engaged. I was mentally and often
verbally interacting with him—perhaps challenging him…. I remember well a class in OT theology. He spent a semester in Genesis 1-11
and we never got through that passage. He often wanted to present
large ideas—it was not small or trivial stuff, it was sweeping theologically. I was always impressed with his vast knowledge and his experience often illuminated what he had to say. [And] he was personable
and easy to talk to…." At both the Bible Institute and then the Seminary, Peters made missions a major emphasis. Hans Kasdorf, who later
directed the Church Mission Institute at the Seminary, says that Peters
"played a key role in planting a missionary vision and curriculum" in
the Seminary.

Nonetheless, when he ended his years at Pacific College and the
Seminary, his successors felt the Seminary needed to be turned from a
mainstream evangelical orientation toward a more Anabaptist stance,
something that both J.B. Toews in the festschrift to Peters, *Reflection*

*GW at a 1978 church convention—his passion was always mission.*

*and Projection*, and a later dean, A. J. Klassen, in *The Seminary Story*, make quite clear. The extent to which Peters was distanced from the life of the Seminary might have been signalled by a 1967 festschrift to J.B. Toews, *The Church in Mission*, edited by A.J. Klassen, that contained essays by 21 Mennonite Brethren writers, but nothing by G.W. Peters. In it, the origins of the Western Children's Mission are credited to J.B. Toews without any mention of Peters. Only one footnote found by this writer mentions Peters.

## NEVER LOST HIS VISION

Yet GW does not appear to have lost either his vision for missions, his desire to pour his energies into the extension of the gospel, or even his appreciation for the Mennonite Brethren. Nor does he appear to have bemoaned his situation for long. After the Seminary, GW became the pastor of the Buhler, Kansas MB church where Toews had pastored years before. He stayed there two years and then went on to Dallas Theological Seminary. A Buhler deacon spoke of Peters as "a great preacher" who had given "many, many suggestions for the program of the church." Perhaps feeling they were too much for them, he added, "now we need help to evaluate what can be applied."

During 17 years at Dallas, Peters created and led a strong World Missions Department and cemented a reputation as a leading evangelical missiologist. He became known as a "scholar, researcher, lecturer, professor [and] author," wrote a colleague of his. "The scope of his research extend[ed] to India, Indonesia, Japan and South America. Peters' grasp of such social sciences as anthropology and psychology combined with his theological discipline provided him with tools that made him most effective as teacher in the classroom, consultant to mission board and author of missiological writings." GW also helped give direction to Trinity Evangelical Divinity School's doctoral program in missions as it was being shaped.

Even retirement from Dallas did not spell the end of active engagement. He stepped into a dearth of missions education in Europe when he accepted the invitation of the Liebenzell Mission to assist in the formation of a curriculum for a new missions academy in Germany. That school opened in 1979 with Peters as dean and matured into the Freie Hochschule Fuer Mission (now Academy for World Missions) in Korntal, sponsored by the German Association of Evangelical Missions. He stayed till 1987. Today a special prize in his name remembers his legacy. A history of the school says it was Peters who gave it its "profile" and brought together a strong team that has since prepared hundreds of men and women for cross-cultural mission.

## TIES TO MENNONITE BRETHREN

Even though GW worked almost entirely in inter-denominational settings after 1960, he always kept his ties to the Mennonite Brethren. For more than a quarter of a century from 1951 on, he was a part of the board of foreign missions. There he exercised a strong influence, for at least a decade of which J.B. Toews was the executive secretary. Another member, Herb Brandt, described him as "very progressive" and a "forerunner of mission-missionfield partnership and the need for indigenization." Because he travelled widely, "he always spoke to issues with conviction and confidence. At times he made sweeping recommendations [which] provoked some criticism from long-term missionaries." He and J.B. Toews were not always on the same page, said Brandt, but, remarkably, the two great men of "strong conviction and many ideas…could come to consensus." GW helped shape modern missions for the Mennonite Brethren. "Directions the board took usually had GW's mark on them," said Brandt.

GW also wrote a very fine book, *Foundations of Mennonite Brethren Missions*, during his latter years. Published in 1984, in it he says missions were a part of Mennonite Brethren thinking from their beginning in Russia and explains how it evolved over the years. One of its traits, said Peters, has been an entrepreneurial approach to new starts—among which the Western Children's Mission would be an example. Others were the A.A. Janzens or the Heinrich Bartsches going off to Congo, and the Frank J. Wienses and the Henry Bartels going to China. He laments the instances when it took decades for the conference to embrace them formally and explores the reasons. While his critiques are strong, he never singles out by name people who might have created roadblocks.

He especially affirmed a mission witness that fostered strong local church linkages to the larger Mennonite Brethren church. A later teacher of missions at Bethany College, Gordon Nickel, said he always reminded students of Peters' emphasis on keeping church and missions together. As he wrote what became his last important statement to Mennonite Brethren, GW named what he thought an MB witness might contribute: (1) an understanding for the believers' church concept pioneered by the Anabaptist-Mennonites, (2) the church as a school of discipleship, (3) the church as an evangelizing body, (4) the church as a functioning brotherhood (rediscovering the concepts of fellowship and body life), and (5) the church as a spiritual home for the family (making the argument for smaller churches). They all sounded very Anabaptist.

A missions colleague of GW, Dr. Paul Hiebert, noted that among the most vivid and prized experiences of his time as Peters' student was the frequent reminder that Mennonites "rooted their beliefs in the Bible and were people of the Book."

George W. Peters wrote no memoirs. For many Canadian Mennonite Brethren he isn't even a memory. But the trail he opened influences us to this day. He planted ideas, inspired young people, and helped create institutions. In the providence of God he became a critical agent of change and growth for Mennonite Brethren.

At his funeral just after the new year 1989, a grandson reflected on the initials carried by his grandfather: GW. They reminded him of George Washington. Like the famous president, George W. Peters "would fight and never give up hope." If we agree that his "fighting" meant passionate advocacy for his convictions, the image was apt. G.W. Peters led well and we owe him a great debt of gratitude.

SOURCES
Important sources for this chapter included books by G.W. Peters, particularly *The Growth of Foreign Missions in the Mennonite Brethren Church* (Hillsboro: 1952); *Foundations of Mennonite Brethren Missions* (Hillsboro: 1984); *A Biblical Theology of Missions* (Chicago: 1976); and *A Theology of Church Growth* (Grand Rapids: 1981). In addition, the festschrift *Reflection and Projection* (Bad Liebenzell: 1988) was very helpful, as was Peter Penner's *No Longer at Arms Length* (Winnipeg: 1987), the story of home missions by Mennonite Brethren in Canada. Interviews with Hans Kasdorf, Elmer Martens and Herb Brandt provided helpful insights. Western Children's Mission files, back issues of *The Christian Leader*, the *Mennonite Brethren Herald* and especially also the *Zionsbote*, which was the major Mennonite Brethren periodical of the '20s and '30s, along with Conference yearbooks, also yielded important information. A footnoted copy of this chapter is on file at the Centre for Mennonite Brethren Studies in Winnipeg.

## B.B. Janz

# ALWAYS WITH "HIS PEOPLE" ON HIS HEART

*By Dora Dueck*

B enjamin B. Janz was well past middle age when he left Russia for Canada in 1926. He was the father of six and ignorant of the English language. He was a soon-to-be farmer although he had never farmed. He was keenly aware, as he put it, that he had "lost an old homeland and was not yet rooted in the new."

He was also a household name among his Mennonite brothers and sisters. It was largely because of him, after all—on the Russian side of the effort at least—that more than 20,000 had escaped the terrors of Russia to immigrate, as he had, to Canada.

So, if everything had changed for Janz, in many respects nothing had changed at all. He had been, it was said, "the man of the hour," given by God to the Mennonite people for a critical period in their history. But he would not and could not rest on his laurels now. The burden he felt for his people, and the convictions and character that bore it, propelled him immediately to further leadership in the new setting.

He transferred his loyalties to his new country. He shepherded his fellow immigrants and helped them get established. He bridged between

*The Writer*
Dora Dueck will be known to many Mennonite Brethren readers for her various stints with the *Mennonite Brethren Herald*, the last as editor. She has also written several books, one entitled *Under the Still Standing Sun*, coming out of years in Paraguay, country of her husband Helmut's birth, and *Willie*, the life of a young Winnipegger, Willie Fast. Her latest book, *This Hidden Thing*, came out in 2010. Dora is a member of the Jubilee Mennonite Church of Winnipeg.

people, between worlds and soon was recognized as one of Canada's dominant Mennonite leaders. Within his own particular group, the Mennonite Brethren, B.B. Janz would be among the greatest of his generation.

## EARLY LIFE

Benjamin B. Janz (or BB as many knew him) was born September 25, 1877, in Konteniusfeld in the Mennonite colony Molotschna, the first of seven children of Benjamin B. and Helene (Penner) Janz. The family made a modest living off a small farm and windmill and the father's work as a carpenter.

The boy was not robust or strong, but he was an excellent student and Benjamin's father wisely realized his firstborn was better suited for teaching than farming. (Indeed, according to those who knew the farmer B.B. Janz in Canada later, he never acquired farming skills in any notable measure.) Father Janz had not been school-educated himself, but saw to it that his son was enrolled in high school (*Zentralschule*) in nearby Gnadenfeld after his basic village schooling.

The tenacity that would become B.B. Janz's hallmark as a leader of his people evidenced itself already in the student. A classmate later recalled a snowball fight on the schoolyard in which the defeated team fled to the side of the playground, all but Janz that is, who was still standing his ground.

Janz himself recalled, in a short memoir he wrote of his childhood and conversion in 1962, his early reputation for honesty: "Whether jesting or serious, he would not lie." An argument among classmates might come down to, "Go ask little Janz, he'll tell you the truth."

The home he was raised in was strict and pious. His father prayed aloud for Benjamin before bringing him to the high school where he boarded—this being somewhat "unusual," Janz recalled: audible personal prayer was at that time a distinguishing mark of the Mennonite Brethren, the group that had broken away in 1860 from the larger Mennonite church of Russia to which his parents belonged. That he was a sinner, Benjamin knew, and also that he needed to be "saved" (*selig*), but they had not spoken to him of how this might happen.

It was in the village of Yalantusch in the Crimea where Janz began his professional life as a teacher in 1896 at 18, that the young teacher, feeling inadequate in his work and needing God's help as he had never needed it before, came to a radical turn within—that is, to conversion.

## "BEING IN CONVERSION"

Janz described the process in some detail later, using the expression "being in conversion." This involved a searching study of Scripture (earlier he had read "every kind of book possible, except the Bible," he said), conversations with older people he respected for their Bible knowledge and faith and earnest prayer. Then revival broke out in the village, but while others were finding spiritual peace and clarity, "everything stayed dark" for him.

One Saturday evening, the reading of Isaiah 43 challenged him to "wrestle through" to find forgiveness and to give himself completely to God. When "the prodigal" finally broke through with repeated surrender, "there was no reaction from above." Disappointed, Benjamin went to bed.

The next day, January 19, 1897, he read Isaiah 43 again, twice, and the second time, the text spoke to him with assurance that his sin had been covered at the cross. Joy flooded his "tormented heart" and the "timid" young teacher startled even himself by breaking into prayer at the end of that day's church service, praising God for salvation. Wonderful weeks, among the best in his life, followed.

When Janz recounted his conversion, he continued with a significant sequel to the salvation breakthrough he had experienced that day in January. A further process of struggle ensued when the joy passed and doubts rose, until he came to the understanding that one's faith rests not on feelings but on the Word of God. It would be an important conviction in his life and later ministry.

The next step was baptism. Janz had earlier concluded that immersion was the right mode of baptism. He was baptized into the Mennonite Brethren church August 8, 1897, following much personal prayer and discussion with his parents, who disapproved of his joining this church.

B.B. Janz's loyalty to the Mennonite Brethren church remained strong throughout his life. Although he served the wider Mennonite community without prejudice, he never wavered from his opinion that the Mennonite Brethren had recovered something vital in their understanding of the church. His ideals for the church rested on what he had discovered in the 1890s during his quest for a spiritual home.

He had received an impression then of its character, "of brotherly fellowship; fear of God; a healthy appetite for the Word; of a sincere, quickening preaching; of work with the faltering one and of the treatment of the unrepentant sinner in the church.... [MBs] believed a man was lost without conversion." This remained Janz's vision of what Mennonite Brethren should always strive to be.

## CALLED TO LEAD

B.B. Janz gave some 20 years to teaching, beginning in Yalantusch, then on a Mennonite estate near Kleefeld, then in Sparrau. At a teachers' conference in the Memrik settlement, he was introduced to Maria Rogalsky, and they married on his 28th birthday, September 25, 1905. The couple lived the first years of their marriage in Sparrau, then in 1908 moved with their young children Peter and Helena to Tiege, where Benjamin taught and also became active in the Tiege Mennonite Brethren Church. (Four more children—Gertrude, Maria, Jacob, and Martha—would be born to them here.)

In 1909, on September 25—a day already significant as his birthday and wedding anniversary—B.B. Janz was ordained and became the leader of the Tiege MB Church.

His local ministry was well received, but it was circumstances rising from the Great War and the Bolshevik Revolution that propelled Janz into leadership on a much larger scale. When World War I broke out, he was drafted and did alternative service, as permitted to the Mennonites by the government, in the forestry camp at Alt-Berdyansk. He returned home in 1917. For some time, he was deathly ill with dysentery.

Minutes of an All-Mennonite Conference held in Lichtenau in 1918, where non-resistance was under discussion, reveal that B.B. Janz spoke up twice. The civil war had unleashed much destruction and suffering as it shifted back and forth across the Mennonite colonies of the Ukraine; organized self-defense seemed a necessary and viable option, especially with the help of the German-backed White Army.

Janz opposed any deviation from the Mennonites' traditional stance. His argument contained two intertwined elements—patriotic participation in the state's fate as much as possible, without weapons, as well as the willingness to suffer for the sake of the belief that, as he would put it more than once in the future, "the shedding of blood is great sin."

When representatives of Mennonites in Ukraine gathered again in February 1921, in Alexanderwohl, to propose the creation of an organization to work on their behalf with the now securely established Communist government under Lenin, Janz spoke up again. There were some matters of conscience, he said, that might need to be resolved first.

Some Mennonite communities had indeed organized military units for self-defense but by now this approach had proved itself a grievous error, damaging both the Mennonites' principles and their reputation. As far as their safety went, it may have made things worse. Janz was elected leader of the new organization but was adamant that the delegates needed to declare themselves on the matter of non-resistance.

But what about those who felt differently? A solution unexpectedly emerged when Elder Plett of Hierschau asked all those who agreed to "attempt" with all their "life and efforts" to remain non-resistant to raise their hands. The declaration was unanimous.

Janz had not won condemnation of the past as he wanted, but he had won a commitment for the future. "This is a good beginning," he realized.

*Emigrants leaving Russia, the second trainload, in early July, 1923. Janz stands in the doorway in the shadows.*

"Don't force the issue; the Lord can continue to help." Janz would have many opportunities in the future to hone this ability to see, then seize upon, what was possible. He was principled, but also pragmatic.

## STRUGGLE FOR SURVIVAL

In appearance, B.B. Janz was unremarkable, his body lean, his face narrow and almost boyish-looking with its full lips and large ears. His personality too was unremarkable in many ways, for he was neither jovial nor particularly charming, nor was he a powerful orator.

He did not have the status of wealth either, for he never owned land in Russia, not even a house of his own. (He had stepped down from teaching in the spring of 1920 and worked as caretaker of the students' boarding house in Tiege for a low salary; the family had a cow but was poor, and would often be in need in the years to come.) Yet B.B. Janz possessed remarkable intelligence, a quiet but dignified and compelling personal presence, and an inner strength that combined tender sensitivity with confident determination.

His first responsibility as chair of the Union of South Russian Mennonites (later Union of Citizens of Dutch Lineage), a post he held until 1926, was to negotiate on behalf of Mennonite men who were being forcibly conscripted into the Red Army. The position soon took on much larger implications, however: namely the survival of his people during famine conditions and efforts for their economic recovery. Janz used the union post, in fact, for unrelenting work on behalf of every Mennonite problem regarding their survival.

He kept up a stream of information and pleas for assistance to Mennonite leaders in North America and Europe, often eloquent in their appeal. In one, he talked about "the desolation of our Egyptian darkness," in another, of the Mennonites' desperate need and their "longing for a man with a donkey, oil and wine, as well as bandages."

Janz was soon convinced that Mennonites had no future in Russia. Not even the introduction of the Soviet state's New Economic Policy changed his mind. He continued his work on behalf of economic recovery but also began to pour himself into efforts for emigration. He persuaded the authorities that it would be good to let some of the Mennonites leave, in order to quiet restlessness in the colonies, and then negotiated for documents of permission, all at considerable risk to himself and at the cost of long absences from his family, as well as criticism and impatience from those he was trying to help.

By the time the emigration movement he led (together with equally hard-working and criticized counterparts in Canada such as David Toews) had been exhausted, some 20,000 Mennonites had been able to leave. Janz himself, already under surveillance for some time, managed to get out in June 1926, just hours before his scheduled arrest.

### DEEPLY INVOLVED AGAIN

In Canada, B.B. Janz and his family, who followed him from Russia after his secret departure, bought a farm in Coaldale, Alberta. Coaldale was a relatively new settlement, engaged in mixed farming that used irrigation because of the dry climate. Except for some two years in B.C. at the end of his life, Janz would live in Coaldale the rest of his days.

The fledgling Mennonite community in Coaldale grew and flourished, and Janz was soon elected leader of its Mennonite Brethren church. This church became one of Canada's leading MB congregations, reaching a membership of more than 600. It established both a Bible school and a high school and thus attracted and produced many leaders for the ministries of the denomination.

Coaldale MB was also a challenging church, formed of immigrants from diverse areas of the Soviet Union. Now "a settler among settlers," as

*Janz with members of the Canadian Mennonite Board of Colonization: rear (l-r), John Harder, C.A. DeFehr, Gerhard Derksen, and J.J. Gerbrandt; front, B.B. Janz, David Toews, C.F. Klassen and J.J. Thiessen.*

his biographer put it, B.B. Janz was subject to the annual and often critical reviews that the "intensely democratic processes of decision-making" deemed the right way to conduct church. A crisis around his leadership led to his resignation in 1933, but Janz was soon re-elected. He spent some 19 years in all as congregational head. Although he himself did not often preach, he arranged for the preachers' list (there were many ministers to choose from), and might close the service in prayer—long prayers that, to younger listeners, sometime felt like a repetition of the sermon they had just heard.

Janz also became heavily involved in conference work. There was hardly a Mennonite Brethren board, it seemed, whether it concerned publishing, education, missions, or "reference and council" on theological questions, that B.B. Janz was not part of or able to influence through his close connections with other church leaders. He was deeply concerned about the welfare of the MB church in Canada, its identity, and its faithfulness, especially in the midst of a surrounding culture more sophisticated than it had been in Russia. Janz knew, from his relationships with American Mennonites, that neither language nor nationality was a critical factor in faith, but he feared rapid assimilation in Canada. He promoted the retention of the German language, cultural traditions and strong institutional growth—locally in burial societies, medical facilities and schools, and nationally in schools, publishing ventures and Bethesda, an Ontario hospital for the mentally ill.

Just as he had in Russia, Janz the immigrant also worked on behalf of the larger Mennonite world. He had barely landed in Canada before setting off on a tour to Mennonite churches in the United States to appeal for assistance with financial obligations the Canadian Mennonite Board of Colonization had undertaken for the migration endeavour. This was only the beginning of decades of travel for meetings or ministry on the North American continent, usually by train. The rolling cars on their tracks of steel must have seemed a second home to him at times.

Whether at home or away, Janz conducted a voluminous correspondence with individuals who sought his help or counsel or with leaders concerning decisions and programs. His letters were usually typed, single-spaced, and often long. With colleagues he moved quickly to the business at hand, but with those in need, or younger leaders he might be mentoring, he wrote with personable warmth and kindly encouragement.

### BEST ON THE BIG ISSUES

B.B. Janz, his biographer John B. Toews wrote, "was at his best on a large stage." In Canada, the events of the 1930s leading up to World War II, and then the war years themselves, put Janz on that large stage again. He strongly defended non-resistance in Mennonite periodicals, especially against those Mennonites who had become enthused about Hitler and Nazism. As keen as he was to retain the German language for their communities, he carefully and insistently distinguished it from the ideology of Hitler's Germany. And, he used every opportunity to praise Canada, its leaders, and the religious liberty his people enjoyed in this country.

He served as Mennonite Brethren representative in the all-Mennonite meetings called to respond to the outbreak of war, and became one of the leading spokespersons for an alternative service position that might include non-combatant medical service such as an ambulance corps. It disappointed him that the various Mennonite groups could not reach consensus on a common approach. His position, described later as "radical pacifism," was to serve the country during wartime by doing everything possible to "provide services in the line of life; reject all services in the line of destruction."

*Janz here honoured the CPR for its enormous support to the 1920s' immigration effort—giving an inscribed tribute to E.W. Beatty, the CPR president.*

Other Mennonite groups insisted on alternative service completely divorced from any military activity and Janz annoyed the other members of the Mennonite delegation to Ottawa when he sought, on his own, to win government approval for his proposal. It was obvious that he still had great confidence in his ability to work with officialdom as well as the rightness of his own convictions. He wanted a medical corps provision for conscientious objectors, while other Mennonite groups were generally opposed to such involvement. Janz knew the medical corps option well from Russia; it fit his understanding of "our definite obligations as citizens toward our homeland, not only in the form of taxes, but also in any service that is not contrary to our conscience."

Although he was not successful in his version of alternative service (though the military did offer something similar later), Janz continued to advocate for and work with young Mennonite men in gaining conscientious objector status. He concerned himself with their welfare in the CO camps, and helped steer Canadian Mennonites safely through the militaristic environment of that period while also fostering the patriotic reputation of Mennonites in the Canadian milieu.

After the war, Janz's energies turned to the needs of refugees. He was a keen supporter of the rebuilding efforts of Mennonite Central Committee (MCC) in Europe. Indeed, the ethos of refugees was always close to his heart. Even the 1920 immigrants were "more like refugees," he said at the 25th anniversary of the Coaldale MB Church. They had not come directly out of persecution, but they recognized it coming, and in their hearts, "it was flight." That had motivated him then, and it motivated him now.

In 1947, at 70, B.B. Janz was given a new assignment, which he described as coming to him as "a bolt of lightning out of the sky." He was asked to go to South America, where MCC was assisting in the settlement of Mennonite refugees, to give spiritual counsel and do a ministry of reconciliation. The Mennonite Brethren churches in both Fernheim and Friesland Colonies in Paraguay had divided over differences around support for Nazi Germany.

In the colonies, B.B. Janz preached nearly every day and spent hours in visitation, always patient but insistent on his goal of confession and re-unification. He saw his efforts and belief in the necessity of repentance bear fruit when the churches came back together after a thorough process of congregation-wide confession.

Back in Canada, Janz stayed involved with the churches of South America through his letters. He involved himself in finding workers for colony schools and churches, and promoted close ties between the Mennonite Brethren churches of the North and the South.

## AT THE END, PAIN AND GLORY

According to John B. Toews, author of the Janz biography, *With Courage to Spare*, Janz the new immigrant was not a legalistic man. In the 1950s, however, that seemed to change. The sharper tones of rigidity and authoritarianism now perceptible in him were probably the result of advancing age, as well as Janz's realization that the assimilation he had worked hard to prevent was proceeding as he had feared. The language of Canadian MB churches church was shifting from German to English, and he himself faced redundancy as a new generation of leaders gained influence in the Mennonite Brethren and wider Mennonite world.

In the 1950s, Janz also became frustrated with MCC, initially over its fiscal policies for the Mennonite colonies of South American, where help was given as loans instead of gifts, and then with its "peace witness" theology, which, to his mind, had lost the biblical foundation of "the new life."

It was, further, a decade of grief and growing ill health. Maria, his wife of 58 years, quiet, uncomplaining and prayerful, died in October 1953. Then, in 1957, Janz got what he called "the severest blow of my life," the sudden death of his oldest son Peter in a car accident, "in the knowledge that he left no testimony of eternal life."

When Janz reached 80 in 1957 and he and his friend P.C. Hiebert, longtime MCC chairman, "retired" from their conference offices and were publicly thanked for their services, Janz declared privately that he felt more replaced and discharged than truly retired.

By the time 1960 opened to what would become a raucous decade of cultural change, B.B. Janz was an old man. His face was deeply lined. What consumed him now was not so much the future or societal upheavals as the very immediate present—and the past. He was plagued with headaches and urinary problems, enveloped in grief and fresh wrestling with God, struggling sometimes with an old temptation to self-pity. ("This suffering, God, after all I've done?")

The one thing he still wanted to accomplish after a lifetime of astonishing accomplishments was to write his memoirs. His body was conspiring against him, it seemed, but his mind was clear, his memories clamouring to be set down. "Everything like your letter or the notation of events or re-reading documents brings life to my thoughts of the past," he told a couple who had written him of their rescue from Russia by his help, "and stirs my soul inwardly with great feeling and gratitude to the heavenly Father, sometimes to the point of falling on my knees."

He managed to get some sections of the story done—about his rise to leadership, and some of his tense negotiations with Communist officials in Kharkow and Moscow. He also started, though he did not finish, a chapter called "My Homecoming," recollecting his early years, the moral training in the family, his conversion and his baptism as Mennonite Brethren. Janz was a good writer, able still to recall details like a meal of horse meatballs, the pose of a Soviet official against a radiator, and his utter despondency one Easter as he waited out the results of a request he had made to Soviet functionaries. He referred to himself, though, in the third person.

Early in 1963, as B.B. Janz's health worsened, he accepted his oldest daughter's invitation to move into their home in B.C. In November 1963, when his needs for care outstripped his children's ability to provide it, Janz entered Menno Private Hospital. He longed to get better but when it did not happen, he became morose.

As Janz suffered, he often found comfort in Scripture and the songs his children sang to him, but both his inner and outer agony were acute. His long dying, with its alternating cycles of despair and faith, finally ended October 20, 1964.

At the graveside service some days later, J.J. Thiessen, a close friend and colleague of B.B. Janz through the Board of Colonization, used the words of 2 Samuel 3:38, "Don't you realize that a prince and a great man has fallen in Israel this day?" to pay him tribute and bid him farewell. B.B. Janz, he reminded, truly belonged among the great.

### SOURCES

Major source for the general narrative of B.B. Janz's life was his biography, *With Courage to Spare* (Fresno: Board of Christian Literature, General Conference of Mennonite Brethren Churches, 1978), by John B. Toews. Some of the quotes come from other writings by Toews such as *Lost Fatherland* (Scottdale: Herald Press, 1967) and *Czars, Soviets and Mennonites* (Newton: Faith and Life Press, 1982). Additional quotes and the description of Janz's early life and conversion, as well as the events of his leadership in Russia, were drawn from Janz's own memoirs and letters, *My Homecoming* [*Meine Heimkehr*], a short, unfinished piece telling of his life from birth to baptism, found in the B.B. Janz papers at the Centre for MB Studies, Winnipeg, and documents and letters contained in *Selected Documents* (Winnipeg: Christian Press, 1975). Other words and sentiments of his were taken from the Coaldale 25th anniversary book as well as several letters among many hundreds of Janz's letters housed at the Centre: letters to Hans Kasdorf, C.A. Defehr and N.N. Driedger.

# C.A. DeFehr

# IN BUSINESS
# FOR THE LORD

*By Harold Jantz*

We may never know whether Cornelius A. DeFehr made it his goal to set an example of how to put one's entrepreneurial skills at the service of Christ and the church. What we do know is that within Mennonite Brethren circles few did it better during a period when they were entering the Canadian business world as never before.

When Mennonite Brethren began launching out into new ventures in the mid-decades of the 20th century, DeFehr invariably was in the thick of them. That was especially true for the MB Collegiate Institute in Winnipeg, the building of the Elmwood Church, the creation of the MB Bible College and the takeover of the Christian Press and the *Mennonitische Rundschau* by the Canadian Conference.

It was true for inter-Mennonite projects like the Mennonite Collegiate Institute in Gretna and the young Mennonite hospital in Winnipeg, Concordia Hospital, as well as relief and immigration efforts that grew into MCC.

It was also true of city missions in Winnipeg, a mission to Africa, as well as the formation of MEDA (Mennonite Economic Development Associates), set up initially to help Mennonite refugees being resettled into Paraguay. And it was true for the whole process of resettling World War II Mennonite refugees in that country under the sponsorship of MCC.

---

### The Writer

During his years as *MB Herald* editor, Harold Jantz would regularly be visited by C.A. DeFehr. Harold spent twenty years in the Christian Press building once created mainly through DeFehr's efforts. Harold and Neoma have been members of River East Mennonite Brethren Church of Winnipeg since the early 1960s.

DeFehr's personal journey—as it did for so many other Mennonite Brethren leaders from the 1930s to the 1980s—began in Russia. He and his young family, together with other relatives, arrived in Canada in September, 1925. It was time to start over again in many things for which DeFehr already had a good deal of experience back in Russia.

## AN ENTREPRENEURIAL FAMILY

They were an entrepreneurial family. Born at Einlage in 1881, CA learned well from a father—Abram A. DeFehr—who was both a farmer and a tradesman. When CA was still very young the family moved onto a farm in the village of Kronsweide, in what is known as the Mennonite Old Colony. That's where his mother Helena had come from and where they could buy some land. But his father also had a workshop where he built furniture and wagons, even taking on larger projects like the construction of houses and windmills. CA says he loved to work with his father's tools, preferred business over farming, and even as a child had the "ambition to enter business."

A very important influence in his early life came from the impact of the renewal that swept the Mennonite colonies and resulted in the Mennonite Brethren Church. It touched the lives of his parents deeply and "had a profound and lasting influence" on young CA's life. He also grew up with the stories of the struggles of the early leaders who were viewed as "trouble-makers by both the civic and religious authorities of the Mennonites."

After a half dozen years in Kronsweide, the family moved to the village of Petrovka in a new settlement called Naumenko, hoping to find better opportunities there. A characteristic of many of the so-called "daughter" colonies in Russia was the higher proportion in them of those who might be Mennonite Brethren. The Naumenko settlement was largely Mennonite Brethren. As a result the church life there became a rich experience for the family. The DeFehrs also farmed a much bigger acreage and prospered.

Young CA's father also did something in Petrovka quite unusual for Mennonites in Russia. When CA had finished his first three grades, his father put him into a nearby school created by a wealthy, highly-educated Russian landowner. There CA and his older brother Abram attended for four years, the only German Mennonite pupils among the 200 in the school. It became an experience from which CA benefitted his entire life. Even the five-kilometer walk in good weather carried lifelong benefits, CA wrote later, not to mention a teacher-principal who was a mathematics expert.

A remark on the first day of school there left a memory CA never forgot. After introducing the two Mennonite students and lauding them as Russian citizens, the principal said that the Mennonites lacked one thing—"they are not as hospitable to strangers as they should be." It was a lesson young Cornelius felt needed to be learned.

## TURNINGPOINTS

CA came to trust Christ for his salvation at the age of 19. Two ministers, Jakob W. Reimer and Abraham Wall, had been conducting a two-week series of Bible studies for the colony in CA's parental home. The last evening came and the meeting that night was to take place in the neighbouring village. As the parents prepared to leave, Reimer said he wouldn't go even though he was scheduled to speak because he noticed the young people of the village weren't going. Despite protests, Reimer persisted and told the DeFehr boys to call their friends together.

That evening he held a meeting for the young people only, and CA wrote later, "the Lord blessed it in a special way." The dozen young people there all decided to follow the Lord, including CA. That decision altered his life forever.

One of the effects was a strong increase in the "missionary interest" within the community. With the encouragement of their minister, and active participation by the youth, they engaged in witness within a nearby Russian settlement and some were converted. Later some of these believers came to Canada and became part of the Arelee Mennonite Brethren Church in Saskatchewan.

At Petrovka, CA also met his wife, Liese Dyck, the daughter of Wilhelm and Maria Dyck. The Dycks only lived in Petrovka for a short few years and operated a mill there. Dyck was a very capable man, possessed a keen business mind, and served the young MB church as an elder (bishop) and itinerant preacher. He impressed CA. Wilhelm's wife Maria had the unusual distinction of having been a teacher, rare for Mennonite women.

Years later, C.A. DeFehr wrote that his father-in-law had a great gift for dealing with the high and mighty, but "he also took special interest in the lowly, the oppressed, and the ignorant, and would assist them wherever possible. Invariably, he would take the side of the right no matter what the odds. He also blazed new trails for the church as chairman of the [conference's] mission board, as an initiator of courses for choir directors and in evangelism. He was an individualist of forceful personality and strong character." [He spent his final years in Niverville, Man. *Ed.*] Dyck's example and Liese's strong moral support, birthed within her home setting, remained a constant throughout CA's life.

In 1903 Dyck moved again, this time to a central railway town called Millerovo, where he with several partners set up a large mill. That fall, CA followed the Dycks and married Liese there. He was 22 and she 18 when they married. For a year they came back to Petrovka but then they returned to Millerovo and went into business on their own—and his life's direction was set. They joined a number of other Mennonite families there with the Mennonite Brethren forming the core.

### IN AND OUT OF BUSINESS

C.A. DeFehr developed a business partnership involving his brother-in-law, Cornelius Martens, and his father-in-law, that was set up to manufacture and sell agricultural machinery: drills, mowers, threshing machines, oil presses and flour mills. They expanded very rapidly and by the outbreak of World War 1, they employed over a hundred employees, which rose to 200 during the war. They did very well. With the coming of the war, however, some of the production of the factory was claimed by the war effort, manufacturing casings for explosive mines, for example, which became a crisis of conscience never fully resolved for its owners.

The Communist revolution followed and eventually, in late 1919, the DeFehrs along with ten other families abandoned their businesses and fled, taking with them the belongings they could pack into a number of train cars. Their destination was the Kuban area in the Caucasus. CA became desperately ill with typhus during the journey and wrote later that a brew of parsley that Liese concocted appears to have relieved the crisis. Through God's grace, the help of a Polish doctor friend and his wife's homegrown treatment, he survived.

Once in the Kuban they set about establishing themselves once more. The church life nurtured them—CA even became the conductor of the church choir—and he returned to business. With a partner he shipped flour in four-pound boxes to Baptists in Moscow who exchanged it for cloth. The business grew till they could ship an entire boxcar of flour.

When he realized the Red government was going to confiscate large amounts of grain, he made sure his own grain was brought to a flour mill the day it was harvested. They never turned in any grain and always had enough to eat and share with others during the famine that followed. DeFehr saw how recklessly and badly planned was the confiscation of grains and meat initiated by the Moscow government, much of which went bad before it could be distributed. It greatly aggravated a famine brought on by drought.

In fact, C.A. DeFehr and another Mennonite were made responsible for the 1922 distribution of American Mennonite food aid in the Kuban

*A family business, Standard Importing and Sale (later C.A. DeFehr and Sons). With CA are (from left), Cornelius, William, son-in-law B.B. Fast and Abe.*

region. He was also given the assignment of assisting young Mennonite men who asked to be excused from serving in the military for reasons of conscience. Their hearings would sometimes take place in front of large groups of onlookers and became occasions for a "clear testimony for God," CA wrote.

Despite the New Economic Policy introduced by Lenin in 1923 and the tangible improvement in conditions that followed, CA and his family became increasingly persuaded that Russia would not provide a rewarding future for them. He was a delegate to the last Mennonite general conference in Moscow in 1925 and came away convinced that the future for Mennonites in that country "was rather dark." They made the decision to leave. In the years that followed he was to discover that "many of the delegates [he] had learned to know at the conference died in exile or [in] Russian prisons. Only a few succeeded in leaving Russia." He never lost a sense of gratitude for God's mercy to his family.

Leaving Russia took a complicated turn for many families because of trachoma, an eye disease. It was detected in CA too, but after making a promise to receive treatment for it in Germany, they got their permissions and visas. In Germany a doctor provided him with eye drops that seemed to work wonders and before long the family was on its way to Canada.

## STARTING OVER

The village of Gnadental near Winkler, Manitoba, became their first home, but before the first year was up, the family had moved into Winnipeg. Within months of coming to Canada, CA was also in business. During the time in Germany he had met with a former supplier of his, Heinrich Schuet, who told him that if DeFehr started up in Canada, he would provide him with products again as he had in Russia. So CA bought a truck and went onto the road peddling cream separators and hardware. He sent his orders off to Germany and in time the products came. It was a difficult beginning, but as orders were filled and he became known, the going became easier. Even so, he wrote that for the first five years in Canada he renewed his Russian passport every year with the thought he might still return.

The next dozen years were filled with strenuous effort as C.A. De-Fehr built his business. In the first years he went onto the road a great deal, often sleeping in farmers' homes, or even in a tent, to economize. Sometimes Liese joined him on the road. The company found a home on Princess Street in Winnipeg and by 1932, it had a branch in Edmonton. Later branches of what came to be known as C.A. DeFehr and Sons were located in Saskatoon and Regina in addition to Winnipeg and Edmonton. The early years started with cream separators and small hardware items; later such goods as sewing machines, plowshares, binder twine and washing machines were added. A seeder plow developed in Europe became an early big seller: by 1930 DeFehr had sold several hundred of them. Most of the business was done across the western provinces.

At the cusp of the Great Depression, DeFehr was already doing over $72,000 worth of business; a decade later, the company reached its lowest point, when it dropped to $33,000. Despite the Depression, the company survived. During the 1930s, a great deal of the inventory came from Europe, especially from Germany and Sweden. When the war came, the company had to switch entirely to North American sources for its inventory. Even then it survived. For a time, the DeFehrs even went back to farming when there was little else to do. But after the end of World War 2, CA and his sons and son-in-law returned with new energy to business and in very short order they were flourishing as never before, thanks in

*Two institution builders—CA with A.H. Unruh, first MBBC president.*

large part to the pent-up demand for consumer goods after a decade and a half of shortages.

### RE-THINKING HIS VIEWS

In his memoirs, CA says that the experience just prior to and during the war forced him to re-think his "pro-Germanism." He had pitched his products to a German-Canadian market and felt German products were much superior to goods made in Canada or the U.S. (as many of them may well have been). But along with many immigrants of that time, his feelings went well beyond that. In late 1937 he and Liese made a trip of several months to Europe, most of it spent in Germany. Later he wrote a long series of articles about the experience. Immediately after disembarking the ship in Bremen and dropping off his wife with friends, he drove to Nuernberg to witness a Nazi *Parteitag* (Party Day) and all the military displays that accompanied it. He also heard Adolf Hitler there. The whole event clearly captured his imagination.

The trip also involved visits to all his major suppliers, including a company in Sweden, and with old friends from Russia and new ones connected to an emerging mission to Congo in Africa. It is difficult, however, reading his reports, to sense any criticism of the militarism he was witnessing, or of the repression of certain groups within German society and of the ideology undergirding it. In an account of a visit with a German family, he stated that the church at home in Canada believed that preachers should not mingle in political matters. It was a position he endorsed.

At the end of his life, however, he realized that his "almost unlimited admiration" for Germany and its culture had been misplaced. He was trying to take the "lessons of World War 2," he wrote, and hoped the German people would too.

In fact, CA's main interests increasingly turned to the work of the church, and there his wife Liese was his strongest supporter. He wrote later, "Not only did she possess a loving heart and helping hands, but a keen mind, boundless energy and considerable determination. With me she was dedicated to the Lord, the Mennonites and our church. She would not allow anything to stand in my way when it came to serving on a church committee or attending a conference. Much of the credit that I have received should have gone to 'Meine Liese.'"

As to where he tried to place his energies, CA wrote, "Beyond attending properly to my business, I have never given much attention to wider political and social concerns....My preoccupation was the immediate needs and the institutional church. World needs for me were the widows in the church fellowship. Reconstruction for me meant the repair of the church and school buildings." He probably wasn't giving himself enough credit, his interests and involvements kept on widening.

## IN THE MIDDLE OF PROJECTS

That is why CA could almost always be found in the middle of projects. When the family arrived in Canada, within three days he had enrolled his sons and son-in-law in the Mennonite Collegiate Institute in Gretna and for years he remained a strong supporter of that school. He became a director on its board and served there for 13 years, helping during a time that a building project gave the school new facilities. When it became clear that Winnipeg Mennonite young people were not likely to attend the rural school, he joined a Mennonite Brethren group who built a high school in Winnipeg. For a time he was a director of both schools. He was part of the first board of Concordia Hospital begun by Mennonites in Winnipeg.

The creation of what was called the "higher Bible school," the Mennonite Brethren Bible College, was a much more ambitious project. CA became a member of its board in 1945 and remained on it for the next 15 years. He spent countless hours securing the supplies to build the first dormitory and repair or erect other buildings. When J.B. Toews came to

*C.A. DeFehr was honoured in 1973 for his role in the work of MCC. With him here was his grandson Albert DeFehr and another veteran of inter-Mennonite aid ministries, J.J. Thiessen.*

become president, it was CA who found the Toews family a home to live in. DeFehr's advice influenced many decisions. (I should know: this writer was part of the MBBC student council in the late '50s who decided to provide curtains and a valence for the chapel stage. When approval for our choice became necessary, it was CA's that was solicited.)

During that time CA also became the Canadian Conference treasurer and for 16 years he kept the books for the growing conference.

He also took the lead in purchasing the Christian Press and its publications when the owner, Herman Neufeld, wanted to sell in 1945. CA made an arrangement with other conference leaders to raise the capital to buy the press, with some of the shares held privately and the rest by the conference. CA became the chairman and held that position until 1961 when the conference bought up all the shares. CA was convinced of the "great importance of Christian literature to families, churches, missions and schools."

But those were also years during which he became increasingly involved on a wider inter-Mennonite stage. In 1940 he had become a member of the Canadian Mennonite Board of Colonization. Fifteen years earlier it was through that board that his own family had been brought to Canada. Now he joined its executive board and in the same year the executive board of the Mennonite Central Relief Committee. Later the two merged and became the Canadian Mennonite Relief and Immigration Council and DeFehr its vice-chairman. The DeFehr warehouse on

Princess Street became its material aid depot and when the CMRIC joined with MCC to form MCC Canada, the first Canadian offices were placed in DeFehr's same Princess Street building. Just after the war, CA's MCRC role brought him into Mennonite Central Committee and that led to a project that was life-changing for him.

## WW II REFUGEES

In 1947 he was asked to go to Paraguay to help settle the more than two thousand Mennonite refugees who fled the Soviet Union toward the end of World War II. The assignment was initially intended to be for five months—it turned into 11 months and was only the first of four times of strenuous effort in the South American country.

When the first company of 2303 refugees arrived aboard the Dutch passenger ship The Volendam, accompanied by Peter and Elfrieda Dyck, it launched a period of intense activity. First, the government of Argentina had to be persuaded to allow them to disembark at the port of Buenos Aires. They were, and then also provided a tent village where the arrivals could stay as transport into Paraguay was sorted out.

The problem in Paraguay was that the country was just then in the throes of a military insurrection. The refugees were forced to wait while the situation settled down. When it eased somewhat, CA and several associates surveyed several large tracts of land to find something suitable to buy and settle. Lesser souls might have turned and run. But with the strong support of Mennonites already there and a great deal of courage from the newcomers—many of whom were widows—sites were selected and a large number of villages laid out. MCC provided much of the initial funding and colonies like Fernhein gave exceptional help.

DeFehr's business experience helped the settlement project through many a difficult decision. But when he spoke to a group of the newcomers, he told them to "direct their thoughts alone to the Lord." Where that wasn't done, he said, there would be "very little prospect for the future." Along with them, CA recognized that eventual survival in that setting would depend on more than human effort.

CA returned to Paraguay again in 1948 and again in 1952 and 1958. The second stint in Paraguay lasted nine months and almost resulted in tragedy. Early on the DeFehrs were in an accident that took the driver's life and left Liese with injuries with lifelong after-affects. Despite setbacks and difficult issues with which to deal, CA's account makes it clear that he saw theirs as a ministry role. He and Liese carried strong concerns not merely for the colonists' material well-being, but their spiritual healing and growth as well. He advocated aggressively for the new

*Liese and C.A. DeFehr in their later years.*

colonists. When they left late in 1948, he wrote later, "a good part of our heart was now in the south. We wanted to return."

One important side-outcome of CA's work in Paraguay, in which he played a major role along with several others, was the formation of MEDA (Mennonite Economic Development Associates). It grew out of the recognition that if the colonists in Paraguay were not to "lose patience in the long run," as CA put it, they needed to be helped to develop thriving economies. They needed industries and access to markets. Only then would their standard of living be raised. After an inspection trip by a team of six, MEDA was born in 1953 and it gave Mennonite business people—initially mainly from Canada and the U.S.—a mechanism to raise capital whereby the colonies could borrow for development purposes. It was, as CA put it, "a miniature alliance for progress."

### HIS ADVICE SOUGHT
During the 1950s, CA also became increasingly engaged in advising Mennonite Brethren missions. During the 1930s, he had been involved in a local initiative to Congo, begun by Heinrich and Anna Bartsch, and for many years he acted as treasurer of the Winnipeg city mission. Now, in 1958, he was asked to review the outcomes of North American support for Mennonite Brethren Bible schools, for students and faculty, and support for "leading ministers, poor and the sick" in Latin America. A year earlier, in 1957, CA spent two months travelling around the globe with J.B.

Toews, the mission board general secretary, visiting the places where Mennonite Brethren were working at the time. CA was 76 years old.

Wherever possible they also visited MCC workers. Days were packed with meetings, often in discussions with other missions, and dominated by attempts to provide counsel and direction. On his return CA commented on his observations. His advice was to encourage stronger accountability of missionaries: each station and every missionary should be required to report regularly, so progress could be measured better and policies be developed based on better information. He also urged more regular visits by mission leaders to the fields so the situations and opinions there could be assessed much better. His experience as a businessman, said DeFehr, prompted his advice.

DeFehr was well up in years when he made the trip around the world, but he said when he came home he felt "several years younger."

**LAST YEARS**

His declining years allowed him to enjoy his family and his church. Both the golden wedding anniversary in 1954 and the diamond in late 1963 became important anniversaries. At the golden, old friends like B.B. Janz from Coaldale, the aging Abraham Unruh, J.B. Toews from Hillsboro, H.H. Janzen of the Bible College, and J.J. Thiessen from Saskatoon, were guests who spoke. He dropped by regularly to see his sons and grandson at the family business. Often he would stop by the Christian Press, the Bible College or his home church. In 1963 he sold his share of the business to his children.

At the end of his life, CA expressed much appreciation for what Canada had meant for his family. It had given him opportunities, but it had also placed on him responsibility to give the employee "the pay he deserves" and a "fair deal to our customers." Nonetheless, he said, "without the blessing of God all our efforts would have been in vain."

CA had always given generously to church and mission causes and he had little patience with those who claimed "bad times" kept them from giving. Attitudes more than "bulging bank accounts" would determine real stewardship, he said. Whatever wealth he might have had, most had been given away by the time he died. "My Liese," as he called her, died after a long illness in 1972 and in 1979 he followed her into the presence of God.

C.A. DeFehr was a model of entrepreneurial ability and wealth devoted to the cause of Christ. He expressed genuine joy in working with others in the projects of the church. He lamented fragmentation from other Mennonite groups where working together could serve the common good and do good for the world, even though he felt great loyalty to his own Mennonite Brethren fellowship. He spent little time looking for attention. He was happy if a project got done well. He kept things simple. Time spent well should pay well. He was in business for the Lord.

SOURCES
Most of the information for this chapter was drawn from C.A. DeFehr's memoirs, *Memories of my Life*, published in 1967. Other sources were the *Mennonitische Rundschau*, Canadian Conference yearbooks, *Mennonites in Winnipeg* by Leo Driedger, *Die Geschichte der Mennoniten-Bruedergemeinde* by A.H. Unruh, J.B. Toews's autobiography, *JB, A Twentieth-Century Mennonite Pilgrim*, *A Time to Remember: The Story of Reverend B.B. and Liese Fast* by Dora Dueck, *Mennonites in Canada 1920-1940: A People's Struggle to Survive* by Frank H. Epp; *Jacob's Journey, from Zagradowka to Zion* by J.M. Klassen, and fonds of the Canadian Conference Board of Higher Education at the Centre for MB Studies in Winnipeg.

# Henry H. Janzen

# BY THE GRACE OF GOD I AM WHAT I AM

*By Vic Froese*

When Henry H. Janzen died on March 4, 1975, he left behind an astonishing record of Christian ministry. He had pastored four Canadian MB churches; helped to found and then moderated the Ontario Mennonite Brethren Conference; served several terms as moderator of the Manitoba MB Conference, the Canadian MB Conference, and once, the General MB Conference; taught at five different Christian schools; ministered as an itinerant preacher and evangelist in Europe for many years; and illuminated the truths of the Bible to thousands of radio listeners in Europe and both North and South America.

Even this brief description only scratches the surface of the many ministry activities of this extraordinary man. His early life, however, showed few signs of what he was to become.

Imperial Russia's glory days were fading when Henry was born in the picturesque Mennonite village of Muensterberg, Molotschna Colony, in southern Russia on October 1, 1901. He was the first child of Heinrich J. and Gertruda Janzen who had married a year or two earlier. He was such a scrawny, sickly boy that no one who laid eyes on him imagined he would ever reach adolescence.

But by age seven he was hardy enough to start school, where he showed that what he lacked in bulk he made up for in intelligence and

---

*The Writer*

Vic Froese is the library director at the Canadian Mennonite University in Winnipeg. He came originally from St. Catharines, Ontario, and lives with his family in Steinbach, Manitoba.

mischievous energy. Although his father was the teacher at the one-room school he attended, Henry was hardly a model of good behaviour. He later recalled that he was a "rambunctious, fun-loving lad," and seldom was something broken at school that he didn't have a part in. Henry's strict father had more than a few occasions to discipline the future "Mennonite Brethren church statesman."

The majority of Muensterberg's roughly 400 villagers belonged to the Mennonite Church. The rest were Mennonite Brethren, and a smaller number, Quakers. The Janzens were among the majority and raised their children to take their faith seriously. Henry received some religious instruction at school, where his father taught his pupils the Bible stories. The subject of spiritual rebirth or conversion, however, was never raised. His father apparently took it for granted that devout parents would raise Christian children. Henry would, before long, bring that naïve belief into doubt.

## LOSING FAITH

The First World War began in 1914 and Henry's father was called up for active duty with the Russian Red Cross. Meanwhile, Henry entered the *Zentralschule* (high school) in Ohrloff where he boarded with a local family. There he became, in his words, a "wild boy," easily lured away from his studies by the offer of a cigarette or the promise of some tomfoolery. By age 15, Henry was losing what faith he had. The school's morning Scripture reading and prayer left him cold. He attended the Ohrloff Mennonite Church on Sundays, but merely out of duty. Henry learned to resist the gospel and later, with some friends, even published a tabloid-type newsletter, *The Anti-Mennonite*, a mouthpiece for his growing unbelief.

Spring 1917 saw Henry finish high school and return to Muensterberg. After the Bolshevik October Revolution that year, Henry's father came home and secured a job as teacher in the Mennonite village of Mariawohl. He moved the family there in August of 1918. It was in Mariawohl that Henry first met Katharina (Tina) Andres, whom he would marry six years later. The terror that hung over the colonies in 1919, thanks to the murderous assaults on Mennonite villagers by Nestor Makhno and his bandits, only confirmed Henry in the belief that God's existence was, at best, highly uncertain.

When the Russian communists finally drove Makhno away in 1920, Henry was enlisted to do clerical work in an unheated Soviet records office. Then in fall of 1922, he was drafted into the Red Army—which he soon deserted, narrowly escaping capture and execution by the military police. His army training, however, included vigorous indoctrination in

*Katharina and Henry Janzen: she helped to nudge him toward faith.*

communist ideology. It dismissed belief in God as a dangerous delusion. Although he rejected the politics and economics of communism, Henry was persuaded by its arguments against religious faith and became a firm atheist. Strangely, his particular brand of unbelief allowed him to pray to the God he didn't believe in. But for the time being, his prayers remained the anguished sighs of an unhappy disbeliever.

### GRACE RECEIVED

In 1923, the Janzens, with thousands of other Mennonites, decided to emigrate to Canada. Henry was happy enough to leave his homeland since there would be no career prospects for anyone not a member of the Communist party. But he could not contemplate leaving Tina behind. After persuading her parents that he would take good care of her, Henry made Tina his wife. They lived on the Andres farm while they waited for their emigration papers.

It was a happy marriage, but Tina was troubled by Henry's unbelief. She stopped bringing the subject of faith up only when Henry insisted that she had to to remain his wife. In 1924, the sudden death of their first child pierced Henry's heart and he started to re-examine his godless personal philosophy. When he and Tina attended weeklong evangelistic meetings later that year (organized, as it happened, by Mennonite Brethren ministers), Henry could resist the Spirit's invitation only so long. It was a Wednesday evening when he finally surrendered his life to Christ. Abandoning forever the opiate of atheism, Henry began what would turn out to be a passionate lifelong discipleship with the Lord. He was baptized soon thereafter.

### ARRIVAL IN CANADA

Only in 1925 did the Janzen clan—including Henry, Tina and their second-born, Rudy—finally leave the Soviet Union. They settled in the growing industrial city of Kitchener, Ontario, where Henry eventually found a job with a mattress manufacturer. Henry and Tina soon connected with a group of Mennonite Brethren and evangelical Mennonite immigrants from the Ukraine who had established themselves as the Molotschna Mennonite Brethren Church (later, Kitchener MB). In August 1926, Henry and Tina were formally admitted as members on their confession of faith. The following day, Henry was rebaptized, this time by immersion, in the Grand River.

It wasn't long before Henry found his niche as an adult Sunday school teacher. His cheerful disposition, earnest faith, and skills as a speaker and Bible expositor made him a popular teacher and he drew the attention of the church's ministers, who invited him to preach. His first Sunday morning sermon was a lively ten-minute homily on 2 Peter 3:17-18, in which (he confided later) he told the congregation just about everything he knew. But he won the congregation over with his insight, humour and passion for the Word. Henry's teaching and preaching gifts were confirmed on April 7, 1929, when the elders ordained him as minister of the gospel.

Much as he wanted to, circumstances didn't allowed Henry to attend Bible school or college. But his desire to learn was intense, so he educated himself. He spent every spare moment studying the Scriptures, and even kept his Bible open beside him at the factory. The prophetic books became a special interest for Henry. Pastor Jacob Friesen gave him some instruction in biblical interpretation as did Rev. Jacob W. Reimer, the noted MB preacher, Bible expositor and proponent of what some today would call "Left Behind" end-times teaching. Reimer's influence on Henry would be lasting.

The economic depression of the 1930s meant that the Janzen family, which by the end of that decade included six children (their last child arrived in 1941), would continue to live in spartan conditions for many years. But as a much-appreciated servant of the church he, along with his family, enjoyed the generosity of church brothers and sisters. It is doubtful that Henry could have served the church effectively without support from its members and from Tina at home. When Henry was not at work, he was preparing a sermon, or visiting church members, or attending a meeting, or—more and more often—travelling to strengthen ties with other Mennonite Brethren churches in Ontario.

### EARLY CONFERENCE WORK

Between 1929 and 1932 Henry helped spearhead a campaign to establish a conference of Mennonite Brethren churches in Ontario, in order to oversee the founding and development of new congregations. The province had six Molotschna Mennonite Brethren churches by this time—one each in Kitchener, New Hamburg, Hespeler, Vineland, Leamington and Port Rowan. They already met annually for business meetings, so relationships between them were close. Joining forces in a formal conference, however, still needed to be justified. Henry, in addition to bringing a contagious optimism and positive spirit to meetings, was persuasive in arguing that larger missions projects required that churches coordinate their efforts.

With the agreement of the other church leaders, Henry called a convention of delegates for January 31, 1932. The convention achieved its objective: five of the six churches united under the conference banner (Port Rowan joining the following year). Its formal title was "The Ontario Conference of Mennonite Brethren Churches." The following November, the new conference held its first annual convention and Henry served as its moderator. He held that position for the next fourteen years. The Conference's many outreach programs—evangelistic, educational, mental health—were a legacy of the missionary vision that brought its churches together.

It was at Henry's prompting that in 1936 the Ontario Conference applied to join the General Conference of Mennonite Brethren Churches, in large part because of the outreach programs it supported. But the terms of membership outlined by the General Conference caused some anguish. Because the Ontario churches accepted as members Christians baptized by sprinkling rather than by immersion and permitted them to occupy leadership positions without restriction, the General Conference would not permit Ontario delegates to participate in conference discussions of constitutional issues or to vote on related questions. Nor would the Ontario Conference be allowed to recommend non-immersed members for missions programs sponsored by the General Conference.

The second-class status the Ontario churches would have to accept did not sit well and, after painful deliberations in which Henry played a major role, the Ontario Conference chose to submit to the terms of full General Conference membership. From that point on, Ontario MB churches allowed only church members baptized by immersion to be leaders or to represent an MB church as conference delegates. The Ontario Conference was accepted into the General Conference as the "Ontario District Conference" on October 25, 1939.

In June of 1946, the Ontario Conference, still under Henry's leadership, also joined the Northern District Conference (made up of churches in western Canada). The Northern District Conference, established in 1910, was henceforth known as the Canadian Conference of the Mennonite Brethren Church of North America.

## OTHER MINISTRIES

But we run ahead of ourselves. As if the work of teaching, preaching, and leading the Ontario conference were not enough, Henry was asked in 1932 to work full-time as pastor of the Kitchener MB Church, for which he would receive a stipend of $70 a month. With additional support from friends, along with gratuities from speaking engagements, and honoraria from the Russian Baptist churches he served, Henry was able to support his growing family and finally quit his job at the spring factory.

Church and conference work and a growing number of speaking assignments kept Henry occupied for the next fourteen years. His renown as a bold and eloquent preacher, fluent in Russian as well as German, brought him invitations from Russian Baptists in New York, Detroit, Kiev (North Dakota), and in the western Canadian provinces. Henry was the natural choice when the Russian Gospel Association was looking for someone to establish and lead a Russian Bible Institute in Toronto. He accepted the offer in 1942 and led the school for four years. Then in 1946, Henry gave up all these involvements and moved his family to Winnipeg.

## COLLEGE AND MISSIONS

The Mennonite Brethren Bible College in Winnipeg was just two years old when Henry became its dean and a teacher of practical theology there. The opportunity to shape future church leaders alongside such notable figures as A.H. Unruh, J.B. Toews, and J.A. Toews was an exciting one. But, for Henry, missions was a passion that rivalled his desire to teach. He had barely begun teaching at the college when C.F. Klassen from Mennonite Central Committee asked him if he wouldn't want to do six months of evangelistic work in Europe with its many Mennonite refugees. Henry was eager to go, and the college, reluctantly, agreed to let him. The experience impressed upon him the burning need on that continent for the gospel. He knew immediately that his first trip back to Europe would not be his last.

When he returned to Winnipeg, Henry had no lack of work waiting for him. Aside from his academic duties, he soon answered a call to be the part-time minister of Winnipeg's South End Church (later, Portage Avenue MB). In the same year he began his first term as moderator of the Canadian Conference (he served in that capacity three more times be-

*Janzen at his desk at the Bible College.*

tween 1948 and 1954). In 1948, he was elected to the General Conference Board of Foreign Missions, on which he sat for six years. Also in 1948, he was made president of MBBC, a position he would hold until 1956.

In addition to discharging the many and varied responsibilities of college president and Canadian Conference moderator, the 1950s saw Henry serve several terms as moderator of the Manitoba MB Conference. Europe called to him repeatedly, and he made a second trip there in 1950, and a third in 1952 as a member of the Mennonite World Conference Presidium. His stint as pastor of North End Church (later, Elmwood MB) in 1953 lasted less than a year but then he took on a three-year term as moderator of the General MB Conference (1954-57). A fourth trip across the Atlantic was occasioned by service in Europe and the Mennonite World Conference in 1957.

### EUROPE CALLING

With Henry's resignation from MBBC in 1956 the path was finally cleared for a longer term of service on European soil. Henry and Tina spent the next five years in central Europe, living in Switzerland, where, among other ministry activities, Henry taught Bible and theology at the European Mennonite Bible School (Bienenberg) and at the St. Chrischona Seminary. The couple returned to Canada where Henry pastored the Clearbrook MB Church in B.C. from 1962-64. But Henry found the European work so gratifying that he returned there as often as he was able in the years that followed.

With each visit back to the European continent, demand for Henry as a speaker at churches, ministers' meetings, Deeper Life services, and Bible conferences grew. Invitations came from Switzerland, France, Germany, Austria, and Holland. And Henry deeply appreciated the opportunities to present the gospel to people starved for spiritual nourishment. His grateful audiences grew even larger when Radio Luxembourg carried his messages. Later he joined the "Words of Life" radio ministry and then the "Springs of Life" broadcast, and finally the "Gospel Light Hour" radio ministry in Canada, which he carried on until his death.

Henry's speaking skills were finely honed by this time. His voice was strong and forceful but completely at the service of his message. A picture of confidence, he was at ease walking away from his notes, speaking extemporaneously without losing his train of thought. His two hundred and thirty pound frame (he was almost six feet tall), always immaculately attired, made him a commanding presence, yet his sense of humour kept him from becoming overbearing. More importantly, his ability to explain difficult biblical concepts simply and elegantly, and his knack for finding just the right application of a Scriptural truth, won him many devoted listeners.

### COMMON SENSE

Henry's appeal also had much to do with the common sense with which he approached practical and theological questions.

For example, on the question of whether "like-minded" Christians must have the same opinion on all matters, Henry said, no, but they must have the same attitude toward Christ. "They must all be motivated by the same faith *in* him, the same Spirit-inspired love *of* him, and the same willingness to be in service *for* him."

On the issue whether a Christian should own a television, Henry believed "that if we shall permit the Holy Spirit to teach us, we will find the right answer to the question which is disturbing us at present."

Should a Christian marry an unbeliever? Henry declared that "in marriage, only believers belong together, otherwise many woes and heartaches ensue, and often the believer then loses his childlike faith." (Of course, he was fortunate that Tina had not followed this advice many years ago.)

To the question of Mary's perpetual virginity (Did she have children after she gave birth to Jesus?), Henry said: "My opinion is that the Lord Jesus grew up in a family with many children and took the experience of its blessings into his ministry."

*Janzen among the World War II displaced people that he shepherded on frequent stints in Europe*

Why had God permitted horrible suffering, especially of believers in Russia? Henry had the pat answers (to teach, to test) but admitted, "Who are we to claim that we understand the ways of God? As far as heaven is from earth, so much higher are God's thoughts than ours."

But his common sense sometime led him to paradoxes and questionable positions. He was known to be "for the underdog," yet Henry was not swayed on the issue of women teachers in church. He defended Paul's prohibition by arguing that "women are more open to emotional influences. [And] ... she carries with her the so-called sexual appeal which will, whether we admit it or not, influence, to a certain extent, those who listen." He supported the work of Mennonite Central Committee, yet believed strongly that the "social gospel" was a stepping stone to atheistic communism. And he was a pacifist, yet had few qualms about capital punishment, which he believed was justified by Romans 13.

## THE BIBLE TEACHER

There is no doubt that Henry always strove to make the Bible his guide. He was, however, always much more a Bible-led *pastor*, concerned with the spiritual welfare of his listeners, than a Bible *scholar* occupied with some academic question or other. Most of his published writings were, in fact, originally studies of a biblical book or theme presented to a church audience, a Bible conference, or to radio listeners. His close and frequent contact with ordinary believers, struggling to find spiritual direction, gave his Bible reading a practical purpose. 2 Timothy 3:16 confirmed him in this practice: "All Scripture is God-breathed and is useful for teaching, rebuking, correcting and training in righteousness."

This principle also gave Henry confidence that the Bible's prophetic writings, especially Revelation, should be important to Christians in the present age, which looked to him so much like the world described in that apocalyptic work. He rejected the idea that its author's intention was merely to comfort his original, persecuted readers with imaginative images of God's ultimate victory over evil. If the visions of Revelation are inspired by an omniscient God, why could they not be literal descriptions of the last days, prepared especially for twentieth-century believers who lived so frightfully close to history's conclusion? Even so, while Henry was certain that time had just about run out for the world and expected Christ's soon return, he acknowledged that considerable time might pass before that glorious event took place.

Whatever one might think of Henry's end-times views, it is difficult to argue against their effect: they ignited in him a sense of urgency to bring God's saving Word to spiritually dying people far and near, while there was still time.

## FINAL THOUGHTS

Henry would have been the first to admit that, intelligent as he was, he was not original in his expositions of the Bible. He relied heavily on the thoughts and insights of others. He was, however, an extraordinarily gifted communicator and a deeply spiritual man, who clung to the Scriptures fiercely, loved God with all his heart, and sought to serve Christ obediently and well, as long as it was in him to serve. And because he was a servant of God he was also a churchman: he was convinced that conferences were an especially effective way to advance the Kingdom through the missions and evangelistic work they helped support.

As for his own passionate involvement in both conference and missions, he seems never to have forgotten that he could easily have missed it all. He had once given up on God and could have been left in that sorry state forever. But God had pulled him away from the abyss and given him a life that not only gave him deep joy but also brought encouragement, wisdom and wholeness to countless others. He knew that he had done nothing to deserve this life, this gift. It came from the benevolent excess the Bible calls grace.

That he saw this clearly we know from the verse he adopted as motto for his life: "By the grace of God I am what I am" (1 Cor. 15:10a). With this profound truth, Henry H. Janzen continues to teach us what it means to be people who know and follow Jesus.

SOURCES

An uncompleted autobiography by H.H. Janzen, begun as a series of instalments in the *Mennonitische Rundschau* (1976-77) and completed by his wife, Tina, together with the editor Erich Ratzlaff, and translated by Hans and Tienne Janzen (1988), provided much of the background for this chapter. Other sources included correspondence in the Heinrich H. Janzen files, Janzen's reel-to-reel sermons, and David Ewert's *Honour Such People* at the Centre for Mennonite Brethren Studies; books and pamphlets by Janzen: *A Brief Outline Study of the Seven Churches: Revelation Two and Three*, *Jesu Rede ueber die Letzte Zeit*, *Von der Herrschaft des Geistes*, *Und ich Sah*, and *Der Roemerbrief*; Caribbean Call interview with H.H. Janzen, World Radio HCJB, Mar 4/67; and several items from *Global Anabaptist Mennonite Encyclopedia Online (GAMEO)*, "Chiliasm as Accepted and Taught in the Mennonite Brethren Church," and "Janzen, Henry H. (1901-1975)" by Bert Friesen and Richard Thiessen.

# John A. Toews

# A MAN OF HIS WORD

### By Rudy Wiebe

*No one may truly know Christ except one who follows him in life.*
Hans Denck (1525)

Taste is the most vivid sensory memory, and all his life John Toews will remember being nine years old and the taste of a *zwieback* [double bun] in the Mennonite village of Friedensruh, Molotschna, Russia. He is in the farmhouse of his once well-to-do grandparents, Johann and Agatha Harms, which in March, 1922 has been turned into an emergency food centre where starving people from area villages come every day to eat one *zwieback* and a scoop of beans or rice, and every second day drink a cup of cocoa.

This food, sent from North American churches by the Mennonite Central Committee, will save the boy's life during the devastating famine which follows the years of Russian Revolution and Civil War.

And many years later, when in Canada this boy has become the Rev. John A. Toews, PhD, moderator of the North American Mennonite Brethren Conference and a world-travelling minister on the presidium of the Mennonite World Conference, he will still talk of that childhood experience. It will be his lifelong testimony to what he considers the basic Anabaptist/Mennonite Christian doctrine: "For by grace you have been saved through faith; and this is not your own doing, it is the gift of God—not because of works, lest anyone

---

*The Writer*
Rudy Wiebe was John A. Toews's student in the late 1950s and already knew him from his home community of Coaldale, Alberta. Wiebe has authored a number of award-winning novels and is recognized as one of Canada's leading writers. He and his wife Tena are members of the Lendrum Mennonite Brethren Church of Edmonton.

should boast. For we are his workmanship, created in Christ Jesus for good works, which God prepared beforehand, that we should walk in them" (Eph. 2:8 -10).

For John, his "walk" will always be the most profound evidence of his "gift of faith."

## A WORLD ENDED

John Aron Toews was born on August 15, 1912 in the Molotschna Colony village of Rueckenau, now Kozolugovka, Ukraine. His father Aron Aron Toews was the Rueckenau school teacher, son of well-to-do farmers in near-by Alexanderkrone, and his mother Agnes Harms, the daughter of a wealthy farm family in Friedensruh just three kilometers away. Besides a large school and a home for the aged, Rueckenau also had a Mennonite Brethren church that served some 3000 affiliated members in the area, and both the Toews and Harms families were members there. In 1918—Aron was spared military or alternative service due to weak lungs—the family moved to the Harms estate in Friedensruh so Agnes could care for her widowed father and Aron teach in the village school.

Soon alternating armies of Red Bolsheviks, White Czarists, Ukraini-an Independents, and bands of largely criminal Anarchists were ripping southern Russia to pieces; cholera epidemics and starvation followed the "triumph" of Trotsky's Red Army in 1921. The affluent Mennonite world had also been destroyed, with well over two thousand of its people killed; as a Christian, Aron Toews could no longer teach children, and he be-came a travelling minister/evangelist in the spiritual revival that helped the Mennonite community grapple with its suffering.

Young John's life and that of his parents and three siblings had been spared, but numerous uncles, aunts and close relatives were dead; a dozen times armies had rolled back and forth over them and they had seen mur-dered and famine-swollen bodies lying in ditches. Life had become violent, inexplicably dreadful and, as Elfrieda Toews Nafziger would later explain in her biography of her father:

> On March 12, [1924] he approached his father for [spiritual] help. Aron took out his Bible and read Isaiah 53:5, inserting John's name. "He was wounded for John's transgressions…and with his stripes John is healed." There was no dramatic crisis experience, [simply] a personal appropriation of faith and a commitment to be Christ's disciple…. John credits the civil war and famine with paving the way for such a decision …. He wanted his life to count for God. [p. 13]

*In Nettie Willms, John gained a strong-minded, supportive wife and partner.*

## STARTING OVER

The Aron and Agnes Toews family were six of over 20,000 Mennonites who escaped the continuing chaos of Communist Russia for Canada in the middle 1920s. By spring 1927 they were on 320 acres near Namaka, Alberta, breaking prairie sod on the former Lane Ranch and building a grain farm. Together with other immigrant families homesteading in the area, they formed the Namaka Evangelical Mennonite Brethren Church with Aron Toews as its leader. On August 4, 1929 the church celebrated a baptism service that included John and also Nettie Willms, the young woman who later married him.

John went to public school, learning his third written language and, though barely fifteen, as the oldest son a great deal of farm work depended upon him. And like all immigrant teenagers, between farming and school he "worked out" at any labour job available. But the extended Toews/ Harms families had a strong teaching tradition and so, despite hail and drought and the setbacks of the beginning Depression, his parents encouraged him to attend the five-month Bible school in Coaldale, Alberta, where his uncle Johann Toews was the leading teacher. Instruction there was largely in German.

For three years, fall 1930 to spring 1933, John attended the Coaldale Bible School every winter after harvest was completed, and returned to Namaka every spring in time for seeding. After years of drought, in 1932 the crop grew superbly, but the price of wheat fell to 28 cents a bushel. Nettie Willms also attended Coaldale and in spring 1933 she and John made a commitment to each other. Nettie had a good position as a house-keeper in Calgary and they carried on a letter courtship while John worked on the farm and completed grade nine. He preached on occasion and was involved in Sunday school, choir and youth work, but he knew that for service in Canada he needed theological training in English.

The Moody Bible Institute in Chicago was too costly, but nearby Calgary offered the Prophetic Bible Institute with William Aberhart. John attended there in 1934-35, and he and Nettie often spent Sunday afternoons listening to Aberhart's popular radio Bible classes. The English instruction was good, but Aberhart's rigid dispensational dividing of biblical history seemed too programmatic to accommodate the immense teachings of Jesus. While John did vote Social Credit in September, 1935 when Aberhart to his own astonishment was elected premier of Alberta, he was never active in politics.

Hail destroyed the 1935 crop. However, Nettie had saved $250 and so she and John could marry on Saturday, November 9—a fierce prairie blizzard blessed their wedding celebrations.

### OFF TO TABOR

For two years the young couple lived with his parents and struggled with Depression farming. In 1930 the U. S. Mennonite leader H. W. Lohrenz had advised John's Coaldale cousin, John B. Toews, to attend Tabor College, the Mennonite Brethren school in Hillsboro, Kansas, and after several years at Tabor, by 1936/37 the gifted John B. was both principal of the Bethany Bible Institute in Hepburn, Saskatchewan and leader of the Hepburn MB Church. Christian ministry was calling John and Nettie and they decided to try Tabor as well. They sold their few belongings and arrived at Hillsboro in October, 1937. John discovered numerous relatives there, including the venerable John F. Harms, cousin of his Friedensruh grandfather and founding editor of the *Zionsbote* (1884), the official weekly of the MB Conference. And he was immediately invited to preach: twice on his first Sunday in Hillsboro, once in English, once in German.

During 1937-38 John completed three years of high school while both he and Nettie enrolled in Bible classes. He pastored a bilingual church and preached at Bible conferences. During 1938–40 he earned his BTh degree; by then World War Two was raging in Europe, and the *Tabor Bulletin* focused much student discussion:

> While soldiers are courageously fighting…for their country, it is only fair that Mennonites risk their lives for God. This privilege can be accomplished only by giving first aid and ambulance services at the front line trenches.

*JA speaking from the floor at the 1975 Regina conference: it was likely to be a persuasive argument.*

How a committed Christ-follower should live in a violence-filled world grew larger in John's thinking, especially regarding non-resistance, and years later he testified:

> [At Tabor] I learned to appreciate our spiritual heritage...by [observing the faculty's] life-style and involvement in service.... What I appreciated...was the balanced emphasis on evangelism and social concern. This blending and balance has been one of my major concerns in my public ministry.

By spring, 1940 John had invitations to teach at three Bible schools. They chose their alma mater in Coaldale, Alberta, founded by the 600-member MB church whose leader, B.B. Janz, had negotiated Mennonite emigration out of Russia in the 1920s. One Coaldale student was teenager David Ewert, who later recalled:

> Naturally we looked the new teacher over rather carefully. Among the things that struck us were his curly hair and his laughter. In

my youth, laughter was not thought of as the best expression of godliness, and perhaps that was why his friendly demeanor struck us. On one occasion that I remember vividly a student had given a less than adequate answer to a question in church history, and Toews turned away to the blackboard and exploded in hilarious laughter.

Ewert and Toews would become outstanding teaching and preaching colleagues, close friends for life.

War was devastating Europe and it affected John strongly. As an active, ordained minister (Namaka MB Church, Sept. 27, 1942), he had Canadian military exemption, but thousands of Mennonite war resistors were working in isolated Conscientious Objector Camps; during the summers of 1942 and 1943 John visited the western camps, ministering to men from 28 different orientations. As John Fretz noted, "We were all treated as equals by brother Toews. He was one of the favourite pastors who visited us." This brotherhood of crucial peace witness in time of war, especially by men from diverse Mennonite groups, profoundly deepened John's understanding of discipleship and Anabaptist community.

During the Toews's ministry in Coaldale, 1940-46, the Canadian MB churches were feeling the stress of an open society; the large, conservative Coaldale congregation felt it especially. Evangelism was unhindered, but how could converts join a congregation whose rigid customs were largely rooted in family and Russian village life, whose language was German? Better education in English was needed, yes, especially for leaders, but education was also dangerous. As B.B. Janz warned his nephew John B. Toews, who began working for a doctorate in theology, "Hans, you are going too far. You will not be accepted in the brotherhood.... You will lose your simple faith in the gospel." Strong mission work in Africa or India was, it seemed, easy compared to the tangled problems of discipleship at home.

## COALDALE CANNOT HOLD YOU

Nevertheless, in September 1944 the MB Bible College had been established by A.H. Unruh with twelve students in Winnipeg, and by July, 1945 John B. Toews was its English-speaking, organizing president. About the same time, Unruh also offered John A. a position at the college: "... in the long run [Coaldale] cannot hold you; every zealous teacher wants to move ahead." John and Nettie agreed; with their three children they moved to Saskatoon; during 1946-47 John completed a BA in History at the University of Saskatchewan while ministering in numerous area churches, and in August 1947 they settled in Winnipeg. John would teach at MBBC for the next 20 years, including seven crucial years as president.

In her father's biography, *A Man of His Word*, Elfrieda notes:

> John's concept of Christian vocation was profoundly influenced during the Depression and World War II.… His emphasis on the Christian's prophetic role in politics and society, on faith as the basis of serving the oppressed, and on the relationship of these to the MBs' Anabaptist heritage, were already recognizable by the mid 1940s.

These formative emphases were certainly there when I took classes with him at MBBC, beginning in 1956.

They were especially obvious in John's favorite courses, Mennonite History and The Acts of the Apostles. My notes of his highly organized lectures on Acts contain comments like:

> Each part of biblical revelation is relative to the setting in which it is given. In much Christian teaching, one of the chief deviations comes from taking a relative truth and making it an absolute.
> In Acts 2 the particularism of the children of Abraham is broken down. The Book of Acts shows us the principle of universalism in God's salvation.

And from Mennonite history, surveying more than four centuries:

> We need a case history of our people to get to the root of their problems, not merely treat the symptoms.… History never expresses the ideal—it is written largely for our warning.
> In 19th century Russia the Mennonite congregation [*Gemeinde*] gradually evolved into a church [*Kirche*], that is, a social and political organization. For example, it refused to marry non-baptized persons, and gradually believers' baptism became adult baptism.

His informed enthusiasm stimulated my own lifelong writing about the Mennonite communal heritage.

By 1956 John was MBBC's President; it seemed his unblinking eye could survey the entire chapel and register if anyone was missing. I was a university graduate, accustomed to going out with whatever young woman was pleased to join me. That fall Tena Isaak, a graduate nurse, and I began going for walks, but after we attended Haydn's *The Creation* together at the Winnipeg Auditorium, President Toews called me into his office. He explained "Sister Isaak" and I must have the Dean's approval to visit, and we must be "more discreet:" stop being so open about our interest in each other. I remember him as understanding, but also immoveable concerning the college's juvenile student rules. Not that Tena and I were deterred; we met less conspicuously (which added to the enjoyment) and by Easter 1957 we had agreed to marry.

### INVARIABLY A LEADER

An outstanding teacher at MBBC was invariably an MB Conference leader; John, together with his contemporaries, H. H. Janzen, David Ewert and Frank C. Peters, was certainly that. From his early thirties until his death, there was never a year that John did not serve on one, sometimes several, Mennonite conference boards:

- Youth Committee, Canadian Mennonite Brethren Conference: 1945, 1946;
- Peace Committee, Canadian MB Conference: 1948-63;
- Committee of Reference and Counsel/Spiritual Concerns, Canadian MB Conference: 1950-62, 1969-71, 1972-76;
- Assistant Moderator, Canadian MB Conference: 1950, 1955, 1956;
- Moderator, Canadian MB Conference: 1953, 1954, 1957;
- Board of Reference and Counsel, MB General (North American) Conference: 1960-63, 1966-69, 1975-78, 1978-79;
- Assistant Moderator, MB General Conference: 1969-72;
- Moderator, MB General Conference: 1975-78, 1978-79
- MB representative on the Mennonite Central Committee: 1965-68, 1969-73;
- Member of Presidium of Mennonite World Conference: 1967-78.

John was also widely invited to preach—including many evangelistic meetings—from Ontario to British Columbia, to conduct lengthy Bible conferences [*Bibel Besprechungen*] in individual churches and special seminars for ministers at the College, and to lecture on Mennonite Brethren/Anabaptist and peace/war issues at inter-Mennonite events. He also wrote copiously. In a selected collection of his essays, *People of the Way* [1981], the list of his publications, a majority in the *Mennonitische Rundschau*, and MBBC's *The Voice*, covers twelve pages. At the request of the MB Conference, in 1955 he wrote a closely argued monograph, *True Nonresistance Through Christ: A Study of Biblical Principles*; four years later the Conference published his history MA thesis: *Alternative Service in Canada During World War Two*. Scriptural exposition and the specific facts of history: the faithful follower [*Nachfolger*] of Jesus needed both.

Above all, he was a powerful speaker which, among the rhetorical traditions of Mennonite church ministry, affirmed his leadership. While not as emotionally dramatic as his cousins J.B. and J.J. Toews, nor as coolly

*With Paul Kraybill of the Mennonite World Conference: an influential voice in the Presidium.*

cerebral as David Ewert, or folksy like Frank C. Peters, John's intense, concentrated convictions made him an incisive orator. He rarely read his messages: he spoke from detailed notes to give full oral scope to his rhetoric. The *MB Herald*, August 17, 1962 prints a picture of John giving an evening address at the 1962 Mennonite World Conference in Ontario. Surrounded by some 8000 listeners in the Kitchener Arena, he is leaning forward into the pulpit and elaborating on the Christian's "Call to Bear Witness." His conclusion was:

> The rediscovery of the church as a brotherhood of believers and as a "community of discipleship" is possibly the greatest contribution of the Anabaptists to the cause of Christ in the sixteenth century.… The Christian community [is where] the Christian graces of faith, hope and love are exemplified and demonstrated. The bane of Protestantism has been its increasing identification with individualism.… Salvation always *begins* as a personal, individual matter, but if it *remains* an individual matter, it is not biblical. The New Testament depicts a Christian life that is lived in intimate interdependence and fellowship with others. A revitalization of our witness will require a revival of our community-concept of the church.

Despite his multiplied ministry in college, North American, World Conference, local church and community settings (as Ewert commented:

"If genius includes the capacity for concentrated work then, I suppose, one could speak of Toews as being one"), John's life also always contained a broad strand of academic studies. He graduated from United College with a BD in 1950, from the University of Manitoba with an MA in 1957, and a PhD from the University of Minnesota in 1964 (at age 52) with the thesis: "Sebastian Franck: Friend and Critic of Early Anabaptism." As MBBC president (1956-63), he expanded its liberal arts offerings and accreditation with what are now Wilfrid Laurier University, Kitchener, and the University of Winnipeg.

## A WIDER FRAME

In 1963 John resigned from the onerous president's role at MBBC, and in December 1966 he resigned as professor. There were many possibilities for wide-ranging service, and with four children now adults, John and Nettie and teenager Irene had more flexibility for worldwide assignments. For ten years John did short-term ministries in the U.S.A., Germany, France, Switzerland, Paraguay and Brazil; while on the Presidium of the Mennonite World Conference he visited Africa, Japan, Indonesia, the Soviet Union and South America on its behalf; he pastored the Fraserview, Vancouver MB Church for three years and taught history at Trinity Western College, Langley, BC for four. He also lectured at the MB Biblical Seminary in Fresno, California and, while there, in 1971, began what could well be his most lasting gift to his community: at the Conference's request, he wrote *A History of the Mennonite Brethren Church: Pioneers and Pilgrims*. The book's editor, historian A.J. Klassen, John's former student at Coaldale Bible School, called it a "fitting sequel" to the first (1911) MB history, P.M. Friesen's massive *The Mennonite Brotherhood in Russia*.

*A History's*... dedication is quintessential John:

> To the "Company of the Committed" in our brotherhood, who with faith and courage under the guidance of the Holy Spirit endeavour to translate the Anabaptist Vision of Christian discipleship and community into the work, witness, and life-style of the church in the contemporary world.

It begins with:

> The name "Mennonite Brethren" which the founding fathers gave to the new church...was a conscious and deliberate identification of the early Brethren with the historic theological position of the Anabaptist-Mennonite movement.

*The General Conference executive for 1975-78: Henry H. Dick, assistant moderator, John A. Toews, moderator, and C.J. Rempel, secretary.*

As such, he sees the 1860 movement as a spiritual awakening and rejects the theory that it was largely an outgrowth of severe social and economic problems within the Russian colonies. With enormous detail, the 500-page history goes on to illustrate how MB congregations, at their core, are the "spiritual heirs of the early Anabaptists." The book ends with the paragraph:

> Compared with the large Protestant bodies...the Mennonite Brethren are but a small and insignificant group. However, to the extent that this worldwide brotherhood remains faithful to its calling and to Christ's teaching, it will continue to hear the words of the Lord in Revelation 3:8 "... Behold, I have set before you an open door, which no one is able to shut; I know that you have but little power, and yet you have kept my word and have not denied my name."

In fall, 1976 John and Nettie left their comfortable Clearbrook, BC home and returned to Winnipeg to teach at MBBC. He wrote, "Our response to the call from the College board was an act of faith and commitment.... We trust that under God we will be able to make a positive contribution to the training program which emphasizes discipleship, service and an Evangelical-Anabaptist theology." And that certainly happened;

John's continued zest for teaching attracted large classes, and on weekends he and Nettie often visited local congregations.

During 1977 and 1978 he was especially active on the Mennonite World Conference presidium; he was also moderator of the General Conference (North American) of the MB Church and was deeply involved with issues as diverse as the place of women in church ministry and the continued use of "Mennonite" and "Brethren" as congregational names.

On Friday, January 12, 1979 he was up early as usual, and preparing to leave for College, when he suffered a heart attack; on Saturday, January 13, he died. A staggering blow to his family and friends and the thousands who knew him, but a good going for a faithful disciple: taken in the midst of service.

Between the time of his first heart attack on Friday to the time it became apparent that the pacemaker that had been inserted was failing, John was able to speak personally with each member of his family except son John, who was grounded in Chicago by a snowstorm. Son David recalls his father's deathbed words: "If you remember nothing else I have said, remember I Corinthians 13. There is knowledge, and faith, and hope, but ultimately it is love that really matters."

As daughter Elfrieda wrote, "For the family his death was so sudden, so brutal." Truly; but beyond that, considering the committed life he lived, to mourn John Aron Toews, the Friedensruh, Molotschna boy once fed by his believer community from half a world away, was to contemplate again the eternal words of Jesus:

"Blessed are the pure in heart, for they shall see God."

SOURCES

This chapter owes particular thanks to Elfrieda Toews Nafziger: *A Man of His Word, A Biography of John A. Toews* (Winnipeg: 1992); David Waltner-Toews; David Ewert in *People of the Way, Selected Essays and Addresses by John A. Toews* (Winnipeg: 1981); and J. B. Toews: *JB, A Twentieth-Century Mennonite Pilgrim* (Fresno: 1998).

# J. B. Toews

# THE LAST OF THE "RUSSIAN" MBs

*By Abraham Friesen*

JB, as he was affectionately known to family, friends and more distant acquaintances alike, was born in Alexandertal, Ukraine, in 1906 to John A. Toews and Margaretha Janz, sister to B.B. Janz, later of Coaldale, Alberta. By the time he left the Ukraine for Canada in 1926 with the help of his uncle Benjamin, JB was twenty years of age, old enough to have experienced the trauma of World War I, the ensuing revolution and civil war, the Makhno terror, followed by disease and famine, and the rise of Communism--enough unsettling events for any man's lifetime.

Many a young man fell by the wayside as these events unfolded; others, however, had their character formed as they rose above the cauldron of their time. The latter, time and again, were forced to make the difficult decision to oppose the flow of their history. To do so, they were compelled to reach deep within themselves, wrestle with their God, and trust in his leading, for they faced a future that consisted of stark alternatives: physical death if they opposed the "powers that be," spiritual death if they capitulated.

Those who came through this hell and reached the other side with life and faith intact were men of strong character, who, like A.H. Unruh, C.F.

---

*The Writer*

Abraham Friesen grew up in Canada but has spent most of his life teaching in the U.S., where he is Professor of Renaissance & Reformation History Emeritus at the University of California at Santa Barbara. He is the author of a number of major studies, the most recent entitled *In Defense of Privilege*, which examines Mennonites and the Russian state before and during World War I. Abraham and his wife Gerry now live in Fresno, California.

Klassen, B.B. Janz, H.H. Janzen, J.B. Toews and others, having made the hard decisions in their youth, became natural leaders in later life. It was no accident that they were given to the church at that time; sad to say, they have seldom been succeeded later by men of equal character and leadership qualities.

## A PRECARIOUS LIFE

JB's father, whose first wife, Liese Janzen, had died of tuberculosis after bearing him three children, was an impractical man of deep yet simple faith. He was a teacher by profession and minister by avocation. His mother, on the other hand, was more down to earth, having married the young father out of a sense of calling after his first wife died. JB, born in 1906, experienced the precariousness of life at an early age. Virtually at birth his body broke out in a rash that turned to festering sores. His case seemed so hopeless that his parents asked God to take the baby to himself. Yet he lived.

On December 30, 1920 he lost his older brother Aaron, a brilliant youth who had just completed medical studies. Later, in 1924, while in his third year at the agricultural college in Gnadenfeld, he was involved in an accident that broke his neck. He lapsed into a coma; the local doctor confirmed the broken neck in his diagnosis, but refused to help. In moments of lucidity, John recalled an oath sworn in anger when some schoolmates had laughed at his expressed intention of becoming a doctor like his deceased brother; he would only be a preacher like his father, they said. But he had sworn he would never be a preacher. The oath came back to haunt him now.

Meanwhile, his family wrestled with his medical condition. After about a week, he was examined by a bonesetter, Dr. Heinrich Wiebe. The latter confirmed the diagnosis but was also reluctant to try to reset the bone in his neck, lest young John die in the process. After several more days of waiting, the family reached a difficult decision: without treatment John would surely die, the risk therefore had to be taken. And it was, under the prayers of the family, successfully. Within five weeks he was back at the university.

Small for his age, young John grew up with a sense of inferiority. During the war years 1914-17, his father was drafted and had to serve in Moscow as chaplain to young Mennonite men serving in the Red Cross. The long absence—the father came home only twice during that time—affected his mother's health as well as his own. He developed a nervous condition that resulted in twitchings in face, shoulders and arms. His sense of insecurity increased, as did his isolation from classmates.

His father's return improved his condition somewhat, but his sense of social ostracism remained. He needed something at which he could excel; he found it in riding horses as yet unbroken, something other boys dared not do. Eventually, at age eleven, his father bought him a bay mare which he rode successfully in a number of village races. A year later, the mare had a colt that promised to be everything a young boy could ask for.

In the meantime (1919) a typhoid epidemic ravaged the villages. Among the many who died was Jacob Wall, a close childhood friend. In the aftermath, a young family man, David Reimer, began to befriend him. He became young John's confidant and counsellor. He helped him with his feelings of rejection, his relationship with his family, his sense of guilt. One Sunday afternoon, he suggested to John that he could rid himself of his guilt and sense of alienation if he repented his past and accepted the forgiveness extended to sinners by Christ. John did so and was baptized in the summer of 1920.

He now participated fully in the church's activities and was even asked to preach at the age of eighteen. He consented, but the sermon appeared too judgmental for a number of older brethren. Their remonstrances, however, only confirmed him in the vow taken at his brother's death to become a medical doctor. Later, as we have seen, he would confirm that decision by swearing, before his comrades, that he would never become a preacher.

No matter the vow, his decision to follow Christ had its consequences, for by now the Communists were firmly entrenched in power. By 1924, it became clear that in order to pursue a medical education he would have to become a party member. His father, a minister, had already been stripped of his citizenship. Although inducted into the army in January 1926, John managed to get an exemption based on his conscientious objection. Others in his class, however, were not so fortunate. Some were court-martialed, others sent to Siberia.

In the meantime, a Dr. Ernst Schrill from the University of Berlin, an ardent Communist, had been hired by the school to indoctrinate the students. In a series of lectures on evolution he, at one point, described the mysterious process of how rotating atoms had created the friction necessary for producing living cells. Unconvinced, Toews asked: "Dr. Schrill, do you have any explanation for what you call an unknown cause?" Upset at such a question by a Christian, Schrill answered, visibly irritated: "No one can answer your question; only God in heaven knows that." Undone before the student body by his own folly, and amidst their uproarious laughter, the teacher stalked out of the room. Within thirty minutes John was arrested, but upon the unanimous defense of his fellow students, who blamed the entire debacle on Schrill himself, he was

released. Nonetheless, he knew his freedom was now in jeopardy; he had
to leave the country.


## FACING RATIONALISM

Shortly after his uncle Benjamin left the country in early June 1926,
John Toews also left, but not without some tense moments, especially
after he met Dr. Schrill at the Melitipol police station where he had just
acquired a travelling permit. In Berlin he and his sister Helen were met
by a Dutch industrialist, George DeJong, who accompanied them to the
Netherlands. There he was put up in the home of George Tigchelhoven,
a foreman on the Rotterdam docks. For 18 months he remained in the
Netherlands until the family was cleared, medically, for entrance to Canada. With time on his hands, John enrolled at the Rotterdam branch of
the Amsterdam Peoples' [Open] University for some courses.

Whereas his classes in the Ukraine had begun to indoctrinate communism, these were riddled with rationalism. More subtly than the former, they began to undermine his pietistic faith. One evening, after wandering all day by the shore wrestling with his spiritual demons, he missed
his 9:00 p.m. train and was forced to walk the four miles to where he was
staying, or wait for the last train at 11:30. He decided to walk.

Crossing the Rotterdam city square John came upon the statue of
William of Orange. Under glass at the foot of the monument was an
open Bible, with Psalm 119: 89 written in bold print: "Forever, O Lord,
thy word is settled in heaven. Thy faithfulness is unto all generations:
thou hast established the earth and it abideth." Rationalism was only a
passing human philosophy; God was the unchanging One. God spoke
to John Toews late that night at the foot of William of Orange's monument, a man who had granted the Dutch Anabaptists religious toleration
so many years before. The conflict between time and eternity had been
settled finally in favor of the Eternal One.

After some time in Southhampton, England with Benjamin Unruh,
in April 1928, John finally passed his medical exam and was allowed to
emigrate to Canada with other members of his family.

John and his family settled on a farm in Coaldale, Alberta, purchased by
four related families. Those first years were very hard, with John having to
do the brunt of the work for the family. His father, already during the winter of 1928, had begun teaching at the Bethany Bible School in Hepburn,
and most of the other family members that were old enough took jobs in
Lethbridge or elsewhere to help meet expenses. In church John became a
youth leader and choir conductor. Under these conditions, medical school
faded quickly as a possibility and the future appeared bleak.

## A NEW HORIZON

Then in July 1930, H.W. Lohrenz from Tabor College came to speak at the Coaldale church. Afterwards he met with John and asked him about his plans for the future. John had none, nor could he see far into that clouded future. But in August, his sister Helen and her husband, who were in Manitoba, expressed interest in moving to Alberta. By the end of the month they had finalized their plans and John wrote to Lohrenz, who advised him to come to Tabor when the crop had been harvested.

Tabor College was both a disappointment and an opportunity. It brought JB into contact with some of the leading members of the U.S. MB Church, but academically the school was not up to the standards he had known in the Ukraine. On top of that, the school was going through a crisis in 1931-32, even closing its doors for the 1934-35 academic year. John also had to go back to high school to make up some deficits before he could enroll in the college's classes.

At a chapel service in the school, he heard and later met Nettie Unruh, his future wife. While in Hillsboro, he was given the opportunity to preach on a regular basis in the Lehigh MB Church. At the end of his second year, having completed his studies, he faced a choice: he was encouraged to join the Shell Oil Company by a certain Sam Schneider of the Buhler MB Church, and about the same time received an invitation to join the faculty of the Bible school in Hepburn, Sask. The one promised a life of relative wealth and security; the other a life of service and relative poverty. Nettie came from a wealthy South Dakota family; how would she respond, and how would her family look on him if he chose the latter? But when Nettie told John it was "okay to be poor," he accepted the call to Hepburn.

Bethany Bible School had been established in 1927, a year before John's father had begun to teach there. At first the school was owned and operated by an association; later, however, it was taken over by the MB churches of Saskatchewan. When JB arrived there in the fall of 1932, the school had two classrooms, with a third under construction. His starting salary was $60 per month for six months. He would be poor! The library had only several dozen books, and until he arrived, every class had been taught in German. The program consisted of a two-year curriculum, limited in scope and depth.

With JB's appointment as principal, changes began to be instituted. In 1934, the year of his appointment, the program was expanded to four years and the classes intensified. In 1935 the school became a member of the Evangelical Teacher Training Association, and by 1939 it had inaugurated a two-year college course, though the latter was already done under the guidance of G. W. Peters, who became president in 1937.

JB's tenure as president lasted from 1934-37, years of academic expansion and intensification. On the occasion of Douglas Berg's appointment as president in 1995, JB wrote him: "How well do I remember when in 1934 at the age of 28, I was given this responsibility at the stage when in Bethany's history the expansion began. God has extended to Bethany special favors in a ministry of many years to the young people of the North."

In the summer of 1933, Nettie Unruh joined JB in Hepburn as his wife. The same year, G.W. Peters joined the teaching staff to replace an ailing Jacob Dueck, and the following year JB's father returned as teacher as well. The latter provided a stabilizing influence; the former, an at times somewhat destabilizing influence. Nevertheless, despite differences of temperament and theology, a relationship developed between the two young teachers that JB described in a later tribute as one of mutual respect. He also stated, indicating the importance of Peter's tenure at Bethany from 1933 to 1942: "In God's providence, Bethany became the platform for Peters to become a leader in world missions."

## ANABAPTIST JOURNEY

For JB, however, Bethany became the place where he began his theological development, for he was responsible for all classes in doctrine and theology, especially the advanced courses in biblical exegesis and theology. Though he sought—and received—advice from A.H. Unruh on what materials he should use, he never felt adequately prepared and in 1938 resigned in order to pursue theological studies, though at the time the primary reason was an illness that could only be cured by relocation to a milder climate.

In January of that year, JB had taken over the ministry in the Hepburn MB Church and became a part-time faculty member at Bethany, so his ties to the school were no longer as close as they had been. Now, in the summer of 1938, he requested a leave of absence from the church as well and set out for Portland, Oregon and the possibility of theological studies at Western Baptist Theological Seminary.

JB came to Portland with every intention of returning to Canada. Yet things changed. After a fall of relaxation and reading in the seminary library, JB's health began to improve. Unlike Tabor College, Western recognized all of JB's previous academic credentials: his 1926 *Reifezeugniss* (certificate of completion) from the Gnadenfeld Secondary School; his two years of study at the Amsterdam Peoples' University (1926-28); his two years (1930-32) years at Tabor College; and his teaching (1932-37) at Bethany Bible School.

His theological studies at the seminary brought him a BD degree in 1940, and a ThM degree in 1941. In 1996, he paid tribute to the education he had received at Western, saying: "Dr. Millikan, then president and New Testament professor—a philosopher-scientist-theologian— was instrumental in helping me find my way, coming to Western with a background of atheism (Kiev), rational humanism (Amsterdam), to a belief in the Bible and conversion to Christ. Western provided the spiritual foundation for a rich, long and delightful ministry—ten years as a pastor, a second decade as a mission executive, college president, seminary president and international ministry up to age 84."

Perhaps more importantly, however, as he wrote in his autobiography, Western "placed a major emphasis on the early history of the Baptist movement, which had its roots in the left wing of the Reformation, namely Anabaptism. They spoke openly of Anabaptism as the womb of the Baptist movement and called for a return to the roots of their faith."

But what kind of an Anabaptism was this and what relationship did it have to the interpretation JB may have imbibed in the Ukraine? It is not enough to speak glibly of "Anabaptism," as many do today without any historiographical or 16th century context. During the years (1975-78) that I worked on the translation of P.M. Friesen's history with JB, I began to realize that his understanding of the movement led back to the Münster archivist, Ludwig Keller (1849-1915). The latter's interpretation glorified the mystical Anabaptist Hans Denck as the most important 16th century Anabaptist leader and sought to establish—like the *Martyrs Mirror* before it—a direct line backwards to the Apostolic Church via the medieval "heretics," especially the Waldensians.

Many Baptists welcomed Keller's studies with enthusiasm. It was this interpretation that came to the Russian Mennonites in the late years of the 19th century via David H. Epp and Heinrich Braun. Only these Mennonites placed Menno at the center of the sixteenth century movement.

It became clear to me during the P. M. Friesen years that JB had absorbed Keller's interpretation already in Russia, and may well have had it reinforced at Western from a Baptist perspective. Over the years his reading of Anabaptist history, especially the more recent studies largely under the influence of Harold Bender, may have modified his interpretation here and there, but the larger picture remained. His Anabaptist theology, however, was not derived from Keller's hero, Hans Denck, but from Menno and later from the Swiss Brethren.

## BEGINNING TO PREACH

Already during his Tabor years, JB had begun to preach, at first as a member of the school's gospel team and mission band. The summer of 1931 was spent working on a farm during the week and preaching on Sundays as interim pastor at the Jansen, Nebraska MB church. The next summer he ministered to churches in North Dakota and Montana. During the summer months of his service at Bethany, JB preached in the surrounding area churches, and in his last year became the pastor of the Hepburn church. Even before graduation from Western, JB spent two years (1940-42) at Freeman Junior College in South Dakota, which allowed him time off to complete his studies at Western.

By the summer of 1941, having completed his BD and Masters in Theology, JB enrolled in the doctoral program in theology at the Southwestern Baptist Theological Seminary in Fort Worth, Texas. While there he received an invitation from the Buhler, Kansas congregation, but turned it down to continue teaching at Freeman and to pursue his doctoral studies in his spare time. The invitation was renewed the following year. In the meantime, an invitation had also come from Tabor College. Eventually, JB turned down the latter because the Bible department, under P.R. Lange's leadership, lacked an Anabaptist emphasis; he accepted the call to Buhler instead.

For JB, his time in ministry—in Buhler from 1942-45, and Reedley, California, from 1948-53—were his best years. When called to the Mennonite Brethren Bible College as president in 1944, he wrote to G.J. Doerksen, "To move from the position of college professor into the practical activity of shepherding a congregation was the best schooling the Lord could have provided for me. Separating myself from this flock is very difficult for me." The same was true when he left Reedley to become general secretary of the Board of Foreign Missions in 1953.

It might be appropriate at this point to say a few words about JB as preacher, for despite the many administrative positions he was to hold in life, JB remained a preacher at heart and continued to preach widely both in Canada, the United States and, later in life, even in Germany. To a degree he became an itinerant minister to the North American MB churches at large, similar to those that had played such an important role in the early history of the Russian Mennonite Brethren Church.

In a 1997 tribute, David Ewert has given an interesting description of JB as churchman and also of JB's preaching style. "I always looked on him," he wrote, "as a man, called of God and anointed by his Spirit, who preached with great passion and served the church with genuine dedication. Yet, I began to feel uncomfortable when he made sweeping

*JB, the young president of the MBBC, with his colleagues (l-r) Henry Wall, Rueben Baerg, A.H. Unruh, Jake H. Quiring and Ben Horch.*

generalizations in his sermons, or when he expounded and applied the Scriptures in such absolutist terms as if there were no other way of reading the text." Despite this criticism, Ewert called JB "undoubtedly one of the most effective preachers in the Mennonite Brethren Church in his generation."

### PRESIDENT OF MBBC

In 1944, the call came to take over the presidency of the new MB Bible College in Winnipeg. As JB wrote G.J. Doerksen, he had "always believed that [his] future [lay] in the North, amongst [his] 'brothers'." But it is unclear whether he would have accepted the call had he not faced the loss of his Canadian citizenship for staying over five years in the U.S. He wondered whether his Canadian brothers would still understand him or he them. Furthermore, his uncle, B.B. Janz, had warned him in 1944 not to pursue his doctoral studies at Southwestern lest he lose his "simple" faith and be rejected by his Canadian brothers.

Now, however, the invitation to become president of MBBC had come from a committee chaired by Janz, and the reason was that they needed someone with a higher theological education to head up their new school! In March 1945, the Canadian Consulate rejected JB's appeal for an extension to his stay in the U.S. and a decision had to be made. He chose the call to Winnipeg.

Initially, the new school was only to add a third year to the theological education offered in the Bible schools, with Winkler acting as model.

But a more advanced theological education was not the only goal: the retention of the German language was to be a co-equal aspect of the program. Perhaps that was at least one reason why A.H. Unruh was appointed president of the new school in 1944: Winkler, unlike Bethany where JB had led the transition to the English language instruction in 1935-37, had retained a German curriculum. Unruh, however, could not function in the English language as president and he resigned after the first year.

It is not clear whether JB was fully aware of the new school's language problem when he was hired, but he must have become aware of it in his first year, 1945-46, for the minutes of the College Committee meeting in Winnipeg on 11 April, 1946, records the following resolution: "We expect that the Bible College will do everything in its power in order to retain and develop the [study of the] German language. We trust that the college faculty will conduct their classes with this congregational goal in mind: that they provide the congregations with teachers and workers who are capable of serving [equally well] in both languages."

But JB's report to the 1946 conference clearly turned this responsibility back to the local congregations and their families. As Gerald Ediger expressed it in his 2001 study, *Crossing the Divide: Language Transition Among Canadian Mennonite Brethren 1940-1970:* "Toews stated flatly that if Mennonite Brethren wanted to retain the German language, they must cultivate German in their homes, religion schools, high schools and Bible schools. The College wanted to prepare graduates able to serve in both languages, but this would only be possible if congregations and Bible schools did their part in preparing prospective students adequately. By implication, Toews was saying that the College was not prepared to accept the burden of language preservation."

Having had to learn English to get into classes at Tabor College, after supervising the transition into English at Bethany, and then having served in English-speaking congregations south of the border, JB was anything but sympathetic to the rearguard linguistic action that Unruh, B.B. Janz and their more culturally conservative brothers were attempting.

When JB arrived in Winnipeg in July 1945, the school had one full-time teacher, A.H. Unruh, and several part-time instructors. There was no catalogue and no coherent curriculum. Already from Buhler, he had negotiated with Jacob H. Quiring and Rueben M. Baerg to join him and Unruh as teachers; the next year H.H. Janzen also joined them. Ben and Esther Horch came on as adjunct faculty. By the time the school opened, the catalogue was ready and a provisional curriculum worked out.

When students arrived for classes on October 1, lodging had to be found in private homes. A house purchased by C.A. DeFehr for the college provided room for some students and kitchen facilities for others. The next year a dormitory was built to house married students, and other facilities gradually begun.

At the same time, JB must have initiated talks with the University of Manitoba to see if some arrangements could be worked out to get university credit for courses taken at the college. The minutes of the College Committee meeting in April, 1946 put it as follows: "The committee agrees with the college's desire to affiliate [*Anlehnung*] with the university, even if the college does what several other [colleges] have already done, i.e., the university prescribes the textbooks, the student receives his instruction from these textbooks in the college and can then write the university exams." But nothing seems to have come from these negotiations.

JB described the first two hectic years of the college's existence as follows in his July, 1947 report to the Canadian Conference meeting in Dalmeny: "The rapid expansion of the young institution created severe internal and external pressures. The arrival of the many students from all the Canadian provinces at a school with inadequate space to accommodate them, a limited number of teachers with differing teaching methods, a largely untested administration but high conference expectations, together with our own inadequacies . . . made us feel like Peter who, when he saw a strong wind arise, took fright and began to sink, cried out and said: Lord, help me!" But before three years were up, when the school was pretty well established, JB resigned to return to the pastorate in the United States, this time in Reedley, California. It is said he did not look forward to a long struggle with Canadian MB language conservatives.

### HARD CHOICES

We need not here address JB's time in Reedley. Suffice it to say that the MB Conference could not do without him for long, even though he served on various boards and committees as pastor. In 1952 he received the call to become general director of the MB overseas missions program. He suggested G.W. Peters instead. But at an April, 1953 meeting of the missions board, he was chosen. Once again JB was forced to choose between service to the conference and his love of the pastorate. He wrote to H.H. Janzen on 14 September, 1953: "It was difficult for me to accept that any assignment would come to my life that would supersede my dedication to the pastoral ministry. The direction, however, as to inward compulsion and circumstantial pressure, was such that it would have meant disobedience on my part not to follow the pathway that we have accepted."

JB had limited preparation for his new position. To be sure, he had visited MB missionaries in the Congo at the request of the board in 1952, had discussed missions with other Mennonite groups at Mennonite World Conferences and consulted men like G.W. Peters, who was a trained missiologist, but he still had a steep learning curve before him. He was coming into the office at a time when missions, in the wake of anti-imperialist and anti-colonial movements, was in a state of flux.

New models had to be worked out, for the old colonial model of the missionary compound, served by locals yet separated from them, with their own schools and "superior" cultures, had to be given up for a greater equality between the parties. Indigenization, the term given to the new direction, was accepted at the General Conference in Yarrow, B.C. in the summer of 1957. But for the missionaries in the field, especially the older ones, it was hard to swallow. Late in life, JB was still getting letters from retired missionaries apologizing for having literally hated both him and his policies at the time. The process, however, remained a work in progress, even at the time of JB's resignation in 1963.

To develop the policy recommended to the 1957 Yarrow conference, JB had consulted both inside the conference, especially with men like Peters, and missions directors of other church organizations or societies outside the conference. When he left in 1963 to begin teaching at the MB seminary, the theology of missions was one of his teaching subjects.

Clarence Hiebert consulted JB's lecture notes in his 1997 tribute, "J.B. Toews as Missiologist." Based upon the book of Acts, they consider the latter "as an encyclopedia of missions...[addressing]...the spiritual, social, cultural and strategy questions of the missionary assignment of the church in the past as well as in its contemporary setting." The sequence here is interesting, perhaps instructive: first there is JB the missionary practitioner; then JB the missions theoretician. Hiebert does not address to what extent the second can be seen as a justification for, or rationalization of, the first.

Whatever the case, in his position as missions general secretary, JB was once again serving both a U.S. and Canadian constituency. He was to do the same as president of the Biblical Seminary from 1964 to 1972 and later as executive secretary of the Historical Commission and director of the Center for MB Studies in Fresno.

His years in Coaldale, Hepburn and lastly Winnipeg, stood him in good stead for he knew everyone of note. His correspondence demon-

*The foreign mission board, ca 1960—the chair was Lando Hiebert, flanking him were J.B. Toews, the general secretary of the mission, and George W. Peters, recording secretary for the board.*

*JB in a setting familiar to many conference attenders. This was at St. Catharines in 1984.*

strates that in all his varied activities he constantly cultivated personal relationships. This allowed him to speak freely and frankly with everyone and under all circumstances. And when he needed to, he could exert pressure to accomplish his goals; the more so since he had served the MB General Conference in virtually all of its most important positions. For this reason, his correspondence makes fascinating reading.

## TWO CHALLENGES

JB had come to the Seminary to teach and to write; with enough administration to last several lifetimes, he sought some respite. But the Seminary faced at least two challenges that many people believed he alone could address. Within a year he had been made president to deal with them. First, was full and equal Canadian participation in the Seminary; the second was the transformation of the Seminary from a Dallas Seminary-oriented evangelicalism to an Anabaptist/Mennonite theology.

The second was achieved first in the early years of his presidency. The first was achieved in 1975. Prepared for the second by his son John's studies at the Seminary (John had complained of the poor quality of instruction and absence of any kind of Anabaptist emphasis in a lengthy letter to his father), JB set about cleaning house and appointing new faculty. With the new faculty came not only a new theological orientation, but better quality that allowed the Seminary to achieve full accreditation with the American Association of Theological Schools. In order to attain the latter, the library also needed building up. With full Canadian participation in the school, the theological course redirected and full accreditation, JB moved on to his last task.

For many years before he became director for the Center for MB Studies in Fresno and executive secretary of the MB Historical Commission—the latter a General Conference entity—JB had become concerned about the theological trajectory of the Mennonite Brethren. To Jacob H. Quiring he wrote in July, 1973 with regard to joint Canadian/U.S. support for the Seminary: "The test which we are facing in the first 25 years of the second century will determine whether we shall be lost in the mainstream of American evangelical Protestantism with a theology of benefit and possession at the cost of discipleship...." Losing ourselves to such evangelicalism, he believed, would affect "not only [our] destiny but [our] character and life in the 'now'." He saw the Canadian Conference decision to join the Seminary as the "answer to many prayers."

*Offering to the church his Pilgrimage of Faith, published in 1993: an attempt to explain the theological identity of the Mennonite Brethren.*

To the Mennonite Church leader George R. Brunk, he wrote in October, 1984: "[Our] commitment to the Scriptures remains solid. The problem of hermeneutics, however, poses a danger. One senses a tendency to relativism which makes room to interpret the Scriptures in the context of a changing culture. This is the great crisis of our day. The lines of the absolute become vague." It was this concern that led JB, as he wrote Roy Just in September of 1975, to take up the historical work for the conference. He was assuming, he said, a *mission* which the brotherhood had neglected for too long. "Our moorings have become shaky because we have moved *too much in[to] a theological perspective of accommodation instead of seriously deepening our historical roots in [a] scriptural context.*"

JB attacked the problem from at least three positions. First, he made a proposal to the General Conference to set up three archival centers in connection with the schools in Fresno, Winnipeg and Hillsboro. In 1977, JB himself visited the Canadian and U.S. MB churches to microfilm and collect their archival materials.

Second, in 1974 a General Conference Historical Commission was established to nurture a sense of history among MBs. Its first project was the translation of P.M. Friesen's *magnum opus*. And third, JB established an endowment to support research into MB themes in the Fresno Center.

## WAS ANYONE READING?

Having done these things, he then proceeded to do what the conference had long asked of him: in 1993 he completed his *A Pilgrimage of Faith: The Mennonite Brethren Church in Russia and North America 1860-1990,* and in 1995 he completed his autobiography: *JB: A Twentieth-Century Mennonite Pilgrim.* And in his spare time, JB encouraged his South American brothers to follow the North American example and developed a ministry to the *Aussiedlers* in Germany, persuading them to write their own history while in Russia (*Die Mennoniten Brüdergemeinde in Russland 1925-1980 The Mennonite Brethren Church in Russia 1925-1980*).

Was JB as successful in his last venture as he had been in his earlier ones? By the time he entered upon this last part of his calling, was it too late to stem the evangelical torrent within the MB churches of North America? Were MBs even interested in their own history, or JB's interpretation of it? In 1994 he wrote to John I. Block of Ontario, "[From a] survey as to how many pastors of the MB churches have read 'A Spiritual Pilgrimage,' I was informed that less than five percent so far have given any attention to it."

When this writer introduced JB's autobiography to the 1995 General Conference, I suggested that many present might be interested in discovering whether or not their names were "written in this book of life." But I, too, was wrong. As Benjamin H. Unruh wrote in 1909: "No religious group has as little historical orientation, none has as little concern for the past of its own church as the Mennonite [Brethren] people."

SOURCES

This chapter has drawn on J.B. Toews's own writing, *JB: A Twentieth-Century Mennonite Pilgrim* (Fresno: 1995) and *Pilgrimage of Faith: The Mennonite Brethren Church in Russia and North America 1860-1990* (Winnipeg and Hillsboro: 1993); the chapter "Baptist Interpretations of Anabaptist History" in *Mennonites and Baptists: A Continuing Conversation* (Winnipeg: 1993); the author's *History and Renewal in the Anabaptist/Mennonite Tradition* (North Newton, KS: 1994) as well as *In Defense of Privilege: Russian Mennonites and the State Before and During World War I* (Winnipeg: 2006), and a chapter in *The Devil, Heresy and Witchcraft in the Middle Ages: Essays in Honor of Jeffrey B. Russell* (Leiden: 1998), entitled "Medieval

Heretics or Forerunners of the Reformation?"; the J.B. Toews fonds at the Center for MB Studies in Fresno; the Canadian MB Conference Board of Higher Education fonds at the Centre for MB Studies in Winnipeg; and the 1997 (Vol. 26, No. 2) issue of *Direction*, dedicated as a tribute to J.B. Toews.

# Marie Wiebe

# THE WOMAN WHO WALKED ON STILTS

*By Dorothy Siebert*

At the age 70, at the annual picnic of the Westwood MB Church in Winnipeg, Marie Wiebe took note of a competition. It was a race on stilts. Yes, she must try this! Away she went.

Then she took a tumble and was embarrassed to find she had cracked her ribs.

"Marie!" the people said, "you are too impulsive—think before you leap!" But stepping out in faith and courage had characterized all of Marie's adult life.

She seemed unstoppable, always ready for the next adventure. Strangely enough, she never learned to ride a bicycle although she twice broke an arm trying. But cars, cows and tractors—these she could drive to great advantage! There is a photo of Marie behind the steering wheel of a tractor pulling a huge and clumsy load. It's a church building. She was hauling the church to its new location in Ashern where she and her husband Joe were immersed in a mission venture.

Marie Wiebe was born on April 1, 1912 in Steinbach, Manitoba, the tenth of 15 children born to Peter and Elizabeth Toews. The happy part of her childhood, before her mother died, was filled with joyful memories.

*The Writer*
Dorothy Siebert and her husband worked in a church planting team in Latin America for 10 years, planting two new churches with other MBMSI team members. She has been a print editor at Family Life Network for 11 years and is a published author with an MA in Old Testament studies. She and her husband Harold have four grown children.

One of her favorites was of going down the stairs into a cellar heaped with boxes of apples. There she loaded up a knitted toque with the fruit and carried it back upstairs for a family snack.

## FROM FAITH AND BACK

Marie was twelve when her mother died and after that she found life at home difficult. Overwhelmed by loneliness, she turned her back on her parents' faith and left home at age fifteen to work in the city of Winnipeg. There she chose friends with whom she could go dancing and drinking. A few years later, at age 18, she went to hear a "yelling preacher" and turned back to God. She also returned home to Steinbach to finish high school.

Then she launched out on her own, moving to Saskatoon where she lived in the home of a married brother. For four years she worked for the T. Eaton Company, who valued her so highly they offered her a full scholarship to college. However, she became convinced God wanted her in Christian service. With no visible means of support, she left her job and jumped into studies at a Saskatchewan Bible college. She appealed to a well-to-do relative for funding but he was so incensed over her rejection of the Eaton's scholarship that he refused to help her. Government student loans were not available at the time. "I couldn't afford even a three-cent stamp," she recalled. Sometimes a few dollars would arrive in the mail or be pushed under her door at college.

Meanwhile, a high school friend back in Steinbach was praying that Marie would return from distant Saskatchewan. It was Joe Wiebe, studying at the Winnipeg Bible College (now Providence College). After two years of study during which they wrote letters, Marie moved back to Manitoba to continue her studies at the school Joe attended. After her graduation, they were married in August of 1938.

Marriage started with challenges. For three of their early years together, Joe battled an illness. After his recovery, both Joe and Marie were eager to reach out to others beyond their faith community. So in 1943, as a couple with two small children, they were asked to start a mission ministry from scratch in the community of Stuartburn, located south of Winnipeg off the # 59 Highway near the U.S.A. border. This assignment came from the Christian Endeavor Society, composed of six Mennonite churches in their region, including the Steinbach Mennonite Brethren Church.

## A PASTURE FOR A YARD

Stuartburn was a town settled by pioneers from Ukraine and was famed as the first Ukrainian community in western Canada. Joe went to scout out the town and found only a tarpaper shack to rent. He rented it on the spot and returned home to report the news to Marie. There would be no electricity, the roof leaked and cows used their yard as a pasture.

Marie looked around at her modern washing machine and other appliances. They would all be left behind along with many other conveniences. "For two days and nights I cried while God loosed me from my house and things," she said.

The Scripture she clung to then, Psalm 126:6, became amazingly fulfilled in her lifetime, "He that goes forth with weeping, bearing precious seed, shall doubtless come again with rejoicing, bringing his sheaves with him."

*Marie and Joe Wiebe: able to think outside the box.*

"The devil didn't want any to be saved in Stuartburn and withstood us at every turn," reported Marie to their support group in Steinbach. "Many times when coming home, we sensed him standing in the middle of the road about a mile from town. We could only go forward in the name of the Lord Jesus who said, 'All power is given unto me in heaven and on earth.'"

Marie and Joe threw themselves into this work with the abandon to God they showed throughout their lives. To relate more closely to the community, they determined to learn Ukrainian, studying that language with a tutor throughout the winter months. For years they held services in their own home. On Sunday mornings their front yard was dotted with cribs, tables and cupboards, moved out to make room for the seekers who responded to Marie and Joe's invitation.

At the same time they extended their efforts into the neighboring town of Gardenton. When they explored renting a meeting place, the local pool hall seemed the best choice in town. It turned out that the go-to person to rent the facility was an Orthodox priest. When he heard that Marie and Joe intended to hold Sunday school classes there, he gladly rented it to them for a reasonable cost. Marie's thought patterns were definitely outside the box for a Mennonite of the 1940s. She was not shy to mix with those of other faiths or of no faith.

Launching out further, Marie and Joe made visits to dozens of rural one-room schoolhouses scattered all over southeastern Manitoba. The whole family would be packed into the car along with music books and flannelgraphs and off they went—at times spending a week or ten days on the road, sleeping in halls, schools or homes. They visited about 45 schools in this way, telling children about Jesus through stories and songs. Both Marie and Joe sang well and most teachers welcomed them. "There were very few who didn't welcome us. Most said, 'Come any day and any time of the day,'" reported the Wiebes.

By visiting the public schools and holding Sunday schools for neighborhood children, Marie saw the great spiritual and social needs of families. "God naturally burdened us with what we would call underprivileged children," Marie reported. In one case, each Sunday morning they went to a certain family living in dire poverty. They woke the children from where they slept in the straw, dressed them, combed their hair and packed them into their car to take them to Sunday school.

"Oh, what a responsibility we felt for them," Marie exclaimed. During summer they took these and other children to a Bible camp held at the Steinbach Bible School. Later, this humble Bible camp grew, moved to a lakeside site and today is the thriving Red Rock Bible Camp. "God can make great things out of small beginnings," reflected Marie.

During those years when it was slow and difficult work to build a fellowship of believers, one of Marie's favorite verses was, "Cast your bread upon the waters and you will find it after many days" (Eccles. 11:1). And sure enough, over the years many of the young believers from the Stuartburn group became Christian workers, missionaries and ministers.

Slowly their group outgrew their home as well as a local meeting place. Their supporters in Steinbach then constructed a new building for them called the Stuartburn Gospel Chapel. At the back of the chapel was an apartment for the Wiebe family to live in. After all the hard work of building up a group of believers, Marie called that building "a monument to the grace of God."

In his book, *No Longer at Arms Length*, Peter Penner describes Marie and Joe as "…the one couple most successful among the villagers and farming folk of southern Manitoba, and who never used any form of subterfuge.…" He praises them for "their modest ways, kindness, non-resistance to intended irritations and agape love."

*Joe and Marie with the future conference executive director David Wiebe.*

## VERY DIFFERENT COMMUNITY

The leaders of the Mennonite Brethren Conference were impressed with the Wiebes' ability to break down barriers and opposition in new territory. In 1946 they asked Marie and Joe to consider moving north to build up a church in the town of Ashern. This town had a very different flavour from Stuartburn. It was a northern business centre for fishermen and surrounding First Nations communities. The move there was a challenge in itself, a traumatic experience in a vehicle that swung crazily from side to side for hours along a wet and muddy road.

They began their work in Ashern by visiting homes, singing and praying with the people and inviting others to join them in their home for Sunday services. Marie played the piano until daughter Ruth started to play for services at age 11. For about the first four years, church services were held in the Wiebe home where they knocked down a wall to accommodate the group.

At the same time, they also held street meetings in town on Saturday nights. These services, like any others, were a family affair—even the young children joined in singing. Though a difficult venture, the entire family faithfully continued the street meetings for eleven years! Marie managed to instill a team spirit in the family, which had grown to include five children: Ruth, Eunice, Lois, Philip and David.

Throughout the years of their ministry, Joe suffered from stress headaches that were debilitating enough to render him unable to preach. At these times Marie stepped forward and filled in, proving to be a capable preacher and teacher.

Marie seemed to enjoy the work in Ashern. Often groups of college students would drive the 175 kilometers from Winnipeg on Sundays to help. Of course, Marie cooked lunch for them all. The Wiebes' salary would not have extended as far had Marie not worked extra hard. She kept a large garden and canned hundreds of sealers of fruit each year, often with no electricity, as well as vegetables, poultry, and fish from nearby creeks, and game that Joe brought from hunting excursions. The family kept a cow for milk and cream and chickens for eggs. Marie churned all the family's butter and made all their bread.

Not only did she provide for her family, but she opened her home to a number of young school teachers new to the area. They called her house their home on weekends. In fact, a supervisor in Winnipeg assigning one timid young teacher to a northern community, remarked, "Oh, don't worry…there are the Wiebes living up there who take care of all the permit teachers!" Several of these teachers, after joining Marie in her home and in her work, went on into full-time mission work themselves, citing Marie's example as their motivation.

It was a rare day when no guest was added to the number at the table. No wonder Marie once commented, "Hospitality is a test of Christian character." Often a song was sung in place of a spoken prayer to begin the mealtime. One day Marie suggested the song, "Five thousand, Lord, by Thee were fed." Instead of singing, everyone burst into laughter as it hit them how true this was of Marie herself!

To make ends meet Marie sewed the children's clothing. When Christmastime approached, often cheques from friends would arrive by mail as well as a ham shipped by train from Winnipeg. With great relief and gratitude she and Joe accepted these gifts.

Looking beyond her home to the community, she reported to their Steinbach supporters, "Our hearts were constantly burdened for the surrounding towns and areas." As a result the Wiebe family expanded their efforts, bringing church services to a town north of Ashern called Moosehorn.

*The Wiebes' Marne home was also the Ashern church's meetingplace at first.*

Most notable were their efforts focused on the town of Clarkleigh. Every second Sunday, after holding the service in Ashern, they drove to Clarkleigh in the afternoon to hold a service, a distance of 77 kilometers. The whole family would go along as well as any guests who happened to be with them. In the car on the way Joe would assign the various parts of the service to family members. "Marie, you'll have the story; Ruth, you play piano; Lois, you sing Jesus Loves Me," and so on. The parents often told the children, "As a Christian, you need to be ready to be called on at any time."

The Wiebe family continued these services year after year. As a result they became the spiritual guides of many who had settled in the area. Entire families in Clarkleigh looked to them for day-to-day spiritual guidance as well as for family occasions such as weddings, baptisms and funerals.

Because of the isolated setting of Ashern, the public school did not attract good teachers. So Marie often filled the void by helping the children to understand their textbooks and to do their homework. Also, the Wiebe children were "foreign" to the community and ostracized for carrying their "foreign religion" into the area. In one of her reports Marie, told the story of a certain girl who made life at school for the Wiebe children "…nearly unbearable; quite often our girls came home crying. But one day this girl told Eunice, 'Tell your mother that I want to talk with her.'"

They met together and Marie ended by praying for the girl. She invited her to open her life to Jesus. "The result," she explained, "was that the Lord gave her rest for her unrestful soul. It was a great encouragement for our girls. That day it was not until late in the night that the girls could fall asleep just for joy."

As a family the Wiebes played many games together: baseball, croquet and table games. In the evenings the parents followed the tradition of a family devotional time. Each child took a turn at leading, but no matter whose turn it was, each one always introduced the story time the same way: "And now we'll have a story by Mom." A great storyteller, Marie always had a story for the children, sometimes with an object lesson as well.

### WORK TILL JESUS COMES

Marie and Joe seemed to work without any breaks. In fact, one of the songs they sang frequently at meetings was titled, "We'll work till Jesus comes." No wonder then that Marie occasionally spoke wistfully about the easier years when she worked at the T. Eaton Company. Through the many moves to different homes she kept some fancy stemware and enjoyed showing her daughters how to set an elegant table. Marie gave the same attention to detail in her personal appearance, keeping her hair neat and dressing well, even if the dresses were usually sewn by herself.

By age 45, Marie showed signs of exhaustion. There were new churches now in all three towns: Stuartburn, Ashern and Clarkleigh. But Marie had worn out. Following doctor's orders, in 1957 the family returned to home base in Steinbach so that Marie could rest and recuperate. This was a Marie that Joe hardly knew. Temporarily leaving ministry behind, he took a job at a creamery and later at an auto body shop to support the family.

After two years, Marie was well enough to take on a gentler assignment. This time they pastored the Lindal Church in the Pembina Valley near Morden. Later on, in 1967, a further assignment took them to Winnipegosis for several years.

It was while they were there that her married daughter Eunice died of illness, leaving her husband with three small children. Marie found that very hard, remembering how her own mother died when Marie was a girl. Her family felt she never really got over Eunice's death—though she worked at keeping a stiff upper lip. On some days, Joe recorded in his diary only the cryptic message, "Marie is in bed" or "Marie is low today."

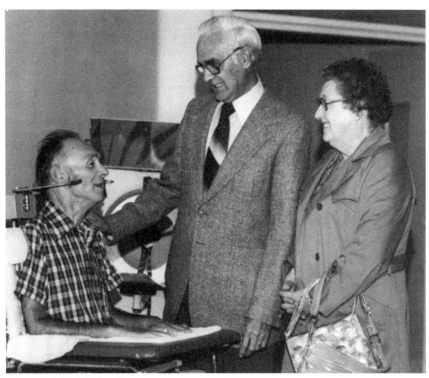

*Marie and Joe did a lot of visitation ministry together.*

Yet, not long after Eunice's passing, Joe and Marie consented to a request from the Mennonite Brethren Conference to move to Mexico, near Guadalajara to minister to Low German-speaking Mennonites. They found it a difficult assignment. Because of the nature of the colonies, they were not permitted to preach or give the Gospel message in the way they had previously done in Manitoba. But Marie discovered a way to do what she did best: storytelling. She donned the typical dress of the colony, gathered the women and told them stories. Sometimes when she pulled the kerchief over her head, she "died laughing" but when she spoke, the women leaned forward with their mouths open, hanging onto every word of the Bible stories.

## SHOWERED WITH LOVE

After their Mexico experience, they settled in Winnipeg. The women of the Portage Avenue Mennonite Brethren Church held a shower for Marie. So used to giving out, not receiving, she felt overwhelmed with the outpouring of love: the cards, money, flowers and gifts. Others did not realize the magnitude of this occasion for Marie. She kept the cards and flowers on display at home for a long time and they would bring tears to her eyes.

Agnes Schmidt, producer of the radio program *Words for Women* recorded at Mennonite Brethren Communications (now Family Life Network), invited Marie to prepare some broadcasts. Marie recorded four programs, relating what she learned from her mission experiences.

In the fourth program she shared her experiences of prayer. "[Over the years] many have come to us asking us to teach them to pray. They had accepted Jesus but found it so hard or impossible to pray. Last year," she said, "I was asked to pray at a function…afterwards five or six ladies approached me and said, 'How can you pray like that? We watched you, you had your eyes closed and were not reading, how do you know all that from memory?'

"'Ladies, I said, it comes from within my heart, born by the Holy Spirit.'

'Would you teach us to pray?' they asked. I said, 'Only God can teach you to pray, but I will give you a start." She stressed, in the broadcast, that prayer should praise Jesus and should name by name those in need around you. "This kind of praying," she concluded, "gives unspeakable joy, confidence and peace."

At age 71, Marie suffered a heart attack. After two years of poor health, she was hospitalized. This woman who earlier had bravely consented to live without electricity was now connected to many machines. Yet she was still the same Marie. On April 11, 1985 she raised an arm and stated with dramatic abandon, "If I perish, I perish!" As she had done throughout her life, she loved and trusted Jesus' words, "Let not your heart be troubled, nor let it be afraid." The next day she died.

Her husband Joe wrote in his private notes, "My Honey went to be with the Lord."

Some 900 people from many regions came to her funeral and spoke of her love for them. Many individuals and families had encountered Christ had found meaning in life through meeting with Marie Wiebe. Today (in 2010), son David carries on Joe and Marie's tradition of church leadership as the executive director of the Canadian Conference of Mennonite Brethren.

Marie was seen by others as walking on a plane higher than most. Launching out on wooden stilts or walking into strangers' homes and communities, Marie, armed with humor and courage, stepped out in faith.

## SOURCES

Much of the information for this chapter came out of the Centre for Mennonite Brethren Studies in Winnipeg, most notably the fonds of Joe and Marie Wiebe: their memoirs; notes, sermons and talks; reports to the Christian Endeavour Society; handwritten scripts for the Words for Women radio program; photos; and obituaries. Other sources were internet histories of Manitoba towns and cities; the *Global Anabaptist Mennonite Encyclopedia Online*; and conversations and email exchanges with friends as well as with Marie's children, Lois Wedel and David. The book by Hedy Durksen, *Along Highways and Hedges* (Winnipeg: 1977) and Peter Penner's *No Longer at Arms Length* (Winnipeg: 1987) were, of course, important sources.

## Katy Penner

# CANADIAN PRAIRIE TO CONGO, A NURSE'S JOURNEY

*By Sarah Klassen*

Katy Penner began her work as a missionary nurse one night in 1953 in a dispensary in Matende, Congo. After a gruelling road trip from Kikwit, she was ready to retire for the night. But the missionary teacher temporarily in charge at the dispensary was also exhausted. "If anyone calls," she told Katy, "don't wake me. Do the best you can."

The call came in the early morning. It was dark and Katy feared venturing into the African night inhabited by unfamiliar peril. Terror threatened to immobilize her until she heard the voice of the Spirit saying: "Do not fear for I am with you" (Isa. 40:10). Not only was she able to walk through the dark to the dispensary where a teenage girl was about to give birth, but also, as she writes in her memoir, "...the deep-seated fear that had been with me since childhood was taken from me that night."

She sums up her first 24 hours as a fledgling missionary like this: "I took my first night call, delivered my first baby, experienced the grief of my first death [the child did not live] and prayed at the first burial I attended."

---

*The Writer*

Sarah Klassen is a poet and writer of fiction living and working in Winnipeg. Earlier she taught English literature in a Winnipeg high school and for a couple of years in Lithuania. She is an award-winning author of five books of poetry and two collections of fiction, among them *Journey to Yalta*, *A Curious Beatitude*, *The Peony Season* and *A Feast of Longing*. One of her reviewers has written, Sarah Klassen "does not flinch for an instant from viewing harsh and gritty realities. But always, embedded in these realities, glows a rich and life-affirming beauty." She is a member of the River East Mennonite Brethren Church.

The journey leading to this dramatic debut into missionary work was fraught with obstacles and challenges. Her fellow missionaries reminded her that "he who hunts a short path through the jungle will be eaten by the evil spirits. He who follows the long prairie path, when the time is right, will arrive." Katy describes her path in her memoir *Diamonds in the Sand,* which has on its cover her personal testimony: "I being in the way, the Lord led me!" (Gen. 24:27). This firmly embedded faith in God's leading was to open up areas of service and influence that neither she nor the sending Mennonite Brethren churches could have dreamt.

### ASKING WHY?

Katy Penner was two years old when Cornelius and Helene Penner left the Ukraine for Canada, arriving in southern Saskatchewan in June 1926, a few years ahead of the Depression. She lived her formative years on the Prairies, an immigrant child growing physically and spiritually, learning to live frugally and to make significant life choices.

She traces her spiritual awakening to a day when she was only five, seated on the knee of a family friend who spoke to her of heaven and Jesus' return—a prospect that left her uneasy. Prompted by the friend, she spoke a prayer for forgiveness. The experience left her happy but doubt reared its inevitable head when she prayed an entire summer for a doll like her friend's. The doll failed to appear. Why? No doubt Katy Penner asked, "Why?" often during the trials and crises that punctuated her years as a missionary.

School was an exciting adventure that she entered with relish. Besides mastering a new language and classroom lessons, she learned about nature on the way to school and about baseball on the playground.

She brought to her grade seven teacher—who was also her Sunday school teacher—her fear of being "left behind" and her spiritual doubt. He pointed her to Acts 16:31: "Believe on the Lord Jesus Christ and you shall be saved." This awakened new trust in God, a trust she would need in abundance. Katy was baptized after grade seven. The practice of personal prayer and scripture reading, deeply ingrained from child-hood, became ever more important in the life of this future missionary nurse.

Although she was a good student, Katy left school after grade eight. She had already learned to do barnyard chores, stook wheat and shovel grain. Now her mother, ill and with a new baby, needed help in the house. Despite these obligations Katy found ways of continuing her education: two winters in the Bethany Bible School in Hepburn, a dress-making course and high school completion by correspondence.

A conviction that God was calling her came when missionary Henry Bartsch spoke in the rural Saskatchewan church where Katy's father was the minister, appealing for a nurse for Congo. But how was she to follow this call, Katy wondered during a fierce prairie blizzard that reflected her inner storm. She felt hemmed in and helpless. Guidance came from Acts 9: 5-6: "I am Jesus...now get up and go into the city and you shall be told what you must do."

Katy eventually moved to Winnipeg where she scrubbed and waxed floors while earning a Bachelor of Religious Education degree at Mennonite Brethren Bible College and a Registered Nurse's diploma at Grace Hospital. When she was offered a scholarship to complete a nursing degree and a subsequent teaching position at Grace Hospital, her calling was strongly challenged. Declining this tempting opportunity—and security—she sailed for Belgium in 1952 and commenced French language studies in preparation for work in Congo.

## KAJIJI ASSIGNMENT

After several months at Matende, Katy was assigned to open a medical work at Kajiji, a station MB missions had taken over from the Unevangelized Tribes Mission. The government had promised funding to replace a burned-down dispensary and unless the construction was promptly undertaken, that money would be forfeited. While the dispensary was under construction, Katy began to treat patients though she had no budget, no familiar medications and few supplies.

When a five-month-old baby was brought in with a raging fever caused by malaria and pneumonia, Katy had no antibiotics, only quinine. But "we have a living God who answers prayer," she said. "Would you like us to pray for her?"

"Yes, please do."

God answered that prayer—the sick baby recovered. Katy would often find herself in situations where she had no recourse except to God through prayer.

Katy's first Easter in Kajiji in 1954 was marked by two events. Before Easter, local pastors and teachers, hoping to pre-empt the traditional practise of initiation rites that took young boys from the village out of school and into the bush for periods of teaching by the fetishers, brought 40 boys to the dispensary to be circumcised. Katy demurred, never having done this before. But her African nursing assistant stepped forward. "We will do them," he said, and to Katy, "I want you to help me." And amazingly, she could.

The other experience was a personal renaming. During the Easter service the pastor called Katy forward and said, "Your name will be Mama

Lobilu." This was a sign of acceptance that moved Katy deeply. "Lobilu" means "prayer" in Kituba. What a fitting name chosen by a pastor who must have understood this novice missionary and observed her at prayer.

With the completion of the dispensary, the number of patients increased. The government intended to build a hospital in the area and chose Kajiji as the site. While the government would fund the hospital, MB missions recruited the first doctor: Ernie Schmidt arrived in 1955. The maternity part was quickly built, but the unrest following Congo's independence in 1960 delayed completion of the hospital until 1963.

### A MODEST START

Katy's remarkable contribution to nurses' education in Congo began modestly. Clearly, if there was to be staff for the Kajiji hospital, there would have to be effective training. So far, training in Congo's isolated clinics had happened sporadically whenever overworked doctors found a minute here and there to instruct assistants. In the 1950s several doctors had suggested that Katy should "write up some courses." The manuals she prepared focused on basic nursing techniques, lab procedures and hygiene. They were written in French, but the five students who formed the first preparatory class in 1955 were instructed in Kituba. The next year's class consisted of thirteen married men. This small start to nurses' training evolved into the Kajiji school of nursing, where Katy worked as instructor, administrator and curriculum writer, always striving for higher standards. Curricula she wrote at Kajiji were submitted to the Department of Health and would eventually affect government legislation. The Kajiji school of nursing weathered many changes, evolved and still exists today.

Katy's work was not confined to hospital and nursing school. She knew that medical work had opened the area to church work in the 1940s and '50s and she remained aware of the larger context of her medical work. Not only did she become counsellor, mentor and Bible teacher to nursing students, but she also participated in the local church, teaching Sunday school and counselling women and children. In later years she participated in Christian education seminars held in various outposts. In medical and church work she was always willing to learn from both fellow missionaries and Congolese co-workers.

Katy demanded a lot of herself, and also of her students. Adingite Bertin, a graduate of the nursing program in Kajiji, later wrote to Katy from university: "If it had not been for your clear, consistent teaching of the Word of God and sometimes difficult discipline in my student days, the Christian community would not have a young man named Bertin to-

*Katy with graduates of the Hospital and Public Health Nursing program in 1983.*

day." This testimony confirms Katy's twofold concern: to raise up Christian workers and train excellent nurses.

The 1960s were turbulent years for all foreigners in Congo. The country was gripped by a war against its colonial overlords and missionaries were told to leave—at least temporarily. By the time the missionaries at Kajiji left their station, many Congolese with whom they had worked had turned hostile. Three men they had treated for severe wounds inflicted by a leopard now helped erect barriers. Others threw stones at the small cavalcade of mission vehicles headed for Angola from where they were airlifted to Europe.

After the 1960 independence upheaval, "Congo did not have single university-trained doctor and few medical assistants or diploma nurses." When the foreigners were forced to leave, nursing aides took over most of the medical work in Congo, including at Kajiji.

The 1960 evacuation was followed by others. In 1964, when rebels of the *jeunesse* movement were terrorizing the country, the Kajiji missionaries, immediately after delivering a baby, were airlifted by Missionary Aviation Fellowship to Kinshasa. Again in 1967, when Katy found herself the only nurse in Kajiji, the MAF plane, instead of bringing the fellow missionaries she expected, brought orders from the American Embassy to evacuate. The reason: the threatening activities of the mercenary army brought in by the president. Every evacuation resulted in neglect of the hospital and nursing school, and depletion of staff and supplies. It meant starting over again.

## HOME EXHAUSTED

The year 1971 marked a turning point in Katy's life and service. With the awareness that "there really was no need for me in the medical work for the time being," she returned to Canada for furlough. Back home, exhausted, she brooded over what she perceived as her own shortcomings and failures, believing she needed to confess them. She found solace—and irony—in the Scriptures: "to keep me from becoming conceited...there was given me a thorn in the flesh" (1Cor 12:7-9). "Conceited" is not an adjective others would have used to describe Katy Penner.

In 1972, rested, she wondered: What next? On the day she read in Acts 16 of the vision that led Paul to Asia, she was invited with a two-year contract from the Congo's President Mobutu's personal physician to set up an education program in the 1800-bed Mama Yemo hospital in Kinshasa. This was a huge challenge in a setting very different from Kajiji. She accepted this invitation, taking a leave of absence from MB missions to become Director of Nursing in a facility with 816 Congolese nurses and 35 European supervisors. Responsibilities for staffing, curriculum development and administration kept her busy. As a result of the critique of health education and suggestions for improvement made by Katy and her colleagues, "President Mobutu in his national speech announced the creation of '*un Conseil Superieur*' for health and education." Could she ever have imagined such influence when she heard the missionary call in a small Saskatchewan church? She began as the lone director, when she left, she had two assistants in place, along with two clinical supervisors and 16 new supervisors.

Katy turned down a second contract at Mama Yemo to return to Canada where her aging mother and disabled sister needed her. After the weighty professional responsibilities in a large hospital and the hectic life in the huge city of Kinshasa, she must have felt severely circumscribed in modest city Saskatchewan. In her memoirs she describes poignantly the marginal position of missionaries: "We live at the boundaries of the cultural life, no matter where we are. In some sense we are never quite at home. In some ways, none of us are ever fully assimilated into the culture where we work. But after spending some time in the mission field, we do not fit into our home culture either."

*Katy with local chiefs, health care promoter Pakisa Tshimika, church pastors and mission leaders Peter Hamm and Henry Dick at the ribbon cutting for a Congolese nursing school in 1986.*

## A WOMAN ON A CONFERENCE BOARD

In 1975 Katy attended the Canadian MB Conference in Regina. She had allowed her name to stand for the Board of Christian Education, but a heated discussion of women serving on Canadian boards left her baffled at the rift over this issue. Prominent church leaders were against it. When the discussion was postponed until after the election, Katy withdrew her name; she did not want to proceed before the conference acknowledged the eligibility of women. According to her niece Gwen Dueck of Saskatoon, Katy was acting on principle. Nevertheless, as a woman accustomed to taking leadership and experiencing collegiality with fellow professionals and missionaries, both men and women, as well as with Congolese pastors, she must have found this deeply disturbing. "On the one hand," says Dueck, "she was acknowledged and celebrated as a woman in leadership in her role as missionary in Congo, yet in her own church community, her potential contributions were not realized."

Only a month later, at the North American MB Conference in Winnipeg, Katy was elected "with grand applause" to the Board of Missions and Services. Ironically, she had been nominated by Dr. Frank C. Peters, who had opposed women on boards in Regina, and encouraged to accept by Dr. John Redekop, who admitted, "The time has come to reconsider our position on women serving with the conference." Katy became the lone woman on a 15-member board on which she sat from 1975-92. She became a forerunner of and model for MB women who would increasingly seek a place in church and conference. According to Gwen Dueck, "She was a role model and mentor for me and for my friends during a time we were searching to...establish our own identities, unique and apart from our families."

The issue of women in the MB church would not soon be resolved. "Little did I realize," Katy writes, "that at the 1999 conference in Hillsboro, Kansas this sticky issue would still need to be "clarified" [to encourage] women to exercise leadership on conference boards, in pastoral staff positions and in our congregations, institutions and agencies." Her sense of dismay is evident and must have increased when the "sticky issue" was carried into the next millennium.

During her years on the mission board her responsibilities included a study of health work in Panama, a review of the literature about the African Independent Church Movement and an evaluation of MB Missions' health and education programs in Congo, all weighty matters that she took on courageously and completed successfully.

The third-mentioned task took Katy, in 1982, once more, and for her last term, to Kajiji. She had used her Canadian interval to upgrade her nursing qualifications and had been teaching at the University of Saskatchewan, where the academic community regarded her work highly, while the church community saw her as "the single missionary from the Congo." Her mother's death and her invalid sister's transferral to a nursing home freed her from family obligations. Now she resigned from her teaching position and returned to Congo, once again under the Board of Missions and Services.

### WELCOME BACK

In Kinshasa, she was welcomed enthusiastically by former students and colleagues from her years at Mama Yemo Hospital. The return to Kajiji, on the other hand, must have been a bittersweet reminder of the 1950s: no classrooms, only an office where her former colleagues attempted to teach. Constant political turmoil and the controversial diamond trade had left the school devastated. Although Katy had come prepared to work on curriculum, she was forced to help find building materials and workers, earning her the name "Nehemiah."

*Katy had very close ties within the Congolese church community.*

In fact, there was talk of moving the nursing program to a more popu-lated area and closing the hospital. However, Doctors Matshifi and Tshi-mika, both Katy's former students, now in charge at the hospital, had no such intentions; instead, they hoped to upgrade the nursing program to a registered nurses' level. With Katy's help the medical work would continue, but with a new focus on community health, a shift the student nurses found challenging. They would have preferred to work in a hospital rather than being sent out to assess health needs in outlying communities. The villagers they interrogated were suspicious of new ways. Nevertheless, the medical work has continued to this day, with Mennonite Mission Health Association (MMHA) and Mennonite Central Committee partnering to provide medications and supplies.

During the thirty-some years Katy spent in Congo, her spirit was regu-larly buffeted. And so was her body. In 1957, when she was only 33, while dispensing medication, she suffered a heart attack. The doctor lacked medicine, oxygen and essential equipment and she was in no condition to be transferred. Like Hezekiah, Katy begged God for time—ten years. After anointing and prayer by pastors and missionaries, the pain subsided. She was reassured by a dream of a beautiful wheat field ready for harvest, each ripe head turning into a black face. She recovered.

When the ten years she had requested were up, Katy, on her motorbike, collided with a missionary van. While the students launched a death wail and attempted to slash the tires of the van that had killed her, Dr. Ferd Pauls was stitching up her nose. A few weeks later, Katy received a letter from Mrs. A.E. Janzen in Hillsboro and another from a student in Winnipeg: both had felt compelled to pray for her at the precise time of the accident.

Another potential crisis concerned her eyesight. Before leaving for Congo in 1982, she received a disturbing diagnosis: a malignant growth in one eye, a smaller one in the other. She proceeded to Congo where an ophthalmologist, alarmed to find the larger growth doubled in size, counselled a return to Canada. Sensing her fear, Pastor Tshimika prayed with her and read Psalm 27:1: "The Lord is your light." The tumour remained but never blossomed into genuine danger.

## INTO UNFAMILIAR TERRITORY

The full reach of Katy Penner's influence on several continents would be impossible to measure. When the MMHA honoured her in 2006, Dr. Ferd Pauls, her co-worker in Congo, said: "I was able to observe the influence she had...not only in the nursing field but also [on] administrators and physicians she worked with. Regardless of where she was, her Christian example was noted by all."

Dr. Pauls, who had been introduced to tropical medicine by Katy, also noted that in her "...relationships with the Congolese she became a close friend of the senior pastor and in this way...influenced him much more than any of us could know. Her personality was such that the male-only church leadership accepted her for her spiritual and wise suggestions."

Dr. Pakisa Tshimika said, "Many of us Congolese will remember Katy as a mother, mentor and teacher. She liked discipline and order. Those who studied under her leadership knew that patients were her first priority. She was a model bridge-maker, able to work within both church and government institutions. She respected both and was herself very much accepted and respected. She amazed many of us in the way she submitted to our leadership later in life, although we were once the little boys she had vaccinated in the clinic."

Katy Penner died in 2008. She was one of a rare tribe of intrepid MB women, single and capable, who, hearing the call of God, left family and friends and set out for unfamiliar territory, bringing healing, education and good news to strangers. These were career missionaries committed not to a "term" but to a lifetime of service. On furlough they told their stories to the churches.

"Aunt Katy was a gifted story teller," Dueck recalls. "Whether it was in a small group, or while speaking (would that be called preaching?) from the pulpit, she peppered her presentation with questions, challenging assumptions long before the rest of us were thinking about what questions we should be asking. She was always provocative, inviting us to make our own meaning of the events we were experiencing or the things we were reading. And she was so well-read herself."

After Katy's death, her niece found a poem Katy had hand-copied and placed between the pages of the Penner family book:

And my heart struggled to walk the way.
It could not understand the Almighty,
As it called in fear and pain:
Even in this must your way be best?

Did these lines recall for Katy her experiences in Congo? Or do they reflect her last long years of failing health and diminished activity when churches and conference lost sight of her?

In the face of changes in MB mission practices, it is essential to keep alive the memory of women such as Katy Penner, by preserving and retelling their stories and by honouring the vital role they played in shaping our MB vision.

SOURCES

Much of the story for this chapter was derived from *Diamonds in the Sand*, Katy Penner's memoirs. Other sources were the *Mennonite Brethren Herald* and conversations or email communication with Anne Tymos, Dr. Ferd Pauls and Gwen Dueck.

# Frank C. Peters

# UNCOMMON LEADER
# WITH A COMMON TOUCH

*By David Ewert*

Mennonite Brethren have rarely had leaders more gifted than Frank C. Peters. He was likely the most sought after preacher during the years of his greatest preaching activity—from the late fifties to the mid-eighties—and in the classroom and as an author, he consistently attracted a strong audience. He used language wonderfully well. He had a remarkable way of engaging people. His hearers always knew that he understood their world, yet his message remained firmly anchored. He was an exceptionally effective witness for an evangelical Anabaptist Christian faith. His way of framing questions and summing up discussions, his ease before a large congregation, his humor as well as his ability to make very serious points, also made him an exceptionally attractive leader. How did he become the person he was?

Frank Peters was born July 5, 1920, the fifth child of Cornelius and Katherine Peters. The Peters family lived in Ekaterinovka, one of the Ignatyevo Mennonite villages in the Ukraine. Only a few weeks after Frank was born, his mother died. She had suffered from heart trouble for some time and died in her sleep with Frank in his cradle beside her bed.

---

*The Writer*

David Ewert was a longtime colleague and close friend of Frank C. Peters. They taught together at the Mennonite Brethren Bible College and served together on a number of denominational boards. David Ewert has taught in at least five Mennonite Brethren schools, authored many books and preached widely, both within and beyond Mennonite Brethren circles. The Ewerts have lived in Abbotsford, B.C. in their retirement.

The care of the motherless infant now fell to his older sister, Justina. It was a sad and difficult time for the Peters family.

Frank's father, now a widower, was a teacher by profession. He soon realized that to carry on with his professional responsibilities and to care for a family of five motherless children was more than he could manage. And so, after a time of grieving over the passing of his beloved wife, he decided to look for a new marriage partner. Anna Reimer, who lived in the community, was willing to become the new wife of Cornelius Peters and the mother of his children. Out of this union one more child, Anna, was born. (She later married Dr. Peter Bargen and passed away in 1997.)

Leninist Russia in the early twenties did not hold out a bright future for the Mennonite colonies. After the Bolshevik Revolution of 1917, the civil war and the famine in the early twenties, the prospect of continuing in his calling as a Christian teacher was rather bleak as atheism became the dominant ideology of the Soviet Union. Also, the economic policies of the Soviets left the Mennonites in Russia with little hope of material prosperity in the future. In 1924 the Cornelius Peters family, like thousands of other Mennonites, decided to leave their Ukrainian homeland and emigrate to Canada.

## A NEW START

Near Langham, Saskatchewan, lived a relative, Johann Peters, who welcomed the family to their new country. It was summer when the Peters arrived and both parents and children did whatever they could to help their kind hosts in their farming operations. After the harvest was completed the Peters family moved to Langham, for it was time for Frank's three older brothers to begin public school in Canada. Justina, however, did housework in various homes in the community. About a year after the Peters arrived in Canada they moved to Davidson, Saskatchewan, where Cornelius tried his hand at farming, but with little success.

Herbert, Saskatchewan, was an important Mennonite center. A number of Mennonite families who had left Russia in the late 1800s had settled here and played host to many of the immigrants from Russia in the twenties. In 1926, two years after arriving in Canada, the Peters family moved to Herbert. That was also the year in which the Ewert family arrived in Herbert. Mennonite churches in the area soon realized that C.C. Peters had great gifts for teaching and preaching and soon he was asked to become what we might call a "circuit preacher" (*Reiseprediger*). It was there that C.C. Peters moved from the Mennonite Church in which he had already been an active worker to the Mennonite Brethren in 1930.

By now it was time for young Frank to begin school. Like most other immigrant families, the Peters were extremely poor. Frank never forgot that he wore girls' shoes when he enrolled in grade one. Justina earned nine dollars a month doing housework in the community, but felt it was her filial duty to give all her earnings to the parents, who needed every penny they could get to put bread on the table.

As the Great Depression exacerbated the poverty of immigrants living in the prairie provinces, Canada's west coast appeared to offer hopes of a better life to many of them. In the early thirties, the Peters family packed up and made their way across the Rockies to the lush Fraser Valley. They first settled in Agassiz, and here Frank completed several more grades of school. However, before he could complete his high school, the family moved again.

At 17 years of age, Frank, like his older brothers, decided to strike out on his own to see if he could earn some extra money. Justina, the oldest in the family, had meantime married Martin Durksen. They lived in Foam Lake, Saskatchewan. Eventually, both Frank and his older brother, Peter, also went to Foam Lake to work for farmers in the community and to earn some money. For a while Frank also worked in the Barkman flour mill in Foam Lake.

When he left home, Frank did not know that God's Spirit was pursuing him. Although he had grown up in a Christian home, he had not yet committed his life to Christ. In fact, he had developed considerable resistance to the gospel. But God's hour had struck. Revival fires were burning in the Foam Lake Mennonite Brethren Church. Martin Durksen, their brother-in-law, took both Peter and Frank to the evangelistic meetings. After a fierce inner struggle, Frank finally yielded to the call of God and surrendered his life to Christ.

Shortly after his conversion, he declared his faith publicly in baptism and became a member of the Mennonite Brethren Church, a church to which he remained true all his life.

## AN URGE TO PREACH

Almost immediately after becoming a Christian, Frank felt drawn to preaching the gospel. Klaus Barkman, in whose mill Frank worked, had promised God that if Frank would become a follower of Jesus, he would bear the expenses if Frank enrolled at the Bethany Bible School. Frank was happy to spend a year in Hepburn, becoming more firmly rooted in the Scriptures. By now his father, C.C. Peters, had been appointed to teach in a new Bible school begun in Yarrow, B.C. It was time to come home.

When Bible school opened in fall, Frank took his second year of biblical studies in the Yarrow school. The move back to British Columbia proved momentous. Melita Krause was his fellow student during that year. Before long it was obvious that Frank and Melita were deeply in love, although dating was considered unseemly by many Mennonite churches. But love can be quite inventive and so there were many "chance" meetings, not to mention the more unobtrusive manner of communicating by letter.

In 1939, Canada declared war on Germany and, like many other Mennonite young men, Frank was opposed to military service and chose to register as a "conscientious objector." The Canadian government established camps in different parts of the country where Mennonites and other pacifists could perform alternative services. For Frank this meant planting trees and building roads on Vancouver Island. (Those small trees, planted by conscientious objectors, have since become a stately forest of valuable timber.) Ministers from the various branches of Mennonites made pastoral visits to these camps from time to time.

One visitor who was greatly appreciated by the boys in the camps was John A. Toews. Not all visiting ministers were received kindly by the young men in Campbell River. In fact, Frank, together with others of like persuasion, sent a petition to Mennonite church leaders insisting that they wanted only such ministers to visit them who knew English (the boys called one visiting minister "Reverend By Gosh," because that was the only word of English he knew) and, above all, who had been genuinely converted to Christ.

Since no one knew how long the war would last, Frank and Melita decided to get married. Long engagements were frowned upon in some Mennonite churches at the time. Frank got leave from camp to travel to Yarrow for his wedding to Melita Krause on August 15, 1943. The wedding took place in the Yarrow Mennonite Brethren Church. Frank's father, C.C. Peters, and Johann Harder, the leader of the church, preached the wedding sermons in which the young couple received instruction and encouragement for their life together as followers of Jesus. Since Frank had to return to his work camp immediately, the newlyweds had their brief honeymoon on the ferry back to Campbell River.

Melita got a job working in the kitchen of the Campbell River Hospital. Their home was a small cabin nearby. Frank had to live at his work camp, about twenty miles away, and came to see Melita at the Denby cabin whenever he had time off. A little better than a year after their marriage their first son, Robert James, was born.

Another year later their second son, Edward Allan, came upon the scene. It seemed a bit ironic, for Melita had shed some tears because the physician, who examined her before their marriage, predicted that she probably would never have children.

*Melita and Frank Peters: a supportive pair.*

## OFF TO STUDIES

It was now 1945 and the war was coming to an end. Frank had long looked forward to the day when he could resume his studies. With very limited finances, they sold their new bedroom suite (Melita's wedding gift from her parents) and decided to move to Hillsboro, Kansas, where Frank enrolled at Tabor College. By the time they arrived the second semester had already begun. Frank found work at a creamery, where he worked the night shift to pay expenses and attended classes during the day.

In the course of finding living quarters in Hillsboro, Frank heard that the Steinreich Mennonite Brethren Church, about eighteen miles out of Hillsboro, was looking for a pastor. Here was a golden opportunity for Frank to exercise his gift of preaching and to augment their meagre income. Since the Peters had no car, the Steinreich church provided them with a vehicle. The Steinreich people fell in love with their young pastor couple and supplied them with meat, eggs and vegetables. It was also in this congregation that Frank was ordained to the gospel ministry.

Frank concentrated most of his energies on his studies and, with some transfer credit, completed the requirements for his BA in short order. After that he commuted to Emporia State Teachers' College and earned his MSc in 1948. Shortly before completing his masters degree, their third son, Gerald Franklin, was born.

Frank had hoped to move directly into a PhD program of studies when suddenly Melita received notice from the United States Immigration Department that she would have to leave the country within six weeks. Although the reason for this order was inexplicable, this meant that the entire family would have to return to Canada. Reluctantly, they returned to Yarrow, B.C., where the economy was in a slump and jobs hard to come by. Without an income, Frank had to take out a small loan to feed his family. This was a difficult and depressing chapter in the life of Frank and Melita. To add insult to injury, some people teased Frank about earning academic degrees in order to cut grass for farmers. Frank finally left for Vancouver, where his brother Peter and his wife lived, and found a job in the fishing industry.

With the approach of autumn and the opening of schools, light appeared at the end of the tunnel. Frank was hired by the board of the Yarrow Bible School to teach for a year. During the course of the school year, Cornelius J. Rempel of Kitchener visited Yarrow on behalf of the Mennonite Central Committee and discovered that Frank might be interested in a pastoral position. The Kitchener Mennonite Brethren Church was looking for a senior pastor.

Rempel returned home and before long Frank received an invitation to come to Kitchener for a weekend visit and to preach in the church. The church responded favorably to Frank's ministry and so in 1949, when the Bible school year in Yarrow ended, the family made its way to Ontario to begin a new chapter in their lives.

The church had rented living quarters for the Peters and generously supplied the family with the necessities of life. After the church built a new parsonage, the family moved into more permanent quarters. A year after they arrived in Kitchener their daughter, Marianne Joyce, was born. Frank enjoyed his pastoral ministry immensely, but he also continued to upgrade his academic credentials. In 1952, he received a Bachelor of Divinity degree from the Waterloo Lutheran Seminary and later a Master of Theology from the Federated Faculty in Toronto. Waterloo College also appointed Frank as lecturer.

Quite unexpectedly, in 1954, Frank got a call from Tabor College asking him to become the president of the college following the death of president J.N.C. Hiebert. This meant uprooting the family once again, but it also promised to open new doors of service and further study, and so Frank accepted the invitation. After the family had settled in Hillsboro, their youngest son, John Wesley, was born. With four sons and one daughter, the family was now complete.

## TABOR, TRIALS AND TESTS

Almost from the beginning of his presidency, Frank sensed that he did not have the full support of the college faculty. Not all older and more ex-

*Frank (back right) with other young CO boys on Vancouver Island during World War II.*

perienced professors took kindly to a 34-year-old president, and for other staff a Canadian leader did not sit well. Even though Frank possessed outstanding abilities, he soon came to the conviction that he would be a short-term president. Frank suffered emotionally from this experience in administration and for years afterwards found it difficult to return to Hillsboro. After two years at Tabor College, he resigned.

Meantime, Frank had begun to work on his Doctor of Theology degree at the Central Baptist Seminary in Kansas City. While still in Hillsboro after leaving Tabor College, the superintendent of the Evangelical United Brethren Church in Kansas invited Frank to pastor two small country churches near Lawrence, Kansas. Preaching in these two churches not only provided the family with a source of income and a place to live, but it also allowed Frank to enroll in a PhD program at the University of Kansas in Lawrence, Kansas.

It was during this time that the Peters discovered to their great dismay that their ten-year-old son, Gerald, had diabetes. They had taken Gerald to the doctor, who misdiagnosed his illness and gave him a sugar solution. When Gerald went into a coma, another doctor was called and he immediately established that Gerald had diabetes. He had to stay in the hospital for a month. This near death experience brought Gerald closer to God. But then came the hospital bills. The family had no insurance. With their meagre income they scraped the bottom of the barrel every month. But God in his mercy intervened. Through the generosity of the doctor and the church community, the debt was completely liquidated.

## WINNIPEG BECKONED

Frank had completed his residence work and had passed his comprehensive exams for his PhD in Psychology when he received a call to join the faculty of the Mennonite Brethren Bible College in Winnipeg.

Frank would have preferred to write his dissertation before he took on a new assignment, but he found the prospect of a teaching position in Canada too attractive. Since by now he had considerable training in two disciplines, theology and psychology, the college was glad when he accepted the invitation. After making his decision, he began to waver and wrote to President John A. Toews that he was hesitant to come if the college's offerings in the area of the liberal arts were not expanded. Toews took counsel with the faculty and we decided (I had by then been on the faculty for several years) that we should let Frank know that we would like him to work together with us in the development of our curriculum. That satisfied him and in 1957 the Peters family moved to Winnipeg.

As one might suspect, they came with empty pockets. They needed living quarters—something the college did not supply. C.A. DeFehr offered them a loan to make a down payment on a house with the understanding that they pay back the money as they were able. Salaries at MBBC were rather low and with five children it was often difficult to make ends meet. They wanted to give their children the opportunity to attend the Mennonite Brethren Collegiate Institute and that meant paying extra tuition. Frank encouraged Melita to go into public school teaching in order to help with the needs of the family. She took teacher training and taught for two years, but it became too difficult to carry on with a full-time job while caring for a large family.

Frank was able to supplement his college salary by taking on a great many weekend preaching assignments for which he was remunerated by the churches. Although this often drained Frank's energies, it was good public relations for the college. Several of Frank's colleagues also spoke

*Frank moderated the convention in 1984 at which Vernon Wiebe, the retiring mission board secretary, was honoured.*

frequently in the churches across the land and this drew students from all over Canada to MBBC.

For eight years Frank devoted himself to the training of young people for church ministries at MBBC. He taught not only psychology but also biblical and theological subjects. The students enjoyed his classes. In fact, his classes were so popular that other faculty members upon occasion suggested that, as registrar, I not put their subjects into the same time-slot as his. Frank was a great colleague: we enjoyed his company; he was fun to be with. His sense of humor was contagious.

## ENJOYED LIFE

Frank enjoyed playing innocent pranks on colleagues and students. We sent each other notes, commended and criticized each other, tossed ideas around at faculty meetings and prayed together. Not only did he laugh with us at the comical aspects of life, but he also cried easily when faced with the tragic side of our human existence.

Having lived in the United States for a number of years, Frank brought several customs with him that were new to the more stolid MBBC staff. Among other things he introduced the coffee break, and it did not take long for faculty members to appreciate the opportunity to meet casually with other colleagues around a cup of coffee. Also, he called us by our first names. That just was not done at MBBC; even students were encouraged to address each other with Mr. or Miss, brother or sister. For some of us this innovation was somewhat harder to accept since several of our senior colleagues had been our respected teachers at one time. For me to call Jake H. Quiring or John A. Toews by their first names was asking for too much.

When Frank was called to MBBC, he made it clear to the administration that he would have nothing to do with administration; all he wanted to do was teach. Besides, he still had his PhD dissertation to complete and defend and that had to be done on top of a regular teaching load. Moreover, as any college teacher knows, regardless of a person's educational background, every subject demands a new set of lecture notes and Frank was teaching most of his subjects for the first time. In retrospect, one wonders how he managed to prepare for his classes, work on his thesis and preach almost weekly in one of our churches. He had an amazing capacity for work, although students thought he was not always as well prepared for Monday's classes as he might have been. But no one complained.

Once Frank had established himself as a gifted teacher, President J.A. Toews drew him into the administration of the College. For about a dozen years from its founding, MBBC had operated without an academic dean; the president and the registrar shared this administrative function. Toews then suggested that we establish a new position and Frank became MBBC's first academic dean.

## LEADER, WRITER, SPEAKER

As Frank became better known in the Canadian Conference of Mennonite Brethren, he not only received numerous invitations to preach in our congregations, his leadership abilities also came to be recognized. Before long, he was elected as moderator of the Canadian Conference and eventually as moderator of the General Conference of Mennonite Brethren Churches of Canada and the United States.

It was my privilege to work together with him in the General Conference Board of Reference and Counsel. Together we worked on a revision of our Confession of Faith, opened up membership in our churches to believers who had been baptized by another mode than immersion, and dealt with numerous other theological and ethical issues. Frank helped our churches in the process of making changes without losing their biblical moorings. And with his training in psychology and counselling, he was able to help numerous individuals for whom the battles of life had become too heavy.

I was editor of the college publication *The Voice* during the eight years that Frank taught at MBBC, and I was always pleased with the articles he submitted. It was expected of all faculty members to make regular contributions to this theological bi-monthly. Not all teachers developed the gift of writing, but Frank certainly did. We had always hoped that he would some day produce major book manuscripts for publication, but Frank could not turn down invitations to preach or to teach and so, unfortunately, he has not left us a legacy in the area of publications. Many of his articles appeared elsewhere, however, especially also in the *Mennonite Brethren Herald*.

Frank preached well. Like his father, he was endowed with a strong, clear and resonant voice. He possessed a very appealing platform presence; he quickly made a connection with his listeners—often with a bit of humor, a quip or an illustration—and never came across as speaking down to his hearers, even when his sermons carried plenty of content. His training in homiletics demanded that his sermons always be well structured. If there was a firstly, there was always a secondly. This enabled listeners to follow more easily as he developed his main topic. He prepared carefully, as his many hundreds of sermon notes attest.

Moreover, he was convinced that expository preaching in which a text is analyzed and expounded would lead to a deeper knowledge of the Christian faith, though he was a master of topical preaching as well. Although he enjoyed counselling fellow believers, he was of the opinion that if good biblical teaching was done in the pulpit, there would always be less need for individual counselling. While he laced his sermons with striking illustrations, often quite humorous, he avoided jokes that had no relation to the message from God's word. At times his emotions got the better of him and he preached with tears in his eyes. Contrary to Mennonite Brethren practice at that time, Frank preached from a manuscript. He claimed that handwritten notes were better visual aids than the typewritten kind, though he prepared many in both forms.

Like most of the other faculty members during the 1950s, Frank was bilingual and often preached in German. When he preached among Old Colony Mennonites in the Swift Current area, he even resorted to Low

German, which greatly pleased his audience. Although he was well educated, he could preach in simple prose and this gave him open doors to Mennonite groups who were suspicious of higher education. On one occasion when he preached to Old Colony Mennonites, a listener expressed his appreciation with these words: "We love to hear you preach, Peters, because you're not as learned as some of those other preachers." Frank loved to tell that story.

Indeed, he enjoyed telling embarrassing stories about himself. Once when the family decided to drive east to Ontario for a visit, Frank suddenly noticed that they were passing through Portage la Prairie, about an hour's drive *west* of Winnipeg. When Frank led a tour group to Palestine in 1953 (my father-in-law was in the group), he did not want to be bothered with much extra clothing. By the time they had toured Israel his clothes were badly in need of cleaning. As they arrived in their hotel in Athens, he saw a sign: "Clothes cleaned while you wait." He gave an attendant his clothes to clean while he took a bath. He bathed and bathed but could not go anywhere without clothes. After what seemed an eternity, he finally got his clothes. When he got home he told his children the story and his son Gerald promptly wrote an essay in English class with the title: "In Greece without Pants." Peters always surmised that the rest of us also had embarrassing experiences, but that we were too afraid (or proud) to talk about them.

Frank admitted later that his eight years at MBBC had been the highlight of his life. But in 1965 he accepted a call back to the Kitchener Mennonite Brethren Church and a teaching position at what became Wilfrid Laurier University in Waterloo. The four eldest children all graduated from this school; John, the youngest, graduated in medicine from the University of Toronto.

## BACK TO KITCHENER

Soon after returning to Kitchener, the university asked Frank to become its president. The university assured Frank that he could do all the preaching he wanted if only he would assume the presidency. Frank rose to the challenge and served the university for ten years from 1968-78. He was an exceptionally good administrator. When he retired the university named a building after him. Several years after his resignation, one of his former faculty wrote him a note calling him an "inspired and inspirational leader...the best president the university ever had" and for giving him "the best ten working years" of his life.

Frank had been instrumental in the affiliation of MBBC with Waterloo College, giving our students full university credit for courses

*Frank loved cars with "features." This WLU vehicle had plenty.*
*Photo courtesy of KW Record, Kitchener*

taken at MBBC. Now that he was president, he alerted us to the fact that out-of-the-province affiliations would eventually come to an end. Due in part to his prodding, MBBC then affiliated with the University of Winnipeg.

By the time Frank resigned as president of the university, he no longer served as pastor of the Kitchener Mennonite Brethren Church and so, beginning in 1978, Frank extended his preaching and teaching ministry far beyond the Mennonite fold. He preached in churches of many denominations, Mennonite and non-Mennonite, both in Canada and the U.S. Already during his years of teaching at MBBC and Waterloo, he visited the mission fields of the Mennonite Brethren in a number of countries. He became a member as well as chairman of the MB Board of Missions. But he was also a member of the Evangelical Fellowship of Canada and in his so-called retirement years preached in countries as far afield as the Philippines where the Mennonite Brethren have no churches.

One of the reasons he kept receiving so many calls to preach or write lay in his ability to strike a real nerve. A few illustrations. In a 1974 article for the *MB Herald* he asked whether "modern evangelicalism would become a success story." He began by describing some of the huge gains evangelicals had been making. But then he named some of the serious weaknesses they were showing: shallow discipleship, uncritical patriotism, the emergence of an evangelical ghetto and the tendency toward an incomplete gospel. The outline of his points easily suggests how challenging he might be.

In another place he wrote about public prayers in Mennonite Brethren churches, calling many of them "weak, if not downright shameful… the orphan part of the service." He didn't mince his language.

A wonderfully rich Easter sermon described Easter as "a signpost." It began with some of the text of a drama by Charles Kennedy, *The Terrible Meek*, and then described Easter as a "signpost in human history (pointing to the fulfillment of the plan of God in history), a signpost of the human mind (pointing to the renewing of the mind through redemption), and a signpost of hope (pointing to the one true hope mankind can know). Expanded, the sermon was a powerful call to come out "of the tombs of indifference and doubt." He ended with, "God is not dead! God lives! It is for us to quit the ways of grief and desolation and sing with all the sons of glory, sing the resurrection song."

An address entitled "Evangelical relevance and youth" asked three fundamental questions: the intellectual question (do evangelicals distrust science, where is God in the material world?), the social question (what shall we do? how shall we live?), and the personal question (do I want to be an evangelical? what do I believe?). Anyone reading his sermon notes or articles today would still find them very challenging.

## THE HOME STRETCH

His ability to speak into many settings opened doors of every kind. However, he always felt drawn back to the churches of his own denomination and in 1980 he accepted a call to pastor the Portage Avenue Mennonite Brethren Church in Winnipeg. The children were grown up by now and so the move back to Winnipeg was not complicated. They rented an apartment in a high-rise and got reacquainted with the Winnipeg community. For three years Frank had the joy of teaching and preaching the Word of God and counselling members of this congregation. He was back with former colleagues on familiar turf.

After three years they returned to Kitchener and Frank continued to serve both at home and abroad. He taught classes at Emmanuel Bible College in Kitchener. The children were married by now and Frank and Melita made a special effort to remain in contact with them. Since Frank was an early riser his phone calls to his children often reached them when they were still in bed. At his funeral, the grandchildren had hilarious stories to tell about grandpa's phone calls.

Frank and Melita had the joy of seeing all of their children accept the gospel and all of them have been active in the life of the church in one way or another. When they were younger, Frank would often take the family out for lunch on Sundays; of course, he placed a limit on what the children could order. To take his family for car rides gave Frank much pleasure. One of Frank's earthly joys was cars, particularly the kind that had "added features." When he bought a car he would take it round to where his children lived to show it off, only to be told that it lacked "certain features"—an error he would vow to correct next time round.

At 67 years of age, Frank was still carrying a full load of speaking engagements. In the spring of 1987 he and Melita traveled to Lake Louise, Alberta, where Frank, together with Philip Yancey, spoke at the Christian Medical Convention. When the children were still at home, Melita usually stayed at home while Frank went on preaching assignments; later she often went with him as he travelled to Africa, South America and Asia. Frank gave much of the credit for his worldwide ministry to Melita, who had been so supportive throughout his years of service in churches and schools.

During the later years of his life, when Frank served a worldwide community, some of us wondered at times whether he had forgotten his own denomination. Some people even wondered whether he had become disillusioned with the Mennonite Brethren and that he found greater acceptance outside his denomination (not an uncommon phenomenon).

When he turned up at the General Conference of Mennonite Brethren in the summer of 1987, held at the Central Heights MB Church in Abbotsford, and permitted his name to stand once again for the Board of Reference and Counsel (now called "Board of Faith and Life"), we were delighted. Since I was then a member of that board, I looked forward to another few years of working together. But God's ways were different and higher than ours.

In September, 1987, Frank flew to Blaine, Washington, for what turned out to be his last preaching trip. Melita was at the Toronto Airport to pick him up on his return. As they waited for his luggage he told Melita all about his trip, as was his custom. But he looked rather tired. On the way home to Kitchener, Frank had a severe heart attack. Melita took over the driving and raced to the hospital. Their son John was with him in the intensive care unit. Frank held Melita's hand and said, "I don't want to lose you." He was in the hospital for two weeks and the family had high hopes that he might recover completely. But it was not to be.

Frank and Melita had just recently purchased a condominium in which they planned to live during their retirement years, but they had not yet moved in. Son John and his wife Becky asked their parents to stay with them for a while. The night before Frank passed away Becky prepared a tasty dinner. After the meal the family listened to Frank as he told them the story of his life. Next morning, after his bath, he lay down on the bed and slipped away to be with the Christ whom he had tried to serve faithfully all his life.

The funeral was held in the Kitchener Mennonite Brethren Church on October 10, 1987. Pastor John Wall was in charge. In order to prevent overcrowding at the memorial service, Wilfrid Laurier University had agreed to have the service videotaped and shown on a screen at the university. The congregation sang several of Frank's favorite hymns and members of the Board of Missions and representatives of various schools and Christian organizations attended the memorial service.

It was my privilege to represent the Board of Reference and Counsel as well as MBBC. A number of us gave brief messages of condolence to the family and expressed appreciation for the life and service of our coworker in the gospel.

For an epitaph on his gravestone Melita chose the verse from Philippians 1:21, "For me to live is Christ, and to die is gain."

SOURCES

Much of the information for this chapter came out of personal interaction with Frank Peters during many years of working together as colleagues. Other sources were drawn from the Frank C. Peters fonds at the Centre for Mennonite Brethren Studies in Winnipeg. The major part of the chapter was originally published in David Ewert's *Honour Such People* (Winnipeg: 1997). Some additional text was incorporated by this book's editor.

## David Ewert
# BIBLE TEACHER AND SCHOLAR FOR THE CHURCH

*By Bruce L. Guenther with Kevin O'Coin*

Few leaders have served the Mennonite Brethren church with greater commitment, sacrificial diligence and longevity than David Ewert. For seventy years his considerable intellectual, public speaking and leadership gifts have been used to serve the church.

His influence has been felt not only among the Mennonite Brethren in Canada, but also in the United States and, to a considerable extent, in Europe and on other continents.

Ewert's years of leadership and influence took place during an important transitional period for Mennonite Brethren in North America. The son of *Russlaender* immigrants, he emerged as a young Bible teacher, preacher and leader during the 1940s as the immigrant German-speaking Mennonite Brethren communities began moving out of their isolated, often rural, ethnically homogenous communities.

---

*The Writers*
Since 1999 Bruce Guenther has been a faculty member at Mennonite Brethren Biblical Seminary (Langley campus), which is part of the ACTS seminary consortium at Trinity Western University. He serves there as associate dean and associate professor of church history and Mennonite studies. Earlier he has been a camp director, freelance writer, researcher and farmer. His experience in and research of evangelical Protestantism in Canada has nurtured a keen interest in understanding the Mennonite Brethren Evangelical Anabaptist identity. This chapter was written with the assistance of Kevin O'Coin, who holds an MDiv from MBBS-ACTS. Kevin currently lives and ministers in Surrey, B.C. with his wife. Evident also in this chapter is the work of Herbert Giesbrecht, whose biographical essay on David Ewert in *The Bible and the Church: Essays in Honour of Dr. David Ewert* (1988) offered many valuable insights.

Ewert was part of a generation that began working and living in more urban centres. They were more interested in doing evangelistic outreach and church-planting that might lead to the formation of multi-lingual and ethnically diverse congregations. And they were more actively involved in all aspects of North American culture, including politics.

As a highly respected Bible teacher, preacher and scholar, he defined and embodied the convictions of the Mennonite Brethren church. His voice spoke into a remarkable number of the theological issues facing the Mennonite Brethren during the second half of the twentieth century. As a full-time teacher in at least five Mennonite Brethren institutions in North America, he shaped the theological views of literally thousands of students, many of whom became pastors, missionaries and leaders within the church. Ewert tried to emulate an irenic balance between denominational loyalty and collaborative, cooperative relationships with a broad network of evangelical Protestants.

His influence helped to move the Mennonite Brethren away from both a particular, and often exclusive, German-Russian ethnicity, and from aspects of American fundamentalism that some had found attractive.

## STEPPES AND PRAIRIES

David Ewert was born on December 5, 1922 on the steppes of the southern Ukraine, in the Memrik Colony village of Alexanderhof. The chaotic aftermath of the Bolshevik Revolution, and the imposition of increasingly more oppressive regulations by communist leaders, prompted his parents, David and Margaret (nee Wiebe) Ewert, to leave Russia by ship in October 1926. In Canada, the Ewert family managed to eke out a meagre living by moving repeatedly in pursuit of employment as farm hands. They eventually settled in southern Alberta, first in the Grassy Lake area, then in 1930 on a well-situated farmstead near Coaldale. Here Ewert learned the discipline of hard physical labour that was part of rural pioneer life on the Canadian prairies.

Ewert's parents were devout and committed members of the Mennonite Brethren church; as a result, young David was exposed during his childhood and adolescence to a large and active Mennonite Brethren community in Coaldale in which he heard some of the most gifted and compelling Mennonite Brethren preachers at the time. "From earliest childhood I loved Jesus," states David, "the thought of rejecting him never really crossed my mind." However, the strong and repeated emphasis on the necessity of conversion, on holy living, and the imminence of the second coming of Christ, left its mark. Lacking clarity and assurance, as a young boy of 12, David, together with his brother John, approached their parents one night to settle the matter.

Four years later, at the age of 16, he enrolled at Coaldale Bible School where he spent three winters (1939-42). Here he was inspired by the teaching of men such as Abram Schierling, Jacob H. Quiring, and John A. Toews, whose well-organized lectures and expressive and winsome manner left an indelible impression on the young student. Bernhard

*David and Lena Ewert, celebrating a long life together.*

W. Sawatsky in particular became a significant mentor at key moments in Ewert's early adulthood. Affirmed and encouraged by his teachers to develop his gifts, Ewert embarked on an educational journey that continued for almost three decades.

The next educational steps included both the Winkler Bible School (1942-43) and Prairie Bible Institute (1943-44), "having been attracted to these schools by the teaching and preaching competence of Abraham H. Unruh (at the former school), and Leslie Maxwell (at the latter)." Both schools nurtured Ewert's love for learning, and introduced him to a larger network of Mennonite Brethren and evangelical Protestant Christians. His time at Winkler was interrupted by a brief stint as a conscientious objector in the forestry service.

His decision to be identified as a CO stood in marked contrast to that of his older brother John, who enlisted in the air force, and whose accidental death in an airplane crash in August 1943 brought intense grief to the Ewert family.

### PROMISING TEACHER...LEADER

"Ewert's lengthy career as a Bible teacher and preacher began with short teaching assignments, during the winters of 1944 and 1945, at the La-Glace (Alta.) Bible School." Coinciding with this appointment was his marriage to Lena Hamm on October 12, 1944, "daughter of Martin and Anna Hamm, to whom he had become attracted while they were fellow students at Coaldale Bible School." Other teaching opportunities soon followed, first at Bethany Bible Institute (1946-47) and then Coaldale Bible Institute (1948-51), where he was also appointed principal. His diligence in these roles helped him to develop his teaching and preaching ability.

His public reputation as a promising leader within the denomination led to both his ordination at Coaldale in 1949 and an invitation in the early 1950s to join the faculty of the recently-established Mennonite Brethren Bible College (MBBC). For the next 19 years, MBBC became the primary setting for Ewert's ministry: it was a time that, despite its difficulties and challenges, Ewert fondly recalls as "the most wonderful years of [my] life."

The new college was strategically located in Winnipeg, a metropolitan area of considerable significance for Canadian Mennonites and for western Canada at the time. Abraham H. Unruh, until then the principal of the Winkler Bible School, was called on to spearhead the new institution in 1944. The declared purpose of the school was to train Bible school teachers, missionaries and church workers to fill positions of leadership in Bible schools, churches and mission agencies.

In three years it became the largest Mennonite Brethren theological school in Canada. By 1960, the enrollment at MBBC equalled almost 50 percent of the total enrollment in the four Mennonite Brethren Bible schools in existence at the time. MBBC became the main centre for the training of Mennonite Brethren pastors and lay church workers in Canada as well as for missionaries and evangelists at home and abroad until the 1970s.

The challenges of classroom teaching quickly intensified a desire for further theological education in order to enhance his own expertise as well as the reputation of the college. Innumerable summer months, weekend commutes and several sabbaticals were devoted to the completion of various academic degrees, often with considerable sacrifice on the part of Ewert and his family. As early as 1947, he began working towards a Bachelor of Arts degree at the University of British Columbia. This was followed by graduate degrees from Central Baptist Seminary in Toronto (Bachelor of Divinity) in 1953, Wheaton College (Master of Arts) in 1956, and Luther Theological Seminary in St. Paul (Master of Theology) in 1961.

The pursuit of a doctoral degree led to one of the darkest moments in Ewert's life. After having spent considerable time and ex-

*David and students at the Coaldale Bible School (ca. 1950), with colleagues Aron Warkentin, P.R. Toews and Bernhard Sawatzky.*

pense over the course of five years tenaciously completing all the requirements for the degree—except for the dissertation—at Chicago Lutheran Theological Seminary, he felt obliged to withdraw from the program after his first advisor imposed a dissertation plan that he felt he could not undertake, and his second advisor refused to sponsor Ewert's dissertation project unless Ewert would agree to accept his theological views. The experience left him with a distinct distaste for the dogmatism and narrow prejudices of theological liberalism. His disappointment in Chicago led him to enroll in a PhD program in New Testament studies at McGill University in Montreal, which he completed in 1969.

## A MEANS OF GRACE

Long-time colleagues noted that "classroom teaching has always been Ewert's most cherished endeavour and pursuit." Within the Mennonite Brethren tradition, teachers, and Bible teachers in particular, were highly revered, and were expected to live as examples for others. Ewert conscientiously attended to such expectations, and was known by his students and colleagues as a person of integrity. Ewert's commitment to excellence in teaching flowed out of his firm conviction that the pursuit of learning is a worthwhile—even vital—exercise for becoming a healthy Christ-follower. He wrote:

> I can see it more clearly now than in my younger years, that intense academic efforts do not endanger a person's devotion to God. In fact, I have found the opposite to be true. When one offers one's academic activities up to God as a daily sacrifice, they become a means of grace. My patience tends to wear thin when I encounter students who in the name of piety shy away from the rigours of study.

Over the years he taught a wide range of courses, but his strongest interests were New Testament Greek, introduction to biblical studies, the Pauline letters and the book of Revelation. As a professor, he acquired a well-deserved reputation for his comprehensive and incisive knowledge of biblical languages and the Bible, and for a lecture-oriented style that was consistently characterized by thorough exegetical preparation, methodically organized presentation and precise punctuality. Despite a certain dignified reserve in his demeanor, Ewert was not averse to occasional touches of humour into his lectures. "Another identifying feature of his teaching was a deeply-felt concern about the ethical and practical implications of the material under consideration," and for the spiritual edification of his hearers.

Adding to the hectic pace of the first several decades of his teaching career was the joy and responsibility of parenthood. Five children—four daughters and a son—were born into the Ewert family between 1947 and 1956. Ewert's dogged determination to complete his theological education, and his numerous preaching and teaching commitments, may have left too little time for family and friends, especially during earlier years. Nevertheless, family members will attest that he was "not merely respected, but thoroughly enjoyed by his children during their growing up years."

Considerable credit for the success of Ewert's public ministry lies with the supportive efforts by his wife Lena, whose capable hands managed many of their household and parenting exigencies. "While Lena may be

Jesus Christus – Weg + Wahrheit + Leben

Bethaus

*In his retirement years, David taught often in settings such as this—among church leaders who came out of Russia to Germany. This was in Detmold in 1999.*

a less public and vocal person than her husband, she is by no means a languid or timorous woman," noted Herbert Giesbrecht. "Although circumstances made it impossible for her to pursue further studies in a formal sense, her own ardent love of reading and powers of perception enabled her to share many of the intellectual interests and concerns of her husband." On numerous occasions, Ewert has recognized and expressed his gratitude for the courage and sacrificial dedication of his wife.

Several other dimensions of Ewert's public ministry emerged during his tenure at MBBC, notably his reputation as a preacher with unusual skill in exegetical preaching, his aptitude for writing with clarity and simplicity, and his capacity for leadership within the denomination at a national level. Ewert had the good fortune of being mentored during his early years by church leaders who closely linked teaching and preaching. Ewert came to love preaching almost as much as teaching, and accepted numerous speaking invitations from congregations and Bible conference organizers because he was convinced that a positive presence in the pulpit on the part of professors helped to build good will towards the school and to recruit students. In time, invitations to teach and to preach came also from non-Mennonite Brethren institutions in North America and overseas.

### WRITER AND LEADER

"The realization that the range of his teaching and preaching influence could be extended beyond the boundaries of classroom and pulpit, and the explicit encouragement of others, induced Ewert to begin writing articles for publication." At the outset, most of his articles were published in denominational magazines such as *The Voice*, the official journal of MBBC which Ewert edited for ten years, the *Mennonite Brethren Herald*, *The Christian Leader* and *Direction*. At the request of Conference boards/committees, he published several short booklets offering guidance to a broader audience on specific subjects.

Adding still more responsibility to the already hectic pace of Ewert's life during his time at MBBC (and after), were the various leadership roles he assumed within the denomination. Because he had lived in every province that had Mennonite Brethren congregations, and had preached in many of these congregations, and because he had taught students from across the country, Ewert was well-known throughout the denomination, and had a well-established network of relationships across the country.

In 1967 he was elected moderator of the Canadian Conference. In 1970 he became a part of the General Conference Board of Reference and Counsel, a body on which he served for two decades and through which he exercised considerable influence in shaping the theological direction of the denomination. The Board was responsible to watch over the spiritual life of the denomination and to give guidance and direction in matters of doctrine and ethics. Their regular planning sessions and deliberations over doctrinal and ethical issues were for Ewert nothing less than "exhilarating." They also had their moments of frustration and disappointment, particularly when recommendations accepted by delegates at church-wide conventions would be ignored by individual congregations.

Ewert regularly wrote and presented papers and conference resolutions on issues under consideration. In 1999, Ewert compiled a selection of the papers that he had prepared for various occasions at the request of the denomination in a book entitled, *Finding Your Way*. These papers span a period of forty years (1958-98) and exemplify some of the issues that faced the denomination during the second half of the twentieth century, and the responses of leaders at that time. Many of the papers featured issues that were, at particular times, highly contentious such as eternal security, eschatology, and the charismatic movement.

Questions about the role of women in church leadership, which Ewert first addressed as early as 1966, have remained a complicated and controversial issue within the life of the denomination. More than most, Ewert wrestled with the exegetical dangers of overlooking passages that point in a direction opposite to one's inclination, or subordinating selected passages to one's preferred texts on the matter. As a New Testament scholar deeply committed to the authority of Scripture, Ewert recognized the dignity of women and encouraged their participation in the life of the church, but repeatedly appealed to an order in creation that, he argued, remains in effect even in the new covenant, thereby requiring the subordination of women to men in pastoral leadership functions. This view served as the basis for Mennonite Brethren polity until very recently.

## AFTER LEAVING WINNIPEG

Attracted by the prospect of working with Myron Augsburger and George Brunk, and disappointed by changes in the direction of MBBC, Ewert decided in 1972 to join the faculty of Eastern Mennonite Seminary in Harrisonburg, Virginia, a school operated by the Mennonite Church. The experience broadened his understanding of the Mennonite constituency, particularly in the United States. He nevertheless remained active within the Mennonite Brethren conference during his three years at Eastern. In 1975, the Canadian Mennonite Brethren Conference officially became a sponsor of Mennonite Brethren Biblical Seminary (MBBS) in Fresno, California. In an attempt to increase the proportion of Canadian faculty, Ewert agreed to join the faculty of MBBS in 1975. His reputation as a Bible teacher and preacher continued to elicit teaching and speaking requests from across North America, and then from overseas.

More conscious than ever about finding ways to have his "voice" heard within the Mennonite Brethren constituency, efforts to publish became more deliberate as he reshaped some of his many lecture notes for publication in book format. Particularly notable was *And Then Comes the End*, a book on eschatology that helped many Mennonite Brethren to become less dogmatic on aspects of dispensationalism and to consider other views. Despite severe criticism at times, Ewert persistently tried to move the study of last things away from speculative and sensational interpretations of current events to a more practical consideration of its pastoral and ethical implications: instead of worrying over signs of famine, we should feed the hungry; instead of looking to escape the Great Tribulation, we should embrace tribulation and persecution as the way of the Christian life.

The response to his early publications encouraged Ewert to submit a manuscript to Zondervan, which was published as *From Ancient Tablets to Modern Translations: A General Introduction to the Bible* and was modestly successful as a textbook in various colleges. Still other books by Ewert, such as *Die Wunderwege Gottes mit der Gemeinde Jesu Christ*, *The Church in a Pagan Society: Studies in 1 Corinthians*, and *How to Understand the Bible*, are either detailed expository studies or handbooks intended for use by students and pastors in their teaching and preaching ministries.

All of his books in the area of biblical studies reflect a careful concern for hermeneutics, which he understood as the "science of interpretation" that is necessary for discerning "true biblicism."

He emphasizes, for example, the importance of reading the Old Testament in light of the New Testament, and the need to discard the naïve notion that it is possible to read the Bible "literally," as some claim to do. He cautions against making the Bible say more than it actually says on issues such as creation, the intermediary state after death, on hell, on the state of those who have not heard about Jesus Christ, and on atonement. Typical of many twentieth-century evangelical Protestants, Ewert's approach to hermeneutics remained focused on the canonical books of the Bible and did not engage the broad range of interpretation theories that are characteristic of post-modernity.

Ewert's books are characterized by the same general features as his classroom teaching and public preaching. Ewert's pre-eminent passion has been to use his education and abilities to bring insight and understanding of the Scriptures to people within the church. As a result, he seldom published with peer-reviewed academic presses, even though evidence of diligent and careful research abounds in his books. Regardless of the issue under examination, as an Anabaptist, Ewert passionately emphasized searching the Scripture as a community, and allowing the Holy Spirit to bring light. Some, however, viewed him as a dangerous innovator who had become "liberal" because of his rejection of dispensationalism and his acceptance of the Revised Standard Version of the Bible. For others he was too "conservative," particularly on issues such as abstinence from alcohol and women in ministry.

## RETURN TO WINNIPEG

In a move that surprised many colleagues, Ewert decided in 1982 to return to Winnipeg to become the president of MBBC. Part of the appeal was the prospect of more extensive preaching opportunities in Mennonite Brethren congregations in Canada, and part was the opportunity to enact a vision for the school that would see it linked more closely to the churches of its supporting constituency. Despite the school's illustrious history, changes in Mennonite Brethren demographics were creating new challenges for the institution. It was Ewert's desire to see the school training young people for life and service in the church, who have a passion for evangelism and mission, but without minimizing the high academic standards that had helped MBBC obtain university affiliation agreements, first with Waterloo College (now Wilfrid Laurier University) and then the University of Winnipeg.

Although Ewert officially retired from his administrative and teaching role at MBBC at the age of 65, he remained as active as ever by accepting an ongoing variety of teaching and preaching assignments. Following invitations to teach in Africa for six months, then in Europe and then a two-year term at MBBS in Fresno, the Ewerts finally settled in Abbotsford, BC in 1992 where they became members of Bakerview Mennonite Brethren Church. Retirement has offered Ewert a new level of freedom that has enabled him to complete an ambitious number of book projects, some of them autobiographical.

The writer of the book of Hebrews encourages Christians to imitate the faith of those who have contributed to the spiritual legacy they now enjoy (Hebrews 13:7). David Ewert has made a significant contribution to the spiritual legacy of the Mennonite Brethren tradition by presenting, as living offerings, his rich teaching and preaching gifts, along with his education, for use in service of the church.

His example continues to shine as a model worthy of honour and imitation for a younger generation of emerging Mennonite Brethren teachers, preachers and scholars.

SOURCES

Sections of this chapter relied heavily on Herbert Giesbrecht's overview of David Ewert's life in *The Bible and the Church: Essays in Honour of Dr. David Ewert*, edited by A.J. Dueck, H.J. Giesbrecht and V.G. Shillington (Winnipeg: 1988). Many of David Ewert's own books and writings were useful sources of information, including *Pilgrims and Strangers: The Story of our Exodus from Russia and Settlement in Canada* (an unpublished manuscript); *Mennonite Country Boy* (Abbotsford: Heartbeat Productions, 2004); *A Journey of Faith* (Winnipeg: 1993); *Honour Such People* (Winnipeg: 1997); *Creation from a Biblical Perspective* (Hillsboro: 1996); *An Approach to Problems of Christian Ethics* (Winnipeg: 1967); *How the Bible Came To Us* (Winnipeg: 1975); *Finding Your Way: Confronting Issues in the Mennonite Brethren Church* (Winnipeg: 1999); *And Then Comes the End* (Scottdale: 1980); *From Ancient Tablets to Modern Translations* (Grand Rapids: Zondervan Publishing House, 1983); *Die Wunderwege Gottes mit der Gemeinde Jesu Christ* (Winnipeg: 1978); *The Church in a Pagan Society: Studies in 1 Corinthians* (Winnipeg: 1986); *How to Understand the Bible* (Scottdale: 2000). Helpful also was Douglas Heidebrecht's STM thesis for the Saskatoon Theological Union, 2003, *"Sisters Leading Brothers? The Hermeneutical Journey of the Mennonite Brethren."* A footnoted copy of this chapter is on file at the Centre for Mennonite Brethren Studies, Winnipeg.

# Nick Dyck

# THE FARMER WHO GREW CHURCHES

*By Jonathan Janzen*

It was late summer, 1921, when Johann Dyck trudged home. The previous years in Ukraine had been difficult. Johann had lost a profitable business, two of his young children had died of black pox, and now the threat of starvation had forced him to go begging.

Just three years earlier, at the age of 48, Johann, along with his wife Katarina, had come to a personal faith in Christ and was baptized into the Mennonite Brethren Church. Discouraged, tired and helpless, Johann summoned his family into the living room. "Let us kneel down and call upon God to see if he will help us," he said.

The family did this. Katarina, who was pregnant, prayed, "Lord, if you will save us and this unborn child, I will give it to you."

On November 5, 1921, Nick Dyck was born.

## GOD REALLY LOVED ME

Less than two years later, the Dyck family arrived in Canada and settled in Drake, Saskatchewan. For young Nick, life revolved around his family, the farm, and church. Nick's father, a lay preacher with an evangelistic concern for people, would travel miles with horse and sleigh in the dead of winter to meet for church services and Bible studies. Nick

---

*The Writer*

Jonathan Janzen grew up in Manitoba. After studies at Regent College in Vancouver, he was invited to be a pastor at the Highland Community Church in Abbotsford. Jonathan is married to Andrea. Their two daughters and one son are keeping them busy.

would later remember that at the end of one house meeting, "Father and another leader pointed at the young men individually and asked, 'Do you want to accept Jesus as Saviour?'"

As a young seven-year-old living in Watrous, Saskatchewan, Nick would hear his parents discussing the age of accountability. When does a child reach that age? Is he saved before then? "I remember thinking about this," Nick once wrote, "and then having a deep sense that God really loved me. When I was nine, I lay awake for some time wondering whether I had crossed that line of accountability. And again after some struggle, some of that assurance of God's saving love returned to me. But there was no public commitment."

Easter of 1937 proved to be a turning point in Nick's life. The Philadelphia MB Church held special evangelistic services during the week. The preacher Dietrich Esau was the speaker. "In response to the message and the prayers of several older members in the meeting," Nick recalled, "the Holy Spirit came upon the entire group. I was deeply convicted. My sister-in-law's father saw me weeping, sat down beside me, shared Scripture with me, and we prayed.

"I felt an emotional release. I had wept and things seemed different," Nick added, "but it was not until we were driving home in our closed-in sleigh, with me taking the reins, that I had a life-changing experience. A sense of cleansing and deep joy filled my heart. I knew I was born again!"

Well into his twenties, Nick often struggled with doubts, however. The earlier joy of the Lord seemed to be missing. Had he *really* decided to be buried with Christ in baptism? Was he *really* a Christian?

In the meantime, Nick's life was changing in other ways. In 1941, at the age of 19, he moved to Yarrow, B.C. He quickly got a job working at the Canadian Hopyards, and used his earnings to rent land on which he could raise chickens and cows. Nick fully intended to be a farmer. But there were other plans afoot. As Nick once put it, "In my life there were so many people who kept egging me on. I was 'body led'...the church sensing, *we feel you can do it*."

Indeed, soon after arriving in B.C., Nick's new friends encouraged him to attend the Yarrow Bible School. Nick was also invited to join a men's group that included the likes of Henry Brucks, the evangelistically-minded co-founder of the Gospel Light Hour, which later became Family Life Network. In the 1940s and '50s, the B.C. MB churches focused their outreach efforts on children, organizing hundreds of vacation Bible school and Sunday school programs in outlying communities. The men's group that Nick joined taught a weekly Sunday school in Silverdale, west of Mission City. Since Nick had never taught Sunday school, Bible school training seemed like a good idea, so he enrolled.

The following years were busy with work, farming, evening classes and teaching Sunday school. Nick's studies became particularly interesting in the winter of 1946-47. Elizabeth Wall sat in the desk next to Nick and a relationship blossomed. On October 7, 1947, Nick and Betty were married.

The newly marrieds settled on nine acres of land they had purchased in Arnold. The

*Nick and Betty Dyck, strong partners.*

following years were difficult financially. After his attempt to grow raspberries and to raise chickens failed, Nick tried his hand at a string of jobs: logging, house moving, blacksmithing, construction—even going door-to-door selling pots and pans. Nothing provided a steady income.

Nick was enjoying successes in other areas of his life, however. Betty gave birth to three children: twins (Carolyne and Robert) in 1950 and a daughter (Lorraine) in 1952. The Arnold MB Church continued to encourage Nick in his leadership abilities, asking him to teach Sunday school, lead the youth Bible study group and sit on the church council. Nick and Betty were also appointed deacon couple.

Through it all, Nick continued to gently invite people to meet Jesus. On one occasion, two boys on bicycles interrupted Nick and Betty's lunch. They were in Nick's Sunday school class. "We want to be saved," they said. As Nick sat on bales of hay in the barn, he prayed with them as they committed their lives to Jesus.

Similar events took place on the job site. While driving truck for Buckerfield's Farms, Nick developed a friendship with one of his coworkers. It wasn't long before Ted moved from a mere interest in Jesus to praying with Nick and confessing Christ as Lord.

## A TRIAL RUN

In late summer of 1955, Nick and Betty found their lives moving in a clearer direction. Because Nick had completed his high school studies in 1951, and had continued to study at the South Abbotsford Bible School in the winters of 1954 and 1955, the B.C. MB Home Missions Committee asked Nick and Betty to start a church in McConnell Creek. The Dycks decided to give it a trial run for a year. In March 1956 they moved into the community, very quickly realized that "this was it," and sold their farm in 1957.

McConnell Creek proved to be an entirely different experience from anything Nick and Betty had ever known. Because McConnell Creek was a logging community, people were transient, coming when the work was good and moving on when the work ran out. Church was low on the priority list for most folks. To top it off, with memories of the war years still fresh in their minds, people were suspicious of these German-speaking Mennonites. Nick, being somewhat shy, was encouraged by Cecil Carter, Manville Bedford and Percy Wills—itinerant evangelists with the Shantymen's Ministry—to visit people in their homes, to become friends with the neighbours, and to invite the community to choir concerts and evangelistic meetings. (The Shantymen were Christians who travelled throughout B.C., visiting remote towns and logging camps, where they held evangelistic meetings. The Shantymen's Christian Association is now known as SCA International.) Slowly but surely, the church grew.

Nick very quickly arrived at two conclusions. First, the Mennonite Brethren name carried ethnic connotations that were barriers to the gospel. Newcomers to the Christian faith thought that only German-speaking Mennonites could join the MB church. Second, Nick realized that Mennonite Brethren had become complacent when it came to evangelism. They were content to leave the reaching out to non-Christian and non-Mennonite people to the little mission churches scattered throughout the province. Nick was convinced that this "arms length approach" needed to change. At the 1960 B.C. MB convention, Nick stated, "We have integrated as far as economics, education and culture (to some extent) are concerned. Why not integrate socially? We must have the friends across the street into our homes... and into our hearts. Jesus did." Nick added, "The minds of the citizens of our communities are filled with prejudices because of our segregation practices. This prejudice can only be broken down by proving to them that we really want them in our homes and in our churches."

In the years to follow, Nick would persistently work at motivating Mennonite Brethren churches to actively invite their Canadian neighbours into a relationship with Jesus.

*Nick, praying for church planters at the 1994 B.C. conference.*

## THE CENTRAL HEIGHTS EXPERIENCE

In 1962, Nick resigned from the church at McConnell Creek. The previous six years had been busy. Two more children had joined the family: John (1956), Evelyn (1959) and a third (Charles) was on the way. Nick had also spent three summers (1959-61) directing Columbia Bible Camp. Nick had a desire to complete his degree, and was planning to enroll as a full-time student at Northwest Baptist Theological College in Burnaby. That summer, while he was directing Columbia Bible Camp, members of the Abbotsford MB Church paid Nick a visit.

"We want you to be our pastor," they said.

Nick refused. He had already declined invitations from two smaller churches in northern B.C. To say yes to this invitation would not look good. Furthermore, Nick was intent on studying.

The Abbotsford church, however, was similarly determined. A few weeks later they returned. "Please reconsider," they asked. After several days of prayer, Nick and Betty had a sense that this was a call from God, and said yes, but on two conditions. First, Nick insisted that he be allowed to complete his studies. This was granted. Second, Nick wanted assurances that the church was ready to reach into the community. The leadership assured him that this was the case, pointing out that the church had switched from German to English worship services for precisely that reason, and that children from non-Christian homes were being picked up and brought to Sunday school.

The work of studying and of local outreach proved to be more difficult than Nick imagined. Juggling the demands of church, school and family pushed Nick to the point of burnout. Nick would later say, "That was an unknown term in those days, so I just carried on as best as I could, and by the grace of God survived!"

Nick found himself sustained by the charismatic movement. In the fall of 1962 Nick, along with Herb Neufeld, Jake Friesen and Vic Stobbe, visited the charismatic revival that Dennis Bennett was leading at St. Luke's Episcopal Church in Seattle. Nick went out of a desire for personal renewal. "I wanted more of whatever God had for me," Nick said.

At the same time, Nick was meeting regularly with a charismatic Anglican priest in New Westminster for times of prayer. "I never spoke in tongues," Nick later said, "but one time I was driving home from school, and somehow there welled up within me this deep sense of praise. I felt like I was about to burst. Ever since then, it's been easier for me to praise the Lord."

While Nick sought out a deeper experience of God, he was striving to open the church up to the community. Nick used a variety of tactics: he joined the local ministerial—something that was unheard of among MBs at the time; he led the church to change its name to Central Heights Church as a sign of openness to the community; he chaired several community-wide evangelistic campaigns conducted by Barry Moore and members of the Billy Graham team; he began Burden Bearers, a counselling and prayer ministry, with a handful of other Christian leaders; and he began promoting Campus Crusade for Christ materials and methods. More importantly, it seems, Nick made sure that new children in Sunday school and new families in church were visited immediately. As one person noted, "Nick pastored people who weren't in his church."

Of course, there was some opposition. One year Nick encouraged the ladies' groups to invite their neighbours to their Christmas banquets, but with little success. The solution, Nick thought, was to start earlier. The next year, Nick started talking to the ladies groups about their Christmas banquets in August. At least two of the women were unimpressed. "Can't we ever be by ourselves?" they asked.

*Two men of mission, Nick with Victor Adrian (at left).*

Needless to say, the answer was "No." When Nick resigned after 11 years at Central Heights, the church had virtually doubled in size, and stood at 380 members.

## THE RIGHT MAN

When it comes to Nick's work as director of the B.C. MB Board of Church Extension (BoCE), it appears that he was the right man in the right place at the right time. By 1973, three major shifts had taken place. First, an increasing number of Mennonite Brethren felt that their efforts at building churches through VBS and Sunday school programs were both ineffective and inefficient. They were calling for change. They wanted "more bang for their buck." Second, the population of B.C. was on the upswing. Sociologists have noted that newcomers are naturally open to fresh ideas. It was obvious that the time was ripe for MBs to pursue innovative ways of inviting a growing population of transplants to put down their roots in the Gospel and the church. Third, by the early '70s, B.C. MBs had "arrived." They were prosperous and professionalized people with whom suburban Canadians could identify. The upshot was that many MBs were ready to follow a leader who wanted to pursue the Great Commission, not just overseas, but in their neighbourhoods and in their home churches as well.

In Nick, B.C. MBs had found their man. Over the next 14 years, Nick would repeatedly call each B.C. MB church to "consider community evangelism and discipleship as its highest priority" and to "be willing to pay the price in terms of hard work, innovative approaches, investing much prayer, time, energy and money." Nick extended this call in a variety of ways: personal counselling; preaching at churches; recruiting pastors and workers; leading workshops and seminars; meeting with church boards and leadership teams; fundraising; serving as an interim pastor for new church plants; and so on. Nick would also insist that new church plants call themselves a "Community Church" rather than a "Mennonite Brethren Church" to be more open to newcomers.

Though he was never a captivating speaker, Nick was persuasive. Under Nick's leadership the B.C. MB Conference added 31 new congregations. In 1986, shortly before he retired, the B.C. MB Conference stated that it would "make evangelism and church growth a priority in all its ministries."

In his efforts to kick-start MB evangelism and church planting, Nick championed the Church Growth Movement. The Church Growth Movement insisted that churches should be effective and growing. In other words, people should experience life-transforming conversions because of the churches' efforts, and churches should therefore increase in size as more and more people accepted the invitation to meet Jesus.

The Church Growth Movement encouraged a number of strategies that Nick, ever the pragmatist, aggressively promoted in B.C. MB congregations. One strategy was to set goals. For example, Nick insisted that the B.C. MB Conference ought to have an annual growth rate greater than 3%. Accordingly, in 1980, Nick and the BoCE recommended that by 1990 the B.C. MB Conference double its membership, and that each church start a daughter church. The conference would start 24 new churches in the next seven years.

Another strategy of the Church Growth Movement was to use sociological methods to maximize evangelistic efforts. For example, in planning for new church plants, Nick and the BoCE would priorize areas where the population was rapidly growing, or an evangelical presence was limited. In addition, as B.C.'s population became increasingly multicultural, Nick encouraged the development of "ethnic" churches, so that by 1985 B.C. MBs worshipped in seven different languages.

A third approach of the Church Growth Movement was to rely primarily on the church planter or church growth leader to motivate the local congregation for success. Nick agreed. In 1974, he launched an internship program that would test for pastoral ministry and preaching skills, and would equip leaders in the areas of setting priority goals for the church, working with volunteers, and developing evangelism and Bible study programs. As Nick wrote in his conference report, "Our congregations must recapture the principle that God causes things to happen through leaders." Churches, Nick added, "must be prepared to give liberty to its leaders and accept their leadership for church growth. This is a biblical mandate to leaders and congregations."

At the same time, the strategy for starting church plants changed. In the mid-1970s, Nick would wait for groups to say that they wanted to start a new church. By the 1980s, however, Nick would call a meeting where he would present a person who would lead. Those who were interested were invited to align themselves with that leader.

## ASSESSING THE EFFECTS

Nick's efforts had both positive and negative long-term effects. On the positive side, Nick corrected and enlarged the Mennonite Brethren vision of mission. MBs had always been active in overseas mission. Nick successfully reminded MBs that they needed to also reach out to their co-workers and neighbours. Indeed, because of Nick's encouragement, churches *did* grow because people *did* give their lives to Jesus! In addition, by 1987, the Canadian MB church had become a multicultural family.

On the negative side, Nick's promotion of the Church Growth Movement appears to have been the most troublesome. While Nick brought a renewed emphasis on the Great Commission, it seems that the pendulum swung so far it tended to exclude the First Commandment. In other words, priority was given to evangelism over social ministries. Indeed, there was a tendency to shift outreach to the more affluent, suburban segment of society, bypassing the disadvantaged. For example, in 1975 the B.C. BoCE terminated Grace Mission in downtown Vancouver, and in 1985 a ministry with First Nations peoples was terminated.

There was another interesting problem that emerged. On the one hand, despite the fact that they used sociological methods to achieve their goals, MB proponents of the Church Growth Movement—including Nick—would claim that their successes were "simply God honouring our faith." On the other hand, those same proponents pointed to rapidly growing MB churches as successes, and insisted that other congregations should "be and do like them." Case in point, Nick would later admit that he was initially disappointed with churches that did not grow as quickly as, or in the way that, he envisioned. "In those days," Nick has said, "it seemed to me that those churches didn't seem to want to go anywhere."

These curious oversimplifications left smaller churches with the impression that they were inferior, and that there was something wrong with them—either they didn't have enough faith; or they were running the wrong program; or they were running the right program but in the wrong way; and so on. Reality, of course, is more complex. For example, churches in small, northern communities found it difficult to grow because people were more transient. In some instances, there was good evidence to say that a church was fulfilling its God-given mandate as a small congregation. In short, the mysterious workings of God cannot be evaluated according to numbers. Nevertheless, the truth that small can be beautiful tended to go unnoticed. To his credit, Nick's perspective has changed. "Looking back," he would say, "I bless those [smaller] churches because they fill a certain need in our society."

### NICK RETURNED THE FAVOUR

After retiring as executive director of the B.C. BoCE in 1987, Nick spent a handful of years working as a church-planting consultant for the Ontario and Kansas MB Conferences, followed by stints as interim pastor for congregations in Ontario and B.C. Nick also worked as the B.C. Conference pastor for a year in the early '90s. By this point, Nick was content to pursue other interests. In between overseas trips with Church Partnership Evangelism, Nick and Betty continued to build friendships with their non-Christian neighbours in Abbotsford.

Looking back on Nick's thirty-plus years of ministry, Nick did for the church what the church did for him. Nick had intended to farm crops and livestock. As it turns out, he was a farmer, but the Mennonite Brethren community made sure he was a farmer who grew churches. From his parents, to his friends, to his teachers, to conference leaders, the MB Church called Nick to be a farmer who would cultivate the church's evangelistic efforts. More specifically, individuals within the church modelled for Nick, and inspired in him, a passion to share Good News with his neighbours.

Having had his life changed by the church, Nick returned the favour. Nick changed the ethos, identity and future direction of his Canadian Mennonite Brethren community. For example, when all was said and done, Nick's efforts contributed to a greater dependency on the Spirit of God. After all, church planting and church growth required the faith to take bold risks. Inviting neighbours to church required a new kind of openness. In addition, Canadian MBs were now an increasingly multicultural family. MBs thus found themselves more diverse, and more hospitable to the charismatic and evangelical dimensions of Christianity.

Interestingly, there were some unexpected weeds. In their desire to be welcoming, B.C. MB churches often downplayed their Anabaptist-Mennonite heritage. B.C. MB churches eventually discovered that they had gone too far and jettisoned important Anabaptist theological distinctives, such as a biblically-grounded peace witness. In other instances, while they had emphasized conversion, some MBs had forgotten the Anabaptist emphasis on daily discipleship.

Furthermore, with the emphasis on leadership, the Anabaptist understanding that God was encountered and followed together as a community was undercut by a growing individualism. There is a particular irony in this because Nick, whose life was profoundly shaped by grassroots Christians and a group of lay leaders, spearheaded the move towards a kind of top-down leadership structure. He seems to have undermined the very thing that had been extremely important in his personal journey.

Nevertheless, Nick gave the MB church a valuable gift. The MB church gave Nick a passion for outreach, and Nick turned around and gave that passion back, leaving the MB church much richer than before.

Nick was once asked to reflect on where his passion for reaching the community originated. He paused. There were individuals—such as the businessmen in Yarrow—who had modelled outreach. There were also churches—like Arnold and McConnell Creek—that had created opportunities for Nick to simply "put outreach into practice."

After some thought, however, Nick replied, "In 1997 I returned to the room where my parents called out to God so many years earlier, and I gave thanks. I suppose my passion for outreach was a result of my mother's prayer back then. I'll have to thank her when I get to heaven."

Canadian Mennonite Brethren will want to do the same.

SOURCES

In addition to interviews with the subject of this chapter, Nick Dyck, background and other information were obtained from John Redekop and Mike Klassen; Peter Penner's *No Longer at Arms Length*; the article, "Biblical Perspectives of Church Growth which Mennonite Brethren Should Embrace," in *Direction*, written by Herb Kopp; and "Burden Bearers." Nick and Betty Dyck's memoirs were also consulted. A copy of this chapter with footnoting is on file with the Centre for Mennonite Brethren Studies in Winnipeg.

## Herb Neufeld

# HE OPENED DOORS AND PUSHED OUT WALLS

*By Andrew Dyck*

At the 1960 Mennonite Brethren centennial conference, with delegates from Canadian and American churches assembled in Reedley, California, speaker after speaker named key issues facing the denomination. The earliest MB believers were known for their personal experience of conversion, now they needed a fresh encounter with the Holy Spirit. Mennonite Brethren once lived in villages where everyone spoke German, now they needed to engage their English-speaking neighbours with the gospel. The first Mennonite Brethren pastors were working men who volunteered their time for the church, now a new relationship was needed between paid pastors and congregations.

### THE START

That same fall, a 22-year-old man moved with his family to Regina, Sask., to study at Canadian Bible College. Herb Neufeld didn't know that in the next half-century he would help the Canadian MB churches change along exactly these lines: experiencing the Holy Spirit, evangelizing their neighbours and redefining pastor-church relations.

---

*The Writer*

Andrew Dyck lives in Abbotsford, B.C., where he co-pastors the Highland Community Church (MB), is writing a doctoral dissertation on Mennonite Brethren spirituality and teaches a course at Columbia Bible College. Andrew and his wife Martha have three sons. Previously, Andrew has pastored at the King Road MB Church, studied at Eastern Mennonite Seminary, was active in Westwood Community Church of Winnipeg and worked as a physiotherapist.

Herbert Dietrich Neufeld was born in 1938 in Namaka, Alberta, a tiny community east of Calgary. His parents, Dietrich and Aratina Neufeld, operated a small grain farm. They belonged to the Namaka Evangelical Mennonite Brethren Church, a congregation of three Mennonite groups who worshipped together under the lay leadership of Aron A. Toews and others. The expression of unity was not lost on young Herb.

When Herb was nine years old, his family (including older sister Martha and younger brother Abe) moved to Chilliwack, B.C., where his parents became charter members of the Broadway MB Church. The move was difficult for Herb. During these years immediately after World War II, anti-German sentiments were still strong. Mennonite school children faced rejection and cruel taunts. As a result Herb hated going to school and did what he could to blend in with the non-Mennonite students. Although he continued attending worship services and Sunday school—and later youth programs—he began hardening himself against his parents' faith. Herb and his close friends began distancing themselves from anything Mennonite.

When Herb was 16, an evangelist came to Broadway MB Church for a week of evangelistic services. Herb realized that he was approaching a crossroads in his life. He sensed that unless he decided to become a Christian, he might cross a line beyond which all the best preaching might leave him unmoved. As Herb explained later, "That particular week the Holy Spirit just nailed me." In the company of two friends, Herb attended the Friday night service. The preacher's scripture text (taken somewhat out of context) was Genesis 6:3a: "And the Lord said, 'My spirit shall not always strive with man'...." The message hit home, but Herb was too afraid to raise his hand in response to the evangelist's invitation. As the three friends left the church, John Friesen, a local store owner, met them: "Wouldn't you like to accept the Lord tonight?" Herb and one of his friends turned around and did just that.

One sign of Herb's conversion was his subsequent involvement at Harrison Gospel Chapel, a project of the Mennonite Brethren home mission board. Each week, he would join others from Broadway Church, take the ferry across the Fraser River to Harrison Hot Springs and teach a dozen 11-year-old boys. Herb also preached his first sermon at Harrison.

Herb expected to follow his parents into farming once he had finished high school. But his aspirations began shifting when he heard Henry Warkentin, field director for B.C. home missions, tell stories about adults becoming Christians in outlying areas. He was moved to hear about non-German-speaking people coming to faith in Jesus. That night, Herb knelt beside his bed and prayed, "Lord, if you should ever call me, I just want you to know that I'm available." In the next few years people who

*Herb and his wife and partner, Adeline Neufeld.*

heard Herb preach would say, "Are you sure you haven't missed your calling?" But he didn't tell anyone about his prayer.

Because farming was not very profitable when Herb graduated, he worked for four years in a branch of the Bank of Nova Scotia. Here he developed self-confidence as he learned not only accounting but also how to work with people. (In 1957 he also studied at East Chilliwack MB Bible School.)

While in high school Herb had met and begun dating Adeline Marie Nessel, after her father hired him to transport raspberries. The family belonged to a German Baptist Church. When Adeline's pastor tried to compel the church to resume using only German instead of English, her family moved to the Chilliwack Christian and Missionary Alliance Church. That's where Herb and Adeline married in 1958 and made a public commitment to serve the church. In 1960 they sold their house and with one-year-old son Allan moved to Regina to study. Herb expected to become a pastor in a Christian and Missionary Alliance Church because few Mennonite Brethren churches were then hiring pastors.

## SETTING DIRECTIONS

Herb's two years at Canadian Bible College laid important foundations for his future ministry. He found himself associating with Christians from various church backgrounds—including Alliance, Baptist and Presbyterian. He was introduced to a church leadership structure based on selecting men of godly character who would guide the church, rather than on a council comprised of representatives from each church ministry (considered the "brotherhood" pattern in many Mennonite Brethren churches). He heard teachings on living in the fullness of the Spirit and met Christian teachers who demonstrated it by the sparkling vitality of their lives.

In 1961 Herb specifically asked God for the opportunity to preach, though this was rare for second-year students. To his delight, he was invited to be the interim pastor for the Baptist Church in Edenwold, a nearby town originally settled by German immigrants. Not only could Herb preach regularly, but the congregation provided his family of four (Caroline was born that year) with a fully furnished parsonage, donations of farm-fresh groceries and a weekly salary of $20.

During the summer between Herb's two years at Canadian Bible College, he received an invitation that changed the direction of his pastoral ministry. The MB churches of B.C. were operating mission churches throughout the province. The mission at McConnell Creek (18 kilometers northeast of Mission) needed an interim leader because its pastor, Nick Dyck, had agreed to be the summer director of the fledgling Columbia Bible Camp. Herb was invited to come to McConnell Creek that summer. He came and one year later accepted the invitation to be the full-time pastor there. Herb would serve within the Mennonite Brethren Church for the rest of his full-time ministry.

Herb was in a hurry. Only 24 years old, he wanted to turn the entire McConnell Creek valley and mountainside upside down for God. He threw himself into his work. He preached twice on Sundays, and again at the weekly youth meetings and midweek Bible studies. That summer he led 300 children in Daily Vacation Bible School programs at McConnell Creek and in Dewdney. He visited people in their homes, especially wanting to win men to the Lord. The congregation began to plan for a church building closer to Mission and to become a full-fledged Mennonite Brethren Church. By fall, this inexperienced pastor was burning out emotionally and spiritually. Herb realized that he needed the help of the Holy Spirit: "Lord, unless you do something fresh in my life, I may just be the shortest term pastor this conference has ever seen."

## A NEW SPIRIT

Herb began praying and fasting and reading about the Holy Spirit. He read Acts in the New Testament, stories about the evangelists Dwight L. Moody and Rueben A. Torrey and *Nine O'Clock in the Morning* by Dennis Bennett. Bennett had recently become vicar of St. Luke's Episcopal Church in Seattle, Washington. Every Friday evening he held information sessions in the church's basement, at which he taught from scripture about the "baptism in the Holy Spirit," led a time of worship during which gifts of prophecy, speaking in tongues and interpretation of tongues were welcomed, and finally gave people the opportunity to encounter the Holy Spirit.

In fall of 1962 Herb with three other MB pastors—Nick Dyck, Jake Friesen and Vic Stobbe—drove to Seattle to attend one of those sessions. Each of them was "blessed," although in different ways. Herb returned to McConnell Creek that Sunday and shared what he had learned about the Holy Spirit. In Herb's own words, however, "Monday was one of those days that you never forget." He was fasting and praying and "it was like heaven came down. My life was absolutely transformed. It was amazing. My wife wasn't sure if I'd lost it, or if I'd just got it." This encounter would shape Herb's character and ministry from then on.

The next year McConnell Creek Mission joined the Conference with the name Mountainview Gospel Chapel—one of the first Canadian MB churches not to have "Mennonite Brethren" in its name. Its new building was completed in 1964. As the congregation gave more attention to the work of the Holy Spirit, the worship services became livelier. Pastors and others from Mennonite Brethren churches would visit Mountainview to find out what was going on. One visitor recalls that the services were more like a jamboree than a traditional service. Some of Herb's fellow pastors were censured by the B.C. Conference leadership for their charismatic views, though Herb would not resign even when a prominent MB leader suggested he should. The Mountainview congregation grew from about 40 to 175 attendees per Sunday. Each family committed itself to reach another family for Christ and to increased financial giving. Eventually two missionaries were sent out.

## WILLINGDON CALLS

In 1968 Herb, Adeline and their four children (Cheryl and Geoff were the youngest) left Mission so Herb could further his studies in Fresno, California. Over the next three years Herb completed a BA degree at Fresno Pacific College and a Diploma in Practical Theology at Mennonite Brethren Biblical Seminary. Waldo Hiebert, a seminary professor, and Dan Friesen, a local pastor and conference leader, encouraged Herb's charismatic direction, because they had had experiences similar to his. Others, like D. Edmond Hiebert, spurred him to study the Bible carefully on the matter of speaking in tongues.

During their time in Fresno, Herb also pastored Raisin City Church of the Brethren, a congregation of about forty people. Inspired by a pastor from Cedar Hills Baptist Church in Portland, Oregon, whose church had thirty home Bible study groups, Herb decided to implement such groups in Raisin City as a way to do evangelism. The first group met in a church member's home. Of the first four couples to join the group, several became Christians.

On one occasion, a young couple—both new Christians—began attending the services at Raisin City Church. Herb was eager to include them in the congregation because most of the church members were over sixty years old. However, when the couple heard Herb mention Anabaptists in his sermons—he had picked up this term from seminary professors like Abe J. Klassen—they asked, "What have you got against the Baptists?" Herb never forgot that exchange and from then on avoided using the term "Anabaptist" in his preaching.

In 1971 Willingdon Mennonite Brethren Church in Burnaby, B.C. invited Herb to be their next pastor. Willingdon had begun in 1961 with goals that were grounded in Christ's great commission (Matt. 28). For this reason, the church used English instead of German. It also began accepting as members adults who had received believers' baptism in a mode other than immersion. In spite of these changes, some people were afraid that if Herb became their pastor the church would split because of his charismatic leanings. However, Herb did come and Willingdon did not split. Instead, by 1986 when he left, it had grown from 242 to 938 members, to become Canada's largest Mennonite Brethren congregation. Fifty-five cell groups were meeting regularly, each led by an elder. More than two thousand people from various ethnic backgrounds considered Willingdon to be their home church.

Herb, 33 years old when he came to Willingdon, began immediately to introduce innovations based on his previous experiences. That fall he facilitated the development of home Bible study groups. Soon, 12 groups were active with 120 adults involved. Throughout his time at Willingdon, these cell groups studied the scriptures and topics that were being preached in the Sunday morning services.

Rather than dividing the church by his convictions about the Holy Spirit, Herb helped people overcome their fears. He preached about the Holy Spirit and invited speakers such as John Wimber to tell their own stories about lives transformed by the Holy Spirit. Later, he introduced a practice he had witnessed at the Christian Life Assembly, a Pentecostal church in Langley, B.C. While Herb would offer a pastoral prayer, people in the congregation would be invited to come forward and pray with elders who were waiting at the front of the platform. People came with struggling marriages, illnesses and the desire to receive Christ—and all this before the sermon!

Music was another means by which the Spirit's ministry was welcomed. Throughout Herb's time at Willingdon, he worked hand-in-glove with Bill Klassen, a high school teacher and volunteer musician who had been at Willingdon from the start. Herb encouraged Bill to follow the example of churches in California that were restructuring their worship services to begin with an extended block of singing and music called "worship time."

Herb's preaching was marked by story-telling, emotional impact, extensive quotes from a wide range of preachers and writers, and liberal references to scripture. Although not an in-depth Bible expositor, as some prominent Mennonite Brethren travelling speakers of that day, Herb communicated effectively with his audiences. He held their attention and offered clear answers to the questions of the day.

One of Herb's most remembered sermon series dealt with elders in the church. Herb had experienced the shortcomings of church councils and became convinced that the biblical pattern of church governance was to have elders. Each would be a gifted leader (Herb especially appreciated leaders who valued goals, not only process), an active shepherd of a home group, known for his godly character and committed to the spiritual growth and goals of the entire church. Herb spent four months preaching about biblical leadership. The home groups studied the topic as well. In 1977, the church was presented with a threefold motion that every church member should belong to a home group, an elder would oversee each group and a board of elders would replace the church council. Ninety-five percent of the congregation voted in favour.

**BUILDING ON TRUST**

Although a few people criticized the change, the church's trust of its leaders grew. The elders committed themselves not to bring any recommendation to the congregation unless they themselves unanimously favoured it. In 1978 they initiated the Positive Christian Singles ministry, inspired by the stories Herb told about such a ministry at the Crystal Cathedral in California. As a result, increasing numbers of divorced Christian adults began inquiring about remarrying. After intensive study among the elders (writings by Charles Swindoll were especially helpful), Herb presented the congregation with a paper that outlined under what conditions and after what process a remarriage would be considered. A thousand people attended that evening presentation and the congregation embraced the elders' direction.

Herb came to Willingdon with a commitment to evangelize the people of Burnaby. In the early 1970s many Mennonite Brethren were still thinking of evangelism in terms of overseas missions, outposts in outlying towns in British Columbia, or local evangelistic crusades. Herb, on the other hand, worked to help the people of Willingdon themselves do evangelism. Home groups were organized to do visitation evangelism. Willingdon's large choir began performing musicals and large-scale seasonal events at Christmas and Easter, to which the congregation would invite unsaved neighbours and friends. Specific Sundays were devoted to honouring local civic workers such as police officers, firefighters and nurses. Svend Robinson—Burnaby's local, gay MP from the New Democratic Party—and other politicians were invited to attend the services and on occasion addressed the congregation.

Herb was convinced that it was more important that people be introduced to Christ than learn about being Mennonite. He met people who were reluctant to attend Willingdon Mennonite Brethren Church because they associated "Mennonite" with Amish-style horses and buggies. For this reason he removed the sign that said "Mennonite Brethren" from the wall of the church. Later he asked for and received the elders' approval for this change.

Herb introduced many other innovations during his time at Willingdon. The church began holding multiple services. In 1982, when Canadians were struggling with a recession and extraordinarily high interest rates, Willingdon built a new and larger sanctuary. Although the sanctuary was large enough to seat the entire congregation at once, they continued with multiple services in order to keep pursuing their goal of church growth. Telecare, a 24-hour telephone crisis line, began in 1983. A social ministry for seniors began in 1984. Spanish and Korean congregations began meeting at Willingdon in the mid-1980s. Willingdon hired a growing number of associate pastors; Herb personally recruited some of them. Many fledgling pastors completed internships under Herb's tutelage and then became pastors elsewhere.

All these innovations did not go unnoticed. Herb believed that Willingdon could "serve as a model regarding church growth basics, leadership structure, as well as development of home Bible studies." Together with Nick Dyck he vigorously pushed smaller churches to set goals for growth. They promoted the eldership form of church polity. Herb encouraged other Canadian MB churches in this direction through personal contacts

*Herb chairing a meeting of the Canadian Council of Boards in 1989.*

and speaking engagements. The Mennonite Brethren Biblical Seminary in Fresno invited Herb to teach seminars on these topics. During a sabbatical in 1981, Herb preached in MB churches in Spain, Germany and Austria.

During these years Herb also sat on many committees beyond Willingdon, usually several at once. In 1982, for instance, he was moderator of the B.C. MB Conference, a member of the Canadian Board of Evangelism, assistant moderator for the Canadian Conference, and a member of the Seminary's board. He was often elected to chair the committee to which he belonged. While at Willingdon he at various times belonged to the local ministerial association, the Burnaby Justice Council, the advisory council of Youth for Christ, the council of the Evangelical Fellowship of Canada and the board of directors for Haven Ministries. He also served as a spiritual advisor for the chapel at 108 Mile Ranch, B.C., even though the group there did not join the Mennonite Brethren Conference. (Herb enjoyed moose hunting when he visited 108 Ranch.)

Herb has quoted Wayne Gretzky, hockey superstar, as saying, "One hundred [percent] of the pucks you don't shoot won't go in." This was part of Herb's self-avowed philosophy of church work: "If you don't try anything, you can bet it won't work." At Willingdon, many of Herb's initiatives seemed "to score." People placed their faith in Jesus, were baptized and joined the church. Leaders were trusted. Bridges were built from the church into the community. Broken, hurting people were loved and served. Then in 1986 Herb, now turning forty-eight, notified the congregation that he was resigning; a month later he was gone. His next efforts at innovation would seem less successful.

## COMING TO CENTRAL HEIGHTS
In 1987 Herb became the senior pastor at the large and highly organized Central Heights Mennonite Brethren Church in Abbotsford, B.C. Each Sunday 800 adults met in classes of 70 for instruction. The teaching and soul care in each class was led by an elder. Elders served as *couples*. Care groups were drawn out of these classes. Herb came with the intention of working with the elders to lead the church into further growth through evangelism.

However, Herb found that he had walked into a situation more complex than he had expected. First, the church leadership's handling of the senior pastor transition from Rudy Boschman to Herb had been problematic. Second, the church's elders weren't filling the same role that elders had at Willingdon. By Herb's second year, the church elders were redefined as men; the heads of the adult Sunday school classes were renamed "class leaders." Third, Herb began facing disunity among the church's lay leaders. This led to increasing conflict among the elders and pastors. A few church members left Central Heights as a result. This resistance caught Herb off guard. He began feeling insecure and defensive. So, when the B.C. Conference asked him to become the province's conference minister, he accepted the invitation after completing only two years at Central Heights. Herb had misjudged the congregation's readiness to change. Later, however, he felt that he tendered his resignation prematurely, because during his last six months there the conflicts seemed to be overcome and the church was growing in numbers.

## OUT OF THE PASTORATE AND BACK
Herb served as the conference minister for B.C.'s MB churches from 1989-92. With the children grown and married, Herb and Adeline relished the opportunity of serving together. Adeline had always been active in the churches they attended. She shared her musical abilities by singing solos and in choirs. She used her training in early childhood education to develop ministries to pre-schoolers. But with Herb's many commitments, she needed to shoulder extra responsibilities caring for their family. (Herb did, however, work at keeping Friday evenings as family night.)

Herb's deepest desire, however, was to be a pastor. For all his conference involvements—he was now moderator of the Canadian Conference—his heart was with the local church, where evangelism takes place. As he said to a group of pastors with their spouses in 2009, "It is better to visit one person seven times than seven people once."

*Speaking to the B.C. convention in 1993.*

When the leadership of the B.C. Conference asked Herb to start a new MB church in the eastern part of Abbotsford, an area where suburbs were growing, he jumped at the opportunity. He recruited Walter Janzen, still serving as music director at Central Heights, to be his associate pastor. A few people from Central Heights decided to join the new church. Others were displeased with this development. In the end, however, Central Heights gave its blessing to the new congregation. In 1992 Mountain Park Community Church held its first service at Yale Secondary School. Almost four hundred people attended.

Once again Herb was innovating. Everyone who came was given a name tag. The services felt fresh and unique. Herb's warm relational style was unmatched. People who had not attended church since their childhood said, "If this is church, we're back in." Walter recalls that never before in his ministry did he have the opportunity to lead so many people to the Lord as when he was visiting newcomers at Mountain Park. Within two years Mountain Park had built a new church building. Six hundred people attended the opening service. The financial risks of borrowing at high interest rates for the building's mortgage seemed legitimate in light of the church's rapid growth, which continued, but only for a few more years.

But once again Herb had to face his two greatest nemeses: the intense workload of serving a new, growing church and leadership conflict. MB churches were no longer filled with people who had grown up sharing a common culture and common assumptions about church and the Bible.

The chairs of Mountain Park were filled with people who represented a variety of viewpoints, priorities and church histories. Whereas Herb had led Willingdon from a core of uniformity outward into a broad, inclusive embrace of its neighbours, now he needed to lead a large, diverse group inward to identify its core values and priorities. Some people wanted the church to be more explicitly charismatic. Others wanted the church to be "seeker-driven," in the style of Willow Creek Church in Illinois. For six months Herb led the church in Bible studies and Sunday evening round-table discussions.

By the fifth year of Mountain Park's existence, the church decided it would be "seeker-friendly," while also offering spiritual nurture to Christians. Some people left. Some elders resigned. An associate pastor graciously moved to another city to begin a church on a different model. And Herb was closer to burnout than ever before.

He was scheduled to have a three-month sabbatical, but because of an unexpected staff resignation, he was only granted a few weeks off. During these weeks he visited Saddleback Church in Lake Forest, California. Through the unexpected generosity of strangers, Herb was able to attend a conference for pastors. Pastor Rick Warren preached on the topic, "Ten reasons why you shouldn't quit." Herb later recalled with tears how that sermon renewed his trust in the loving God who is Lord of the church. Once again, God's Holy Spirit had restored Herb's soul.

Herb returned to Mountain Park for another year. At age 60 Herb retired from Mountain Park and from full-time pastoral ministry. He had always intended to retire at that age because he wanted to make room for younger leaders and because he never wanted anyone to say of him as an aging pastor, "He didn't do anything dumb [enough to be fired] but he didn't do anything brilliant."

## ACTIVE RETIREMENT

In his retirement, Herb began enjoying the solitude and rest that he had so often missed. He accepted a part-time job developing support for the Mennonite Brethren Biblical Seminary. Between 2000 and 2004 he worked part-time as the interim senior pastor at East Aldergrove MB Church. The church flourished under his leadership. It grew in size, in trust for its leaders and in unity. The growth seemed to result from the same features that characterized Herb's other pastorates: warm relational skills, personal recruiting of first-time leaders, a renewed evangelistic purpose, increased visibility in the community through media advertizing and a name change to the Ross Road Community Church, home groups, "ministry times" in the services, a building renovation, an elder-based polity and frequent invi-

*Herb always engaged easily with members in the church or delegates to conventions*

tations to be baptized. Although Herb's style of leading behind-the-scenes through one-on-one conversations sometimes frustrated committees, the church as a whole flourished. Herb's final pastorate came as interim pastor for one year at Olivet Mennonite Church.

### LOOKING BACK

Between 1964 and 2005 Herb served on 10 conference committees at provincial, national and binational levels. He was either moderator or assistant moderator for 11 years in the B.C. Conference and for nine years in the Canadian Conference. Herb led innovations at the conference level, just as he did in local churches. Eventually Herb would participate in changes that reined in some excesses that resulted from his earlier innovations. He also played a part in some conference-wide controversies.

Not surprisingly, Herb's commitment to evangelism shaped his conference involvements. In his sermons as Canadian moderator, he always emphasized personal evangelism. Convinced that "the greatest resources for church growth and outreach [are] in the local church," he promoted personal friendship and home Bible studies as the best methods of evangelism. He helped initiate church growth seminars. These included two national conferences, Disciple-Making '85 and '88. Herb helped bring in speakers such as Gene Getz, Myron Augsburger, C. Peter Wagner, Robert Coleman and Michael Green. Herb promoted church growth banquets, conference purpose statements and church growth strategies.

As a conference leader, Herb cut a wide swath. In his efforts to help people see the big picture, he expressed his opinions strongly—sometimes with words, other times by shaking his head or rolling his eyes. As a result he needed secretaries and assistants to nuance what he sometimes overstated, and to complete details that he had glossed over. In the 1980s, the number of church members in the B.C. Conference was rapidly becoming more than half of all the members in Canada's MB churches. Herb was willing to be outspoken on behalf of B.C. perspectives at a time when most conference decisions, staff and activities were still centred on Winnipeg.

Some of the innovations that Herb promoted in his early years later required reining in. Herb helped make the necessary adjustments. Between 1983 and 1985, when he was volunteering as conference minister for B.C., he used the General Conference's 1972 statement about the charismatic movement to help calm the waters in churches that were in conflict because of the movement. In 1990, while Herb was employed as conference minister, he acknowledged that church leadership styles were contributing to increased tensions. As a result he recommended better mediation processes, better ways of evaluating pastors and approving new pastors, and an orientation seminar for pastors new to the MB Conference. During his retirement, Herb continued to teach biblical principles of elder-based leadership as a correction to the distortion he was seeing in some churches (for example, elders becoming "yes men" to pastors or managing instead of shepherding).

In 1992 Herb supported a B.C. resolution that stated that churches which no longer included "Mennonite Brethren" in their name should, for the sake of integrity, "clearly identify their affiliation with the MB Conference in their membership orientation classes and in their weekly bulletin." (The Canadian Conference's Board of Faith and Life issued a similar statement in 1988, when Herb was conference moderator.) In 1994 MB leaders met for a study conference in Denver, Colorado, to work at rewriting the Confession of Faith. Biblical scholars argued that only baptized believers should receive communion whereas church planters wanted a more open approach. It was Herb who averted division by proposing an additional sentence that is in the present Confession of Faith: "The normal pattern in the New Testament was that baptism preceded participation in the Lord's Supper."

Herb's conference involvements also led him into controversies. In 1989 Herb was the moderator of the Canadian Conference and conference minister for the B.C. Conference. The Canadian Conference's Board of Higher Education was asking the provinces to give it coordinated oversight of all Mennonite Brethren Bible schools and colleges across Canada. The B.C. Conference, however, had a long history of concerns about the Mennonite Brethren Bible College in Winnipeg—the one educational institution supported nationally instead of provincially. Herb supported the position of the B.C. Conference, which voted against the Canadian resolution and in favour of withdrawing national funding for MBBC.

A major conflict involved women serving in leadership ministries in MB churches. Herb always valued the gifts and contributions of women in the church and during his time as Willingdon's senior pastor, it became one of the first MB churches to hire a woman onto its ministry staff. Herb's understanding, however, was that the New Testament teaches that elders should only be men. Thus, at Central Heights, women who had served on the church council were not permitted to serve on the new board of elders. In 1993, the Board of Faith and Life of the MB General Conference brought a resolution to the convention that would have given each congregation freedom to permit a woman to be the leading pastor based on its understanding of the scriptures. Herb was then the moderator of the B.C. Conference and didn't support allowing women to be lead pastors. Prior to the convention, the B.C. executive gathered the province's pastors and spouses to hear presenters contend that leadership in the church and home should be taken by men. The motion of the Board of Faith and Life was defeated.

However, debate and frustration continued. From 2000-2002 Herb was the chairperson of the Board of Faith and Life as it was revisiting this topic. He was one of the last of the board members to oppose giving each member church freedom "to call and affirm gifted men *and women* to serve in ministry and pastoral leadership." In 2006 the Canadian Conference gave local congregations the freedom to call and affirm gifted women and men to all ministry and leadership positions.

### HELPED REDEFINE US

After Herb retired from the pastorate in 2005, he continued to preach at churches, banquets and seniors retreats. He was called on to give guidance to new congregations who wanted to learn about biblical leadership and church growth. He sat on the board of International Christian

Ministries and led a home Bible study group within his home church, North Langley Community Church. In 2008, after months of being ill "for the first time in my life," he was eventually diagnosed with a rare and often fatal fungal infection in his lungs, for which he was treated successfully. In late 2008 Herb and Adeline sold the Christmas tree farm that they had enjoyed operating for three decades. Herb took particular joy in spending time with his children and grandchildren. Although he was present less often at MB conference events, he continued to cheer for the MB family and its growth.

Herb's business leanings undoubtedly contributed to his zeal for innovating. Some people, especially those who didn't know him well, criticized him for devaluing transparent, participative process in favour of outcome. His zeal for promoting change and his preference for working through personal channels meant he sometimes bypassed policies and procedures. However, his relational warmth endeared him even to those who disagreed with him.

Herb's innovations were clearly directed toward church growth. He wanted to remove perceived barriers to evangelism and implement church goals, celebrative worship and home Bible study groups. Some might criticize Herb's focus on the local church as undermining conference solidarity, or as being insufficiently community-based (as the missional movement stresses). However, this was Herb's way of helping Mennonite Brethren, steeped in an Anabaptist sense of community, to bring mission outreach back into their own homes, neighbourhoods and ultimately congregations.

By removing barriers and embracing people of varied backgrounds, Herb helped to redefine and broaden Mennonite Brethren identity. Although Herb consistently served the Mennonite Brethren conference and held to its Confession of Faith, his overarching priority was evangelism in the power of the Holy Spirit. Herb wanted the MB church to have a broad ethnic make-up. He therefore felt free to learn from and associate with believers of many different denominations and traditions. In this way Herb helped position the MB family as one among many evangelical denominations.

Through all his innovations and evangelistic efforts, Herb's experience of the Holy Spirit was his motivating centre. The Holy Spirit is the One who changes people's lives. This happens not only at conversion, but whenever believers humbly pray to God for help—as Herb experienced repeatedly. The Spirit is the One who invigorates true worship. Herb has credited the Spirit of Jesus with whatever innovations were fruitful during his ministry.

Herb Neufeld is no longer in the eye of most Mennonite Brethren. Many people miss feeling his arm around their shoulders. They miss hearing the catch that creeps into his bass voice. They miss his large presence behind the pulpit.

However, the work of God's Spirit in the past half century among the Mennonite Brethren—and through Herb Neufeld—will continue to bring change, as the gospel of Jesus Christ is introduced to the people of Canada.

## SOURCES

Much of the background for this chapter was obtained through interviews and correspondence with Herb Neufeld, supplemented by interviews with people who worked with him in congregations and conference committees. Other sources included the 1961-2005 conference yearbooks of the General, Canadian and British Columbia conferences of Mennonite Brethren churches. The published histories of the Willingdon and Central Heights Churches were consulted. Herb wrote 11 articles for the *Mennonite Brethren Herald* and *Direction*, plus an unpublished study conference paper. Other articles in the *Herald* and in the *Global Anabaptist Mennonite Encyclopedia Online* furnished helpful details.

David Poon

# Not I, but Christ

*By David H. Leung*

On December 31, 2007, after serving as the senior pastor of the first registered Chinese Mennonite Brethren church in North America for 29 years, David Poon retired from Bethel Chinese Christian MB Church in Vancouver, B.C.

While David's 40-plus years of ministry abounded with blessings, there were also moments of fiery trials and periods marked by hard labor and major challenges. Yet God has been faithful and gracious and David can truly echo the wonderful truths and lyrics of the hymn, "Not I, but Christ."

Born to second-generation Christian parents in Canton, China in 1942, David Poon was the youngest in a family of nine. His grandfather was led to the Lord in 1916 by Ruth Hitchcock, a missionary from California. The testimony of his grandfather was so striking that he led 40 of his relatives from his village to know the Lord. This passion for evangelism seems to be a trait of the Poon family. Among David's siblings, their spouses and children, there are nine ordained pastors.

David's father was a medical doctor who was killed in a freak accident when David was only 15 months old. This brought about much hardship to the family. David's family subsequently moved to Hong Kong and his mother worked long hours to make ends meet. David's poor childhood left

---

*The Writer*
David Leung is a member of the Stewardship Ministries team of the Canadian Conference of MB Churches. David is a retired businessman, a chartered accountant and a certified management consultant. He lives in West Vancouver with his wife Ruth and two children.

## THE LIFE OF DAVID POON

| | |
|---|---|
| 1942 | Born in Canton, China |
| 1957 | Baptism |
| 1964 | Commitment to ministry |
| 1968 | Receives Bachelor of Religious Education from Hong Kong Alliance Bible Seminary |
| 1968-69 | Pastor at Wah Kee Alliance Church in Hong Kong |
| 1969-71 | Studies at Canadian Bible College |
| 1971 | Ordained to ministry |
| 1971-78 | Pastor at Christ Church of China in Vancouver |
| 1972 | Marries Esther |
| 1978-2007 | Pastor at Bethel Chinese Christian MB Church in Vancouver |
| 1993-97 | Serves on the Board of MB Missions/Services |
| 1995 | Receives Masters degree in Christian Ministry from Hong Kong Alliance Bible Seminary |
| 2006 | Serves as an advisor to MB Chinese Church Association |
| 2008 | Serves as Honorary Itinerant Minister for China Evangelistic Mission |

him feeling insecure and depressed and he had very low self-esteem. While going to elementary school, David stayed with his sister and brother-in-law, Pastor Andrew Leung and his wife. Their selflessness, faithfulness and non-worldly mindset inspired him spiritually. In 1956, David came to faith in Christ as his Saviour and never looked back again.

Throughout David's time in high school and his years at the Alliance Bible Seminary, he was blessed with unusual successes in a variety of ministry undertakings, including vacation Bible school teaching, doing evangelism among prisoners, conducting worship teams and preaching in rural villages. These preparatory years cemented his sense of calling from God to become a pastor after seminary training. "Trailblazing, long-suffering and zealous devotion," a motto upheld by the Alliance Bible Seminary, best captures David's pastorate experience at three different churches in the ensuing 40 years.

### CHURCH STARTER, A TRAILBLAZER

Shortly after David Poon graduated from the Seminary in 1968 and before his further studies at the Canadian Bible College a year later, he was invited to plant a church at a new government housing development (Wah Fu Estate) in Hong Kong. This residential area had a population of over

20,000 but no church. The Christian and Missionary Alliance, together with a local Alliance church (C&MA North Point Church), saw the need and appointed David and Pastor Charles Fowler to begin planting a church and spreading the gospel to over 2500 households. This initiative led to the establishment of the Christian and Missionary Alliance Wah Kee Church.

As a trailblazer, David quickly learned that there is no substitute for hard work and innovation in reaching out. Every month, invitations were mailed to every household in that area.

*David and Esther Poon, a ministry marked by trials and blessings.*

Since door-to-door flyer distribution service was not available through post offices during that era, the only acceptable practice for mass mailing was by sending out individual letters. This meant David had to manually personalize addresses for over 2000 households per month. Together with the mass mailings, a community hall with seating capacity for 400 was rented every Sunday for worship services, and for evangelistic meetings and children's Sunday school. The time and effort involved in setting up and taking down chairs and banners was significant. Given the long commute to the community hall, it was not unusual for David to leave home at 6 a.m. on Sundays and not return until 1 a.m. the following morning.

### HEARD GOD'S WORD

While studying at the Canadian Bible College, the Lord called David to serve at a small, independent church in the heart of Chinatown in Vancouver. Christ Church of China had a history of 60 years but had been without a pastor for many years. With a congregation of about 40, mostly seniors, it was more like a clannish club than a church. After his candidating sermon, David still vividly remembers overhearing an elderly woman say to another, "I did not sleep during the sermon today because I heard God's word." To David this clearly meant God was calling. David dropped his studies in Regina and moved to Vancouver.

In his seven and half years as senior pastor at Christ Church of China, David faced numerous challenges as he worked at changing some of the deep-rooted ritualistic traditions among church members and leaders. Each time the statement he overheard from the elderly woman gave him the burden, impetus and courage to stand firm for the truth and to lead by example.

## GATHERING FUNDS

Immediately after David took up the pastoral position, he was asked by the church council to go door to door among Chinatown merchants to raise funds for the church's operating budget. Apparently this practice had netted about $1000 annually. But David rejected this tradition because he firmly believed the Lord would provide and did not think believers should be yoked together with unbelievers (2 Corinthians 6:14). Facing strong opposition from church leadership and stern warnings that his salary could be jeopardized, David not only preached the message of tithing, but also set an example for others to follow. Contrary to their expectations, church giving increased and the church did not experience any further deficit.

## INFANT BAPTISM

Another early controversy David faced involved the baptism of little children. In spite of David's teachings that infant baptism did not fit his convictions about the Bible's teaching, and that a baby dedication was more appropriate (Luke 2:21-23; 3:21-23), one church family insisted upon baptizing their children. As a result of David's refusal and his uncompromising stand for what he understood the Scriptures to teach, this family stirred up dissension among church leaders in an attempt to force David to resign. It took a lot of prayer and counselling before the matter was settled. In hindsight, David wished that he had shared his statement of faith before accepting his pastoral position.

## BUILDING SOLD FOR $1

Perhaps the most explosive challenge of all during his tenure was a two-year-long legal battle over the ownership of church property. With a growing number of newcomers becoming church leaders, a small faction of old-timers felt threatened and devised a scheme to sell the church building for a dollar to a new organization controlled by them. Security guards were brought in by the new owners to lock out members of the congregation from entering the church facility. For four weeks in a row, Sunday worship services were held in the open air and once along the hallway at a nearby senior citizens' home. The incident made headline news in the local *Vancouver Sun*. A legal challenge was launched and a court injunction was granted to reopen the church while the case was being processed at the B.C. Supreme Court.

David was in his early 30s then, and he struggled between fighting a full-fledged court battle for God's sake and abiding by the apostle Paul's teaching about letting God take revenge (Romans 12:19; 1 Corinthians 6:6). In the end, he resolved to trust in the Lord and take steps that were both biblical and legal. He rallied the congregation to pray and live by faith. He also taught them to overcome evil with good through re-

*David: a passion for church growth.*

spect, acceptance and love for others who held different views. David's actions paid off and the court case was settled in favor of the church after a long and arduous two years. Not only that, in the midst of those tumultuous years, his ministry continued strongly and the congregation grew in numbers and reputation. They cared for one another and provided financial support to cover legal expenses.

## TIME TO MOVE ON

Less than two years later, the church was blessed with exponential growth to 400. It became evident that additional pastoral resources and building facilities were needed. A pastoral search committee was formed. Unfortunately, the search process led to misunderstandings between David and the moderator, and criticism from a few church members. David agonized over the strained relationships and concluded that rather than be preoccupied with personnel issues, his time could be better utilized on ministry matters. After much praying and fasting, and with the support of his family, he decided to tender his resignation. Despite numerous attempts made by church members and the moderator to change his decision, they failed to dissuade David from leaving.

David was 36 and he rededicated himself to the Lord. He hoped to serve in an established church denomination with practices and beliefs closely identified to his theology.

## GOD'S TIMING

God is faithful and his timing is impeccable. Within 12 days of David's resignation, on May 12, 1978, David met with Herb Neufeld (chair of the Board of Church Extension of the B.C. Conference) and Nick Dyck (general secretary) to explore church planting opportunities. After much consideration and research into the history, the confession of faith and organizational structures of the Mennonite Brethren, he sensed God's calling. During the B.C. Conference annual convention in June 1978, David was formally accepted as a church planter and pastor of the Richmond Chinese MB Church (subsequently known as Bethel Chinese Christian MB Church). This marked the beginning of David's 29 years of service with the B.C. Conference of MB Churches. At Bethel Chinese Christian MB, David experienced God's miraculous provision and great blessings. His distinctive way of leading—constantly encouraging people to embrace new ideas within the confines of the Scriptures, learning incessantly and taking steps of faith—were evident throughout his ministry. It bore fruit.

The newly-formed church relocated three times from one rental facility to another during its first two years. In 1981, despite skyrocketing housing prices in Vancouver, a small church with seating capacity of 120 was purchased. This building was soon outgrown and an extension was constructed in 1984, accommodating a total of 170 attenders. By 1993, with a steady increase in congregation, another expansion plan was conceived.

In 1995, while David was finishing his post-graduate studies in Hong Kong during a sabbatical, a church building with a price tag of $1.2 million and a seating capacity of around 400 went up for sale in Vancouver. It was strategically located, close to bus routes and mass transit, and with a high Chinese population nearby. It would provide a great locale for evangelism. After sharing his vision and the financial need, God inspired a Christian couple in Hong Kong to pledge $200,000 towards the pur-

*David and fellow Chinese delegates Yu Cheng, Aymon Chu and John Redekop at the 1982 Canadian Conference in Three Hills.*

chase of the property. David relayed this news to the deacons. To his surprise, they expressed no interest in pursuing this opportunity: David was out of the country and, more importantly, the church building fund had a mere $44,000. With the firm conviction that the building was in the right neighborhood, David encouraged the deacons to be faithful and courageous servants. Once again, by God's grace, a unanimous decision was reached to move forward and the property was bought for $1.13 million.

This building, with approximately 14,000 square feet, provided ample room to launch and grow various ministry initiatives. Soon after the move to the new church building in 1995, David decided to formalize the adult Sunday school curriculum and started an in-house Bible school. A full-time director of Christian education position was created to provide guidance to a more systematic approach to biblical learning.

## TRAINING IN EVANGELISM

After years of one-on-one evangelism, David realized that eventually it would be necessary to move large groups. David decided to change his strategy to one of training the trainers. The Evangelism Explosion program was introduced to the church in 1991. Evangelism Explosion (EE) is a ministry that trains people to share their faith in Christ and bring people to God. It utilizes components such as prayer, actual on-the-job training where experienced persons lead the inexperienced, and the principle of spiritual multiplication.

While this program became a core part of the evangelism training among Bethel church members, it was also opened to pastors of other local churches. After becoming a certified Evangelism Explosion trainer in 1992, David conducted eight formal EE training programs for Christians in Vancouver, Venezuela and Calgary, besides within his own local church.

With an ever-increasing Chinese population in Vancouver's suburbs, David had a vision of planting a church in its neighboring North Shore. In 1992, a survey was conducted in the target community. Unfortunately, due to a lack of resources, the plan had to be put on hold. In 1995, with significant growth in the congregation, Rev. Alan Choi was added to the pastoral team and became responsible for evangelism training and church planting. In 1997, about twenty church members were recruited to start the church plant in a rental facility in North Vancouver. Initially, the new church was completely supported by the mother church. In less than two years, North Shore Bethel Christian MB Church became completely independent. The year 2007 marked another major milestone: a church building was purchased in a neighborhood that rarely had church properties for sale.

## FOCUSSED ON MISSION

David has always been mission-minded. From the inception of the church, 10% of church's total income had been designated as a fund for missions. This fund was used to support various missionary organizations and evangelistic ministries. After the church became debt free in 1988, David took further steps to emphasize the importance of supporting missionaries around the world, witnessing for Christ and partaking in short-term mission trips. Annual mission conferences were held along with frequent invitations to missionaries to speak at Sunday services. David led by example by making several mission trips to Venezuela, Surinam, Panama and Thailand. In Venezuela, David assisted missionaries in starting up two MB churches and training local church leaders. He also led short-term mission teams from his church to Venezuela and China.

## SHADOW OF DEATH

During a routine physical check-up in 2003, the lab results showed a higher than normal PSA (Prostate Specific Antigen) reading. Subsequently, David was diagnosed with prostate cancer. Even though he was completely dumbfounded because there had been no prior symptoms, David was very much at peace because he knew God was in control. A surgical operation removed the cancerous tissues.

But after the apparently successful surgery, massive internal bleeding suddenly occurred. Within two days, he was transfused with seven bags of blood and five bags of plasma before his condition stabilized. According to the nurses in the recovery room, David's non-stop bleeding would normally have been fatal. Indeed, God was merciful and accompanied David as he walked through the valley of the shadow of death. After five days he was discharged from the hospital. David slowly recovered and returned to work three months later. His vigour in ministry never abated.

## PASSING THE BATON

In spite of many ups and downs, David Poon's 43-year-journey after accepting his calling to pastoral ministry was filled with affirmations and blessings. In hindsight, David said he found God to be truly amazing in the way he saved, moulded and led a weakling like him all these years. At the age of 65 in December 2007, David retired from Bethel Chinese Christian MB Church and passed the baton for shepherding on to Rev. Wing Wong.

Asked about principles/learning he wanted to share in his pastoral journey, David cited the following:

- It is important to lead by example and be a good witness at all times.
- When dealing with conflicts, focus on facts rather than personalities.
- Always strive for unity.
- Be available and genuine in loving and caring for others.
- Always handle money matters with transparency and full accountability.
- Spousal and family support is vital.

Retirement for David does not mean "not working" anymore. God continues to use him in other capacities, particularly building upon his experience and passion for mission. Since 2008, David has been on the road again, serving as an honorary itinerant minister with the China Evangelistic Mission (CEM). His role involves caring for, supporting and encouraging missionaries of CEM in South Africa, Hong Kong, Macau, Thailand, Taiwan, Myanmar, Cambodia and Germany. David is also an advisor to the MB Chinese Church Association, a fellowship of pastors among over 15 Chinese MB churches in Greater Vancouver.

## HIGHLIGHTS OF BETHEL CHINESE CHRISTIAN MB CHURCH
### 1978 TO 2007

Nov 5, 1978   First Sunday worship service held at Fraserview MB Church in Vancouver with an attendance of 62.

Jan,1979   Moved with Fraserview MB Church to Richmond.

Feb 11, 1979   Rented Richmond Bethel MB Church for church services.

Nov 4, 1979   First church board inaugurated.

June, 1980   Church formally accepted as a member church of B.C. Conference of MB Churches.

Aug 10, 1980   Moved again to a rental facility at Wilson Heights United Church in Vancouver.

June 22, 1981   Purchased own church building at 235 E 15th Ave, Vancouver.

June 19, 1988   Paid off all bank loans.

Nov 4, 1988   Began first annual mission conference to promote and support missions.

June 3, 1994   Rev. Poon led a mission team to Venezuela.

June 28, 1995   Purchased the building of Collingwood United Church at 3215 School Ave., Vancouver.

Aug 13, 1995   First Sunday worship service at new location.

Sept 7, 1997   Planted North Shore Bethel Christian MB Church and began first Sunday worship service at Sutherland Bible Chapel in North Vancouver. Rev. Alan Choi was appointed as pastor of the new church.

Mar 19, 2000   Paid off all loans from offerings and sale of old church.

Aug 11, 2000   Rev. and Mrs. Poon led a mission team to China

Aug 2007   North Shore Bethel Christian MB Church purchased a church building in North Vancouver.

Dec 31, 2007   Rev. Poon retired and Rev. Wing Wong was installed as senior pastor on January 1, 2008.

## SOURCES

Contents of this chapter were based largely on interviews with Rev. David Poon and several books, articles and church records. These included the *Vancouver Sun* (May 6, 1974), *The Province* (June 11, 1977), the *Mennonite Brethren Herald* (Feb 9, 1996), the 1978 yearbook of the annual convention of the B.C. MB Conference and Ruth Hitchcock's *The Good Hand of our God* (Elgin, Il: David C. Cook, 1975).

## Katie Funk Wiebe

# A WOMAN'S VOICE
# TO THE CHURCH

*By Doug Heidebrecht*

As a young girl growing up in northern Saskatchewan, Katie Funk had quietly suppressed the small voice within her that longed to write:

> I'm afraid to be a writer…I'm afraid to put things down on paper, things I might regret later on, as if these things really applied to me. But then they do, these things that I want to write are my thoughts, the things that keep me going, the things that slow me up and make me wish I was anywhere but where I am. I shouldn't be afraid. I know I shouldn't. No one will ever see these things I write. No one will ever know they belong to a girl who once had hopes and dreams, but who never saw them realized.

Yet fifty years later Katie Funk Wiebe was recognized by the editors of *The Mennonite*, representing the largest group of Mennonites in the United States, as one of the top twenty people during the twentieth century who had significantly influenced the faith and life of Mennonite people. Katie was honoured for raising "the credibility of Mennonite writing" and being an advocate for women and widows. Most Canadian Mennonite Brethren are likely unaware of the far-reaching impact Katie Funk Wiebe has had through her writing.

---

*The Writer*
Doug Heidebrecht is the director for the Centre for Mennonite Brethren Studies in Winnipeg, a position he assumed in 2008. Prior to that he taught for many years at Bethany College in Hepburn, Sask. Doug and his wife Sherry are members of the Westwood Community Church [MB] of Winnipeg.

Katie's early interest in writing led her in a direction no other Mennonite Brethren woman had travelled. She recognized the significant challenges she faced. "I realize that in writing anything I have two myths to overcome: first, that God expects very little of a woman, particularly a Mennonite woman, except to sew and cook; and secondly, that evangelical Christianity is really not a thinking person's religion." It was Katie's ability to transcend both these assumptions that enabled her to resonate with readers across denominational boundaries.

At the heart of Katie's writing is her love for the church and her passion for what the church could be. Katie writes from within the church, giving voice to those who are often silent or even marginalized: women, younger adults, lay people, widows and older adults. Even though Katie has lived and worked among the Mennonite Brethren all her life, her own journey among them has been a crucible for addressing critical issues facing the broader church.

## IMMIGRANT CHILD

Katie's parents, Jacob and Anna (Janzen) Funk emigrated from Rosenthal, southern Russia (now Ukraine), to Canada in 1923 as part of a Mennonite exodus following the Communist revolution. Katie was born in September 1924 in Laird, a small village about 40 miles north of Saskatoon, Saskatchewan. A few years later the Funk family moved a little farther northwest to Blaine Lake, where Jacob managed the local OK Economy grocery store. Blaine Lake was an ethnically diverse community of mainly first generation immigrants: Russian, English, Scottish, Irish, French, Ukrainian, Indian, Polish, German and now one Mennonite family. During the summers the Funk family continued to attend the Mennonite Brethren church across the river in Laird.

As a girl, Katie worked in her father's store, read as much as she could and did so well in school that she graduated in 1942 with a 93% average and the Governor General of Canada Bronze Medal. Katie's experience growing up in Blaine Lake provided her with a unique mix of theologies ranging from a forthright Mennonite Brethren evangelicalism, which focused on crisis conversion, missions and eschatology, to the less confining views of the United Church, which centred around loving God and doing good.

Following high school, Katie worked for several years in Saskatoon as a bookkeeper and stenographer, although she was rather directionless, with no goals for the future except the anticipation of romance, marriage and a family. While she called herself a Christian, she reflects later that she wasn't really a disciple until she had a profound encounter with God at the age of 19 through a random reading of Oswald Chambers' devotional, *My Utmost for His Highest*. Katie then began reading her Bible avidly and spoke openly in youth meetings regarding her newfound zeal, so much so that she was soon elected president of the youth group at the Saskatoon Mennonite Brethren Church.

It wasn't long, though, before she was asked to step down at the request of the pastor and church council. Katie readily consented without giving much thought as to why a woman wouldn't be allowed to do the Lord's work if she was the best suited person for the task. Katie was baptized near the end of the summer in 1945, just before she left for Winnipeg to attend Mennonite Brethren Bible College (MBBC).

*As a teacher, Katie was first Mrs. Wiebe, then soon, simply "Katie."*

### RECRUITED BY THE
### PRESIDENT

Katie had been recruited as a student by J.B. Toews, president of the college, who also asked her to serve as his personal secretary. The clear conservative social boundaries, reinforced by strict rules at MBBC, were foreign to Katie's sense of freedom fostered by her experiences growing up in Blaine Lake and her life in Saskatoon. When Katie joined the staff of the student publication, she began working with its new editor, Walter Wiebe, a student from Yarrow, B.C. who had served as a conscientious objector during the war.

Walter proposed to Katie in the spring of 1946, while leaning over the counter in the college office. The next fall Katie returned to MBBC, while Walter remained in Yarrow to care for his parents and to teach at the Elim Bible School. Despite JB's consternation at losing his secretary, Katie and Walter were married on a Thursday evening, August 21, 1947, in the Saskatoon Mennonite Brethren Church.

Following their wedding, Katie and Walter moved to Yarrow, B.C., where Walter continued to teach at Elim and Katie struggled through one of the most difficult years of her life, surrounded by "cramped quarters, limited budgets and lonely days." In the spring of 1948 they returned to Saskatchewan, where their first daughter, Joanna Katherine, was born in June. Walter initially taught a short-term high school program on the campus of Bethany Bible Institute in Hepburn and then grade school for the next two years at the nearby one-room Hudson Bay public school. It was during this time that Katie and Walter spent a lot of time sorting through what they thought God wanted of their life together and one evening they knelt beside the kitchen table and committed themselves to a literature ministry within the church.

In the summer of 1950, Walter and Katie moved to Winnipeg so Walter might return to his theological studies at MBBC. Their second daughter, Susan Helene, was born in Winnipeg in July 1951. After Walter graduated with a Bachelor of Theology degree in 1952, they moved back to Hepburn, where Walter took a teaching position at Bethany Bible Institute. That fall their dream of a literature ministry found expression when Walter began editing *The Youth Worker*, a publication of the Canadian Mennonite Brethren Youth Committee, which sought to support a growing focus on youth work within churches. As a result of Walter's busy teaching and preaching schedule, Katie took on more of the editing work to the point that she was producing the entire publication under Walter's name.

### NO ASSIGNMENT FOR HER

The Hepburn MB Church ordained Walter to the ministry in October 1953, and Katie reflected later that the imprint of the preacher's sweaty fingers on her new black velvet hat left her with the sign of ordination but no assignment or recognition. Their third daughter, Christine Ruth, was born in Waldheim in November 1954. In 1956 the Hepburn Church called Walter to serve as their pastor. Around this time Katie typed herself a little note:

> Today I have been doing a lot of thinking about writing. Is it worthwhile considering seriously or shall I just forget the thing altogether? The whole problem seems to resolve itself around the matter of having something to write about. If I have nothing to say, there is no use in writing that bit of nothing down on paper.

Katie's name was added as a co-editor to *The Youth Worker* in 1957 and she increasingly began to sign her name to the work she was doing, often with a "kfw." In 1958, after only two years, Walter resigned from pastoral work in order to devote himself more fully to his studies and their vision of a wider literature ministry.

*Whether writing or speaking, Katie wrapped words around thoughts well.*

They moved to Virgil, Ontario, where Walter taught at Eden Christian College. That fall, however, he began to feel ill and Katie slowly watched his joy and energy dissipate. James Philip, their youngest, was born in November 1958 in Niagara-on-the-Lake. After Christmas, while in Hillsboro, Kansas for Publication Board meetings, Walter collapsed and emergency surgery revealed a ruptured appendix, which likely had happened already in September. Walter spent that spring recuperating. It left the family without an income and created a lot of soul-searching regarding whether God had actually called them to a literature ministry, despite these setbacks.

In the summer of 1959, Walter and Katie moved to Kitchener so Walter could study at Waterloo Lutheran College as well as teach at the Ottawa Street MB Bible School. Walter finally completed the requirements for a Bachelor of Arts degree in 1961, yet despite this accomplishment, he continued to experience health complications. He had to have a large cyst removed from his abdomen in May and his appendix taken out in July.

Walter decided to attend Syracuse University in New York State in September 1961 in order to pursue a Master of Arts degree in religious journalism, leaving Katie with the children in Kitchener, where she worked for a temporary secretarial service. During this year Katie published several freelance articles in *Christian Living* and *The Canadian Mennonite*. In 1960, Katie had also been invited by Orlando Harms to write a column, "Women and the Church," for *The Christian Leader*. She eventually began it in January 1962 for five dollars a column. Katie launched her column by asking whether the church had a relevant message for women in the midst of a changing society.

As Walter was finishing his first year of studies at Syracuse, Orlando Harms invited him to come to Hillsboro to work for the Mennonite Brethren Publishing House as the book and literature editor. Katie was offered a job with the General Conference Board of Missions as a research assistant, which later turned into bookkeeping. Even though Walter noticed another growth in his abdomen, doctors approved their immigration visas to the United States. So in September 1962, Walter and Katie moved to Hillsboro, Kansas with great anticipation of seeing their vision for a literature ministry finally becoming a reality.

## NEW BEGINNINGS

A few weeks after arriving in Hillsboro, Walter began to feel ill again and a tumour was discovered growing rapidly in his abdomen. In the early morning of November 17, 1962, Walter died at the age of 44. Katie was now a widow in a foreign country, surrounded by strangers, facing the prospect of raising her four children alone. Why did God not heal Walter? Had God really led them to this place only to abandon them? While Katie was plagued with questions, she realized that God had also been slowly developing in her a sense of trust during the last four difficult years: "not as a strong blinding light, but as a glimmer of hope in the gathering darkness."

Initially, Katie's first priority was the care of her family, which meant that she now needed to work full-time in order to pay for groceries and the rent. She began working at the Mennonite Brethren Publishing House as an editorial assistant doing copy editing and proofreading. In the fall of 1966, Katie was offered a position teaching one section of freshman English at Tabor College in Hillsboro, despite having no degree and no teaching experience. Katie embarked on her new career at Tabor College, teaching her first class of English composition during her lunch hour. Katie was soon offered a full-time position in the fall of 1967, which also included the opportunity to continue her own education. Katie graduated with a Bachelor of Arts degree from Tabor College in 1968 and immediately began work towards a Master's degree in English at Wichita State University, which she eventually received in 1972. At the age of 48, ten years after the death of Walter, Katie

*At church gatherings, Katie would seldom be off by herself.*

was in many ways just beginning her work.

In hindsight, Katie recognized that Walter's death was the one "experience that probably had the most far-reaching effect on me, my faith, my outlook on life and my vocation," because "widowhood changed the road signs and sent me down a new path." Katie had experienced a profound loss of identity and began to re-examine not only her role as a mother within her family, but also as a woman in the church. Katie soon realized that her long-time interest in the work of the church had been experienced through her husband's position, and now she found herself completely disconnected from the church's decision-making processes. Furthermore, Katie's resistance to the subtle pressure in the church to accept the inactive and subdued role of a widow encouraged her to evaluate the impact of the church's teaching that women "needed only to be submissive and passive."

Katie had recognized for some time already the "vast reservoir of untapped potential" of women in the church, but it wasn't until after her husband's death that she began to call on the church to stop responding to women—who challenged traditional patterns of ministry—with "a gentle patting into submissiveness back to the kitchen and the sewing circle." She urged Mennonite Brethren conference leaders and pastors to "try to close the gap between what women of the church are capable of doing and what there is available to do." Katie felt strongly that defining "women's roles only in terms of limitations, rather than opportunities, was wrong."

### ASK WOMEN FOR IDEAS

Katie's own perception of her identity as a person, not just a widow or even a woman, presented her with the challenge "to write as a person to persons, not just as a woman to women." On March 28, 1967, Katie changed the name of her column in *The Christian Leader* from "Women and the Church" to "Viewpoint." Her first three columns highlighted three groups of people in the church—women, young adults and lay people—who were often "shut out from the more important decision-making processes of the church or [had] been given only token membership in them." Katie wondered "what would happen if some of the boards and agencies of our church and conferences would ask the women for their ideas and not just their work." She also observed that "when the church is no longer communicating vitally to its young adults, we are simply mumbling to ourselves in a corner."

Finally, Katie recognized the need for the Mennonite Brethren constituency to hear the voice of the lay person "who hasn't all the background information but who is sometimes concerned, sometimes bewildered, sometimes ready to offer an insight." In her attempt to represent different perspectives through her column, Katie stated, "The main reason I write is not to make you come around to my viewpoint, but to cause you to think about the issue discussed."

During the 1960s and early 1970s, Katie was virtually the only voice seeking to prod Mennonite Brethren to address the implications of the changing status of women for life in the church. Katie shared, "As I felt my own pain and that of other women because of the church's disregard for the treasures buried in its own pews—the gifts of its women—I felt compelled to speak out. These gifts lay deeply unused under a pile of proof texts and cultural conditioning." But Katie often felt that "writing about the issue was a monologue, not a discussion."

Katie's practice of submitting her *Christian Leader* columns to other Mennonite periodicals carried her reflections about women in the church beyond her Mennonite Brethren context. In the *Gospel Herald*, Katie's 1970 column, "Liberation—For Men and Women," was "the first article

*Katie with her children, Christine, Susan, Joanna and James. Christine has passed away.*

that made a blatant plea for [Old] Mennonites to consider ideas coming out of the feminist movement." Katie's "invitational approach" that encouraged people to re-examine the church's traditional stance toward women was well received within the wider Mennonite community in a way that did not always happen among Mennonite Brethren.

Katie was involved in the initial attempts by North American evangelicals to address the question of women's roles in the church, including the 1973 Denver conference, "Evangelical Perspectives on Women's Role and Status," and the 1975 Evangelical Women's Caucus in Washington, D.C. Katie was also appointed to the Mennonite Central Committee (MCC) Taskforce for Women in the Church and Society in 1975, where she represented Mennonite Brethren, even though no Mennonite Brethren board took responsibility for her participation. These involvements introduced Katie to women who shared her concerns, yet represented the broader evangelical and Mennonite world.

### INVITED INTO THE DISCUSSION

It wasn't until 1986 that Katie officially became involved in the Mennonite Brethren conversation about women in church leadership. She was invited to be part of the Women in Ministry Task Force, which drafted the first resolution prepared by both men and women. In 1987 Katie was also the first woman to address a General Conference convention as one of the key speakers. Later she would co-edit *Your Daughters Shall Prophesy: Women in Ministry in the Church* (1992), which was used by Mennonite Brethren congregations as a study guide for reflecting on the issue of women in church leadership.

Katie observed that the lack of recognition for women's involvement in the church was linked to the "almost total absence of the contribution of women to the church in recorded church history, particularly Mennonite history." Katie intentionally set out to reveal the "underside" of history by telling stories of women who had often been overlooked because they were not part of official historical accounts. Her first book, *Have Cart, Will Travel*, was a 1974 adaptation of Mennonite Brethren missionary Paulina Foote's autobiography, *God's Hand Over My Nineteen Years in China*. Katie also told the story of the Bethel Deaconess Hospital School of Nursing in Newton, Kansas, as well as stories of Mennonite Brethren and Krimmer Mennonite Brethren women who made significant, though often undocumented, contributions to the life of the church in *Women Among the Brethren*. In *Who Are the Mennonite Brethren?* Katie provided a conversational overview of the history and beliefs of the Mennonite Brethren church, which was used widely by congregations in discipleship.

## BEYOND THE MENNONITE COMMUNITY

Katie's popularity as a writer expanded beyond the Mennonite community, where her regular columns were well-known, when she published *Alone: A Widow's Search for Joy* in 1976. *Alone*, the story of her husband's death and her experience as a widow, sold thousands of copies and demonstrated how readers resonated with Katie's vulnerability and honesty. Katie regularly told her own students, "Writing is often an exercise in self-revelation…the more personal the writing, the more universal." Katie now was giving voice to the widow as she put a human face to a label that was so easily ignored in the church.

*Alone* also reflected Katie's unique autobiographical approach to storytelling, which enabled her to share the struggles of her own journey. Katie maintained, "I cherish the opportunity to share my stumbling through life with others. After I have lived it, why hang on to it?" In 1988, Katie wrote *Bless Me Too, My Father*, which won the prestigious Silver Angel award and featured her reflections about change, particularly theological change, during middle adulthood. During her retirement years, Katie wrestled with her own experience of aging in *Border Crossing: A Spiritual Journey* (1995) as well as looked back on her childhood and Mennonite roots in *The Store-*

*keeper's Daughter: A Memoir* (1997). In 2009 Katie shared the difficulties and joys of her journey as an adult, from a naïve college student to octogenarian in *You Never Gave Me a Name: One Mennonite Woman's Story.*

Katie retired from teaching English at Tabor College in 1990 after a 24-year career and was honoured with the appointment of Professor Emeritus. A year later Katie moved to Wichita, Kansas to begin her retirement years. After thirty years, she completed her last "Viewpoint" column for *The Christian Leader* on December 31, 1991. In many ways, her columns had become a journal of her life and concerns. Katie modelled a deep trust in God's Word, an openness to change her mind when needed, and the ability to invite others to explore the questions she did not flinch from asking herself. She demonstrated that ordinary people can be theologians *par excellence*, when they have the "courage to shape faith by looking honestly for answers to God-questions."

Katie's attention now turned to another group of people who were often ignored or undervalued in the church: older adults. Their gifts and talents, like those of women, often lay untapped in congregations. Katie embraced a new challenge: "I want to be a catcher in the rye for older adults before they fall off the cliff and think of themselves as nobodies. I want them to keep growing." Through writing, speaking and educational programs, Katie sought to create awareness within the church of the needs of older adults as well as the value of their contributions. Katie also shifted from teaching college students how to write to encouraging older adults to write their own memoirs.

## KATIE THE WRITER

Katie and Walter's persistence in following their sense of God's call to a literature ministry took a very different route than they had anticipated, yet it has also borne fruit far beyond their expectations. Even though Katie essentially started writing in her late thirties, she has published over two thousand articles, columns and book reviews, not to mention twenty books. Katie has openly shared her life and by doing so has invited others not only to listen but also to recognize themselves in her story. Perhaps Katie's greatest gift to the church is "wrapping words around thoughts readers were struggling to articulate." Her courage to express the ideas and questions of an ordinary woman continues to challenge men and women to faithful discipleship in the midst of life's struggles.

Despite the longevity of her writing career, Katie's message to the church has remained surprisingly consistent over the years. On the one hand, Katie encourages ordinary people in the church to engage in honest self-examination and deeper theological reflection. On the other hand,

Katie challenges the church to recognize the diversity of God's gifts and to involve all people in the work of the church—women, young adults, lay people, widows and older adults—without distinction. Katie's core message, while prophetic at times, also reveals a deep love and passion for the church, motivating her to write. Katie recently wrote, "Although I am eighty-three [in 2007], it is not yet time to pull back. I tell myself it is important to keep reaching for goals I personally will not win....I want to die climbing."

## SOURCES

Among the many sources for this chapter, the writer drew on many of Katie Funk Wiebe's columns in *The Christian Leader*, books of hers such as *Alone, A Widow's Search for Joy; Border Crossing, a Spiritual Journey; You Never Gave Me a Name, One Mennonite Woman's Story; Your Daughters Shall Prophesy* (which Katie co-edited); *Have Cart, Will Travel; Our Lamps were Lit: An Informal History of the Bethel Deaconness Hospital School of Nursing; Women Among the Brethren* and *Who are the Mennonite Brethren?*; and other of her writings in periodicals such as *The Mennonite, Youth Worker Program Helps, Christian Living, Direction,* the *Mennonite Brethren Herald, The Canadian Mennonite* and *Mennonite Life.* Other sources were found in *The Blaine Lake Echo;* the Saskatoon Central MB Church family registry; a 2006 thesis entitled *Discovering Voices among Peculiar Quietness* by Rachel Swartzendruber, written for a communications degree from Wichita State University; the Mennonite Brethren General Conference 1987 Yearbook and finally Katie Funk Wiebe's own correspondence and papers. A copy of this chapter with appropriate footnoting is on file at the Centre for Mennonite Brethren Studies, Winnipeg.

# John H. Redekop

# ALWAYS A RECOGNIZED VOICE

*By James Toews*

It began as a backroom concession. In 1963 at the Canadian Conference convention in Clearbrook, a 31-year-old John Redekop, the most vocal of the voices calling for change, had been publicly rebuffed. As a demonstration of good faith, why not ask him to write a few words in the newly-formed publication called the *Mennonite Brethren Herald*?

The article ran January 3, 1964 and was entitled, "On Constructive Criticism." For the next 40 years the Personal Opinion of John H. Redekop was an MBH fixture. It was always a "personal opinion," but as a recognized voice. Editors and conference leaders rolled over but John kept writing.

It tracked and commented on the developments in the world of Canadian MBs over seasons of dramatic external and internal changes. John became, arguably, the most well-known Canadian MB and at times the most trusted voice of the conference.

Forty years later, on February 28, 2003, the last Personal Opinion column, entitled "The Iraq War," appeared and a chapter of our history closed.

---

*The Writer*

James Toews has been pastor of Neighbourhood (MB) Church in Nanaimo since 1987. He and Janet moved there upon his graduation from the MB Biblical Seminary. It was their first church assignment and may well be their last. Very few pastors have the privilege of serving in one place during the entire period of their children's lives and they are very thankful for this extraordinary blessing.

## TEACHER FATHER

Like most of the Mennonite Brethren leaders arising from the '50s and '60s, John's origins came from one of the centres of the Canadian MB world. The youngest of six children, he was born to Jacob F. and Agnes Redekop in Herbert, Sask., on November 29, 1932. His father was a teacher in the Herbert Bible School and, as was typical at that time, combined his teaching profession with farming. The commitment that John's father exhibited in this dual vocation was a reflection of the Mennonite Brethren world of the time. It was no surprise that John would commit his adult life to education.

In 1944 Jacob Redekop was invited to teach at the newly-forming Abbotsford Bible School [which later became Columbia Bible College]. Since dual incomes were the necessity of the day, this again meant buying a small farm in the Abbotsford region. The farm and the home were extremely modest but normal within that community.

As John was growing up, the Mennonites of B.C.'s Fraser Valley were an immigrant community carving out their identities in this new land. As such, these Mennonites fit easily into the Canadian mosaic, but with their immigrant identity these Mennonites brought another dimension. They lived with a 500-year-old narrative of repeated uprooting and relocating: Holland to Prussia, Prussia to Russia, Russia to Canada. Countless smaller migrations and displacements between the major ones kept the narrative alive.

The constant winnowing of displacement and settlement produced a community and this community produced John Redekop.

While his father's generation pursued education in the hours left over after the farming was done, the prosperity of the years after World War II afforded a new generation of young men and women the luxury of higher education.

In the Fraser Valley this meant going to the University of British Columbia. And John, with a small army of Mennonite men and women made a new pilgrimage: weekdays were spent in the city and the university, and weekends back home on the farm.

Writing of that time, JR speaks of a disconnect—even a schizophrenia—that he and his colleagues lived with. Every Monday they left behind a deeply interwoven community that worked to create safe and enduring social structures. It was a community searching for stability in an unstable world.

They were then enveloped by an exhilarating world of discovery and change, but it was also a lonely world where survival and failure were very individual affairs. This was the world that challenged every stability and status quo.

These two worlds operated with vastly different standards and values.

Even more disconcerting was the fact that in this weekday world, the belief system of community woven together with biblical faith—that seemed

*John and fellow student Harvey Dyck rewarded themselves after their studies by putting ten thousand miles on this motorcycle on a tour of Europe and North Africa.*

so self-evident and cohesive on Sunday morning—was aggressively challenged.

And when they came home on Saturday the challenge was answered explicitly or implicitly: "out there is the world against which we must stand."

Every seven days they switched between two worlds in tension and each world had its self-serving retorts ready.

Given that the university challenge was directed at the very ideals that had nurtured them—the ideals of faith, family, church—this oscillating journey left deep marks on John's generation.

There were casualties. The schizophrenia left its mark and many of those who left the farm for the university did not come back. In the end it was neither the farm nor their community, but the faith that suffered the most difficult loss.

## NOT A CASUALTY

JR, however, was not a casualty. Looking back, he writes that while, during his time at UBC, his worldview was still in its infancy, his experience there left a positive mark on him. In all likelihood this was due to the strength, support and safety that his personal family and church had given him—and possibly a contrarian streak. That positive, if complex, experience laid the foundation for a deeper plunge into both higher education and church life that would follow.

The memory of his time at UBC still animates JR, and with it the enduring heart for the university student. How does one help the journey of faith that begins in the community we all want to build, but that must navigate a new understanding of faith in the university?

He was, after all, a high achiever and the world of the university rewarded him. Upon completing his undergraduate degree with a B.C. teacher certificate, John accepted an invitation to do a year's study at the Karl Ruprecht University in Heidelberg, Germany.

Completing the year in Germany, he and a fellow Canadian student Harvey Dyck decided they should do a road trip. They bought a used 225cc DKW motorcycle, learned to ride it and then travelled from Germany, through Italy, ferried to Tunisia and rode the motorcycle across the Sahara to Egypt.

John was a certified journalist and had arranged an interview with Egyptian President Gamal Abdel Nasser in Cairo which, in the end, he had to abandon after an interminable wait in the President's waiting room because their ship to Beirut was leaving.

After putting 19,000 kilometers on the motorcycle, John and Harvey returned to Heidelberg to write their exams. The product of this grand adventure was "An Illustrated Lecture" by the two at Clearbrook's Mennonite Educational Institute: "Adults .35, Students and Children .25, proceeds to be divided equally for Relief Purposes and the MEI Alumni Book Fund."

But John did come back to his community both physically and intellectually. His exotic adventures complete, he moved home, was married to Doris Nikkel and took on the safe assignment of high school teacher. For the next four years he taught high school. In the years that followed they would have four children, Wendy, Gary, Heather and Bonnie.

A deeply impactful moment during this time was the sudden and untimely death of his father. Jacob F. Redekop was a leader, both in his home and in the MB community, and his passing had a deep impact on John. It focused John's sense of responsibility first to his mother and then to the Mennonite Brethren community that his father had served with such passion and commitment. This sense of responsibility to his parents and the legacy that they had passed on to him would be an impulse that would carry him through the challenges he would face as a change agent within the church.

*John greeting Jacob Fast, a Baptist leader from the Soviet Union, at the 1978 General Conference.*

## CHURCHMAN WITH QUESTIONS

John came home intellectually. Far from being separated from his community as were many of the young intellectuals of his time, he self-consciously engaged it. It was clear that as an intellectual and a strong personality, John would find himself in tension with the MB community. He saw three choices before him. He could simply live with and accept things he was uncomfortable with. Or he could leave the conference and find another church community. Or, finally, he could stay and work within the structures to bring the changes he felt passionate about. He deliberately chose the latter. This choice would at times be severely tested in the years that followed, but it stood.

Upon arriving back in his home community in 1956, John took on the assignment of English-language secretary for the B.C. Mennonite Brethren Conference. This began a life as a fixture in the MB conferences. John became a churchman.

In another pattern that would follow John, he engaged in several streams of activities concurrently. While managing to remain fully involved in the

Canadian MB world, in 1960 John left for a year of graduate studies at the University of California, Berkeley, followed by doctoral studies at the University of Washington in Seattle.

In fact, it was while working on his doctorate in political science at the University of Washington that John faced the first of the defining challenges of his life as a Canadian Mennonite Brethren. It came around the matter of language.

As a people, Mennonites had moved with their languages. During the 1950s they still remained a predominantly German-speaking community while living in an English-speaking world. But the younger generation was moving on. The language of the home and church might be German, but the language of the city was English. The debates were heated and often divisive.

To preserve the German language in the church community a Committee for the German Language was formed to stem the tide of English, and the debate about the place of German was vigorously engaged.

In 1963, from this place on the "inside," John and a small group decided to publicly question the validity of such a committee and even to propose that its mandate be discontinued. John and the leader would deliver speeches to that end. At the last moment the other withdrew and John delivered the only speech. John was now a lightening rod in a confusing and at times divisive debate.

He was severely criticized for the dissension it caused and the criticism stung him deeply. It is typical of John's involvement as an MB churchman that this crisis and rebuff could launch his career as the most prolific, visible and longest running voice of the Mennonite Brethren in the second half of the 20th century, beginning with the article, "On Constructive Criticism."

The phrase "on the other hand" could well represent a significant part of JR's voice. While not really a genuine contrarian, JR became famous and infamous for always asking detailed questions about the implications of the actions and decisions of the Mennonite Brethren conference.

German had been part of the historic MB identity—but was it a matter of the faith? And if it was not, then why have a "Committee To Preserve The German Language"?

While they were logical, such questions were not always met with gracious responses. Given John's propensity to ask questions of long-standing presuppositions, it is perhaps easier to understand his choice of academic study.

## A POLITICAL SCIENCE CAREER?

Although MBs did have the ambivalence to higher education common to agrarian and pietistic cultures, they also sent their brightest students off for advanced studies. Biblical studies surpassed agrarian pursuits and needed no justification, but it was not just pastors who were sent to the universities. Among John's colleagues were numerous future physicians, business people, historians, philosophers, literary critics, writers, psychologists and even lawyers.

It was the lawyers who pressed the leading edge of the Anabaptist view of church and state. The legal profession, even if it was not directly an arm of the state, was viewed with deep suspicion.

But John chose none of these fields for his graduate studies; he chose political science. Only graduate studies in military tactics would have challenged the Anabaptist presuppositions of his heritage more directly. But there he was, an Anabaptist political scientist, an apparent contradiction in terms. He made it his life mission to reconcile these two.

Even in choosing the subject of his PhD dissertation at the University of Washington, John continued to stretch into territory that was both unusual and applicable to his community. The political science student made American religious fundamentalism and its merger with the political right wing his field of study. While ostensibly apolitical, a significant number of Mennonites were attracted to these two movements.

His specific subject was Billy James Hargis and the Christian Crusade organization that he founded. During the time of John's research the Christian Crusade was at the apex of its reach and power.

What makes this 1965 dissertation interesting is John's willingness to engage this organization as a real voice within American evangelicalism, and to do so in a manner that elicited a measure of respect from the Christian Crusade leaders for the balanced manner in which he dealt with them.

The evidence of this was the fact that, having published a book very critical of them, John was invited back to the Christian Crusade headquarters for a public debate with their leading scholar.

The ability to remain dispassionate in the midst of very heated debates filled with extreme and volatile language served him well in this context. It didn't hurt that he had a rapier-like intellect and a quick access to facts. It also probably served him well that in many cases the complexity and depth of his argument was lost on those he engaged.

It is a testament to John's determination to remain part of the Anabaptist world—and that world's tolerance for diversity—that John the political scientist became one of the best-known voices in the Mennonite Brethren conference and even in the larger Anabaptist world.

In 1964, after completing his PhD at the University of Washington, he accepted a position at Pacific College (now Fresno Pacific University), Fresno.

## RETURN TO CANADA

In 1968 he took on the position of Associate Professor of Political Science at Waterloo Lutheran University (Wilfrid Laurier University after 1973). This was to be his home for his academic career. He became full professor in 1971 and chaired various departments. Partly driven by the memory of his own journey into the academy, John cared for his students, not just for their academic prowess but as people on complex life paths. In 1992 he was given the Outstanding Teacher of the Year award.

Here the Waterloo MB Church became his church home and he served it with the same tireless energy that he gave to all his pursuits.

Back in Canada, established in a solid church home and in a stable employment, John would make his imprint as a mature churchman.

During the years that followed, the annual conventions of provincial, national and bi-national levels were the forums in which MBs most visibly shaped their identities. These being the places of change and conference activity, John threw his considerable energy and passions into them.

As an academic, he was soon asked to sit on the boards of various colleges (1968-77, Mennonite Brethren Bible College, Winnipeg; 1973-87, Mennonite Brethren Biblical Seminary, Fresno). Often John was part of the transitioning discussions that took place in these schools. In the case of MBBS, this involved complex negotiations of the governance of a binational seminary as well as the later partnership that MBBS took on with the ACTS consortium at Trinity Western University in Langley.

John became assistant moderator and then moderator for the Canadian Mennonite Brethren (1980-87). During this time several historic events took place. In 1984 the Quebec conference was accepted into the Canadian Conference and French, not German, became the second language of the conference.

In 1986, John delivered a formal apology to the Mennonite Church of Canada for the practice for excommunicating MBs who married GCs. This took place at his home church, Waterloo Mennonite Brethren, but it was given for all those churches where this had happened.

## ANABAPTISTS IN THE WORLD

John was also involved with MCC and served on its Canadian board from 1983 to 1991. Again he found himself, as a political scientist, uniquely placed in a world that was coming to terms with a shifting paradigm. The MCC was an organization that had risen almost spontaneously from the crisis of Mennonites in Russia in the aftermath of the Communist revolution and over time became an international relief agency. Now it was increasingly engaging with political questions.

*A highlight of the 1984 Canadian Conference, with John as moderator, was welcoming the Quebec churches into the conference. Above, the platform guests including many of the Quebec church leaders.*

*Ernest and Lydia Dyck, below, were recognized for their many years of leadership in the Quebec churches.*

Historically, politics and even governments themselves were seen as part of "the kingdom of this world," a kingdom that Anabaptist theology distinguished as separate from the kingdom of God of which followers of Jesus are a part. The tension between the historic Anabaptist view of worldly society separated from the kingdom of God came head to head during these years.

To this discussion John brought several things. First, he brought the more dispassionate language of the social sciences rather than the charged language of theology. Moreover, he brought an appreciation for the diversity within the political spectrum of the Anabaptist world. John was able to bridge the left and right wing divisions often triggered by the social activism in which MCC was increasingly engaging. It may well be that his experience of respectful engagement with the extremist Christian Crusade gave him a voice that both the left and right could appreciate, even if they were not always sure whose side he was on.

From his unusual place as an Anabaptist political scientist, John wrote, spoke and participated in study sessions that shaped the MCC during the second half of the 20th century.

But John's activities were not limited to the Anabaptist community. His twin convictions that MBs are part of the North American evangelical community and that Anabaptism has an important voice in that community propelled him to engage these connections. Again, because of John's unique position as a Mennonite political scientist and social commentator, the Evangelical Fellowship of Canada was a natural platform. He became involved at every level including vice president and then president from 1985-91.

It is unlikely that without John's drive and persistent hard work that the Mennonite Brethren presence in this national organization would have taken the prominent place that it has today.

It was only natural that a respected spokesman with political insights would be at some point courted for political office and John did have attractive overtures but except for a brief stint as Abbotsford city counsellor he remained on the sidelines of active partisanship.

## IDENTITY ISSUES

John never forgot his roots and the questions that rose from them. The topic that animated him continuously remained the mixing of faith and the ethnic culture from which he had emerged.

By the time he returned to Canada in 1968, the question of German as the language of the church had run its course. But for him the question had never merely been about German. The question was more fundamental: are Mennonite Brethren an ethnic group or a faith community? While few if any MBs identified themselves as essentially an ethnic group, John began to look at the question from another perspective—have others identified us as an ethnic community and having been so identified, has our faith been compromised?

JR's answer on both points was, "Yes!"

He researched the identity question exhaustively and the conclusion from the data seemed to him to be clear. When tested against various definitions of ethnicity, MBs were ethnic.

This led to the second question and here, too, while our Confession of Faith clearly states that MBs are a faith group, he believed his research showed this had been seriously compromised.

Just as he had done in framing the options in the early language debate, he set up the question for this one. "If we are serious about our faith, we must change our name from Mennonite Brethren." Thinking ahead to the question of what that name should be, JR posited "Evangelical Anabaptist."

What seemed so self-evident and so difficult to refute to John did not garner enough support to pass as a convention resolution.

It was as an "Evangelical Anabaptist" that JR worked very self-consciously and often brought his contrarian instincts to bear. He worked with various Anabaptist organizations such as the MCC. There he often was the evangelical voice reminding his colleagues that the early Anabaptists were not merely social activists but concerned too with the spiritual nature of the kingdom of God.

Within the MB conference, JR was the voice that reminded his readers and listeners that as Anabaptists we are not homogenous with the larger evangelical culture in North America. His studies of Billy James Hargis had given him a detailed understanding of a significant segment of the evangelical world. This aspect of evangelicalism represented, for JR, an erosion of the core of Anabaptism, a core that he worked hard to articulate and strengthen.

It was JR's desire to see Mennonite Brethren reach beyond their own Christian communities that motivated John to begin to work actively with the Evangelical Fellowship of Canada.

By the turn of the millennium MB participation in the EFC become normative, but for many years JR was one of the strongest MB voices in inter-church participation.

John taught at Wilfrid Laurier University for 26 years. In 1994, upon retirement from WLU, John and Doris moved back to Abbotsford, the community of his youth. While in "retirement" John did not slow down the pace of activities that had always characterized him. He took on a position at TWU and now engaged the Fraser Valley Mennonite Brethren.

## STILL WORKING

It was from his new base in the Fraser Valley that a whole new ministry engaged his attention, camping. The imagery he liked to use was that of the revival tent meetings of the middle decades of the 20th century. These meetings were the gates through which the community of God's people was renewed.

In John's view, camp ministry is the "big tent" of our time—the place where conversions take place, both naturally and effectively. With this vision in mind, John threw his formidable shoulder behind camp ministries. Stillwood (once known as Columbia Bible Camp) became the specific focus of his efforts and John raised millions of dollars for it from all sectors of the community.

While camp ministry consumed a significant portion of John's time, his passion for the need for an Anabaptist theology of politics remained strong. In fact, appropriately after a lifetime of wrestling with it, he wrote *Politics Under God* (Herald Press, 2007). In this he challenged the association of government with the kingdom of darkness, as spelled out in early Anabaptist confessions such as the Schleitheim Confession. This is too negative, in John's opinion, and has meant that the Anabaptist voice has not been part of political conversations. "Unacceptable!" the Anabaptist political scientist declares and undertook to articulate what he called "Anabaptist Realism."

John also remained deeply involved in the evolution of Mennonite Brethren structures. Now it was the B.C. Conference and Columbia Bible College that had direct access to his organizational, administrative and visionary gifts. During these years huge changes in the way denominations functioned were taking place. This was a time when expertise in political and social structures was desperately needed and John continued to examine and critique the changes. In 2004 his was the strongest voice arguing against structural revisions the Canadian conference had embarked upon.

Among Canadian MB leaders there is a remarkable variety of Kingdom gifts. To these John the writer, the political scientist, the activist and the churchman has added his own rich mix.

In the end, however, it may well be his 40 years as the writer of the Personal Opinion column by which he is best remembered. It is here that he was able to bring the insights of a scholar onto the ground on which Mennonite Brethren Canadians actually lived. For an Anabaptist scholar that is, after all, the ultimate test of credibility: to scratch where it itches. On that score John's place as noteworthy figure in the MB world is unambiguously established.

## SOURCES
Most of the material for this chapter came out of several extended interviews with John Redekop, years of reading his columns and observing his activity, along with reading in works of his such as *A People Apart* (Winnipeg: 1987), *Politics Under God* (Waterloo: 1987), *The American Far Right* (Grand Rapids: 1968), and *Two Sides--The Best of Personal Opinion 1964-1984* (Winnipeg: 1984).

## Walter Unger

# PLAYING THE GAME
# WITH HEART AND MIND

*By David Giesbrecht*

Walter Unger (Wally, as all his friends have known him) comes from sturdy immigrant stock. In 1923 his parents, Jakob P. and Hilda (Wiebe) Unger migrated to Canada, adapting to the rigors of farm life in Saskatchewan. Faced with the difficulties of the Depression years, the Ungers moved to St. Catharines in 1937, three years after the birth of Walter. Jakob and Hilda wasted no time in joining the local Mennonite Brethren congregation.

Little could Walter have known how deeply the ethos of these pioneer immigrants would reach into his life. The Ontario Mennonite Brethren Conference was organized in 1932 with five congregations comprising a membership of 287. For the first several decades of its existence, only few issues dominated Conference agendas. One was the establishment of a Bible school in 1937, "which became the organizing and stimulating institution [for the Conference], at least until about 1957."

As an extension of the Bible school, Eden High School (later Eden Christian College) was begun in 1945. At the same time, concern for an

---

*The Writer*
For 18 years David Giesbrecht was the library director for Columbia Bible College, Abbotsford, B.C., where Walter Unger was dean and president. He has also taught with MCC in Nigeria and Jamaica and has served on the MCC B.C. board, for some of those years as board chair. He is a member of the MB Historical Commission, and locally has worked with the Mennonite Historical Commission of B.C. and the Yarrow Research Committee. David and his wife Betty are members of the Bakerview MB Church of Abbotsford.

evangelistic outreach began to exercise Ontario MBs, resulting in the establishment of a vigorous Daily Vacation Bible School program. This effort peaked in 1967 with some 440 teachers teaching 3,000 children in various southern Ontario locations.

These three ministries powerfully impacted a youthful Wally Unger. As a teenager, he began to participate in DVBS work in Hamilton. Later he would graduate from Eden Christian College, where principal David Neumann and teacher John Wittenberg became two of his trusted advisors. Observing the influence of the Virgil Bible School on young people was a catalyst for Walter's own lifelong calling and ministry in a Bible College setting.

## PREPARING FOR THE TASK

There is little doubt that Wally began sensing a call to ministry early in his life, but not without competing interests. At 17, he became an avid Junior B hockey player in Ontario. He was fast on the ice and loved the competition. "I was in the position where continued participation in organized hockey could lead to a career in the game." These competing interests couldn't long co-exist. As he later reflected, it was the call of Christ that triumphed. He realized that effective ministry would require intellectual and spiritual equipping.

For young Canadian MBs considering ministry, the place to be during the 1950s was the Mennonite Brethren Bible College in Winnipeg, established in 1944. Its purpose was to provide theological education and practical training for ministers, missionaries, Bible school teachers and workers in local congregations. By 1950, the College was in its ascendency, becoming the first Canadian Bible school to be accredited by the Accrediting Association of Bible Colleges. During Walter's student days at MBBC, John A. Toews became president. This appointment proved providential for both the College and for Walter. In short order the College began offering a Bachelor of Divinity Degree. In 1961, MBBC became affiliated with Waterloo Lutheran College, significantly enhancing its academic credibility.

The three years Walter studied at MBBC shaped his interests and calling in definable ways. His appetite for higher studies had been kindled. Walter admired President Toews who was a historian with an earned doctorate. From Toews, Walter imbibed not only a love of history, but also a deeper understanding of historical writing. Toews impressed on his students the difficulty of objectivity, especially "when writing about the brotherhood to which one belongs." A critical approach notwithstanding, Toews also conveyed to his students a deep love for their Anabaptist heritage.

*One of Walter's early mentors was David Neumann, the Eden High School principal, here at the school's homecoming with three other classmates, Herman Wallman and Art and Fred Andres.*

If Walter absorbed his love of history from John A. Toews, it was David Ewert who taught him to love the Scriptures. Ewert had become an expert in biblical languages as well as the history of the English Bible. He taught his students the exacting skills of biblical hermeneutics. Here was another indispensable skill that Walter would further hone and use extensively in his own later teaching and preaching.

After MBBC, Walter continued his studies at the University of Waterloo, graduating with a degree in history and philosophy. After a further year of professional training at the Hamilton Teacher's College, he began a ten-year stint teaching in the Ontario Public School system, including seven years in a junior high school. During those years he also met and married his lifelong partner, Laura Redekopp, who has been his strong supporter and mother to their three children. She, like him, had her roots in the Scott St. Church of St. Catharines.

While public school teaching provided a dependable career path, Walter's yen for graduate studies became irresistible. In 1968 he enrolled in an MA program in Church History and Christian Thought at the Trinity Evangelical Divinity School in Deerfield, Illinois. TEDS is one of the largest theological graduate schools in the world, with an emphasis on developing servant leaders for the global church. At the heart of the divinity school lies the Master of Divinity degree, preparing pastors, teachers and missionaries for many kinds of service. The spirit and culture of this school connected with Walter's own sense of values, particularly the institutional emphasis on engaging contemporary culture spiritually, biblically, and theologically.

Very significantly, for his MA thesis, Walter examined the social views of Charles G. Finney. It would be hard to overstate how deeply Finney's convictions and contributions became imbedded in Walter's consciousness. Finney was a passionate 19th century evangelist who held that indifference to moral reform revealed a seared conscience. Most profoundly, Finney abhorred "a piety that had no humanity in it." From this study, Walter concluded that Finney did not preach a social gospel, but a gospel with "definite, practical social implications." Such emphases would come to characterize Walter's own ministry.

Walter completed his MA in 1969. Approximately a decade later while teaching at Columbia Bible Institute, he undertook doctoral studies at Simon Fraser University in Burnaby, BC. His dissertation was entitled, "Earnestly Contending for the Faith: The Role of the Niagara Bible Conference in the Emergence of American Fundamentalism, 1875 – 1900."

This very thorough study of the Niagara Bible Conference equipped Walter to understand the phenomenon of American Fundamentalism. Here was a formidable spiritual convergence that brought together "a new love for Bible study, but also a militancy for defending the Bible's inerrancy." Fundamentalism, further, produced a great zeal for evangelization and missions, since separation from the world became more important than social reform. From this study Walter concluded that this fundamentalist-evangelical tradition "still shapes the American temper in many significant ways." But it was also a breeding ground for tension. How could these believers "hold to a gospel of hope which was coupled with prophetic despair?"

It was not lost on Walter that a profound impact of American Fundamentalism has been the spawning of numerous Bible institutes. Schools such as Moody Bible Institute emerged in the 1880s and rapidly multiplied. "So rapid was the spread of the Bible institute movement that by the 1930s there was one Bible school in every large American city."

*Celebrating the 10ᵗʰ anniversary of the Fairview Church of St. Catharines, Walter and Laura (at right) with the pastor and his wife, Harvey and Agatha Gossen.*

With a trained army of zealous believers, interdenominational faith missions proliferated. Moreover, Fundamentalism also gave birth to evangelicalism, resulting in an expression of the Christian faith that allowed intellectual and theological respectability. Walter's vision for a credible Christianity mediated through Bible school training was in no small way energized by this study.

## CONSUMMATE CHURCHMAN

Walter Unger grew up in a home where his parents nurtured in him a sense of significance of the local fellowship. In his adolescence, the St. Catharines (later Scott Street) MB Church provided opportunities for young people to discover and exercise their ministry gifts. Pastor Henry

Penner, not averse to sharing the pulpit with aspiring preachers, invited Walter to craft some of his first sermons. And when in 1964 this congregation decided to plant a daughter church, it was Walter who provided the initial leadership for the Fairview MB Church. Not long after, Fairview called Harvey Gossen to be their lead pastor. For the next four years, Walter served this congregation as the assistant pastor, being mentored by a "true and loving shepherd."

Fairview quickly became a dynamic fellowship with thriving ministries. A dial-a-meditation service attracted 63,000 calls in 1969 alone. Members were encouraged to participate in missions. Deeper life meetings brought many prominent preachers to the Fairview pulpit, including Frank C. Peters, J. J. Toews, Ralph Bell and Louis Paul Lehman. The experiences at Scott Street and Fairview excited a love for vibrant congregational life in Walter Unger and introduced him to compelling Christian leaders of the era.

With their move to British Columbia in 1969, Walter and Laura Unger joined the Bakerview MB Church. It was at once apparent that here too he was willing to share his gifts and participate in the life of this congregation. Over the past several decades Walter has been valued as a member of the Bakerview preaching team, assisting with the development of preaching series. Walter has also served as an encourager to younger preachers, offering encouragement but also critique.

Over a lifetime of service, Walter has cultivated a high view of the church. In a very illuminating contribution to *Direction* magazine, he noted that maintaining a biblical understanding of the church seems like a continual challenge for Mennonite Brethren. Unger emphasizes that the ideal of being a disciplined, visible believers' church still remains at the heart of MB ecclesiology. However, he also candidly allows that this high view of the church forces believers realistically to embrace "the pilgrim/process nature of those within the church." If the gospel is indeed a gospel of grace, then perfection is sought in the central message of Christ's grace.

Walter Unger's contribution to the church has extended far beyond the congregations where his membership resided. Provincially, he has served on the B.C. Board of Pastoral Ministries, influencing pastoral selection and training, particularly for leaders joining the Conference from non-MB backgrounds.

Walter has also contributed prominently at the Canadian MB national level as chair of the Board of Faith and Life. This Board as no other articulates the theological identity of Mennonite Brethren by providing spiritual guidance and direction in matters of faith, theology, ethics and

*Walter and Columbia Bible College chairman Vern Heidebrecht cut the ribbon for the new resource centre in 1992. With them, Ed Enns (l), project supervisor, and Gary Loewen (r), vice-chair; and rear, Herb Thiessen, CBC vp, and Art Block and John Redekop (r), campaign co-chairs.*

Christian living. He is especially gratified that during his tenure as chair of this Board, he was able to advance the cause of freeing those MB women for ministry who are called and gifted for a spiritual vocation.

Beyond formal committee work, Walter brought a respected theological voice to national debate through the force of his ideas in more than a dozen papers he has presented at meetings of the Canadian and U.S. MB conferences. As a theologian, he has also written several definitive entries for the *Global Anabaptist Mennonite Encyclopaedia Online*, including the statement on "The Holy Spirit."

## PROLIFIC WRITER

Inside and outside of the MB church, most people have come to know Walter Unger through his prolific writings that have appeared in some twenty journals and magazines, principally the *Mennonite Brethren Herald*. Over the last forty years he has submitted approximately 300 entries on issues often at the core of current community interest.

In his columns Walter reflected a deep love not only for his own Mennonite Brethren denomination, but also for the global church of Christ. He didn't skirt around the issues as he addressed questions of practical morality, particularly over the inroads of secularism into Christian thinking. He forcefully exposed shallow arguments that masqueraded as anti-intellectualism, tersely noting: "Although it is true that faith can be established in the heart by faith alone, it is absurd to assume that faith can precede reason."

Perhaps owing to his personal interest in the arts, Walter often commented on secular films portraying Christian themes. He characterized the very popular 1970s musical, *Jesus Christ Superstar*, as "a gold rush to Golgotha." Or Martin Scorsese's film, *The Last Tempation of Christ"* as presenting "a Jesus who never was." Knowing that these films were widely viewed, Unger insisted that inaccurate departures from historical accounts could not "be glossed over in the name of artistic licence." Walter's opinions never came across as ideologically confined. When he found a deserving production, he was not averse to commending it to others. With respect to the film *Man of Two Worlds*, he saw "God at work in the theatrical world."

He took very sharp issue with stories in the secular press that satirized Christian faith, noting: "When we dethrone God, we kill man."

With his wide historical awareness, Walter enjoyed celebrating the contributions of notable historical persons, such as Finney, Martin Luther, William Wilberforce and D.L. Moody. Summing up their lives, Walter wrote: "Men are God's method." At the same time, he expressed his remorse over the "sanctification gap" all too often characteristic among contemporary evangelical leaders. In the column, "When Saints Sin," he mourned fallen fellow pilgrims, humbly calling to mind his own "potential for similar sin and worse."

Frequently his columns weighed in on the consequences of shifting spiritual trends. With timely insights, Walter provided vigilant commentary concerning the seemingly insatiable public interest in occultism during the 1970s; the embrace of the "Signs and Wonders" phenomenon in the 1980s; or more recently, the consequences of the Emergent Church movement, in what he refers to as the post-Evangelical world.

As a long-time *Mennonite Brethren Herald* columnist, Walter Unger served a wide constituency as a teacher of the church, consistently reflecting an Anabaptist understanding. The tilt of evangelicalism towards a right-wing militarism makes Anabaptism more relevant than ever before, he reasoned. "We need to hear of a higher way of discipleship." For him, Anabaptist Christianity seeks a balance between the contemplative and the activistic, and a spirituality that never fully trusts individualized experience. In each age, it is inside community that Scripture must be discerned.

### AT COLUMBIA BIBLE COLLEGE

By the time Walter Unger graduated with his MA degree from Trinity Evangelical Divinity School, he was already becoming widely noticed in the North American MB world. John B. Toews, then president of Mennonite Brethren Biblical Seminary in Fresno, had a particular intuition for finding and promoting promising young leaders. On the recommendation of Toews, Walter was hired to a teaching position at Columbia Bible Institute in 1969. A year after his arrival, Walter was appointed as the academic dean. It was the beginning of a ministry that, by the time of his retirement as president of Columbia Bible College in 2001, would leave an indelible imprint on the school.

At the time of Walter's faculty appointment, discussions were underway to unite two Abbotsford-area Bible schools. Walter provided energetic leadership to the completion of this merger, with the new school known as Columbia Bible Institute. This was no small achievement, as it became the first inter-Mennonite Bible institute in North America, promoting an evangelical Anabaptist/Mennonite theology. The *Canadian Mennonite* observed that while other Bible schools in Canada struggled to survive, these two schools chose a bold route. However, given the historic distance between the two Mennonite conferences, such a merger seemed "as unlikely as snow on a mid-summer day." To his great credit, Walter cultivated the confidence of both the Mennonite Brethren and Mennonite Conference constituencies, a trust that would become indispensable to the survival of Columbia Bible College.

One of Walter Unger's great gifts to Columbia was his ability to administer the school with a consistent, lucid vision. At the 1989 annual meeting of the CBC Society, Walter passionately reminded delegates that his role included "the development of Christian character, the learning of practical obedience to the Word of God, the development of skills in biblical interpretation and equipping [students] for service." At the AGM two years later he again spoke his conscience about a consistent vision: "I believe that it is crucial that we constantly keep the vision before us, not only of what we want to do, but what we want to be as a college. I believe that being motivates doing."

As president, Walter saw it as his responsibility "to facilitate a wholesome spirituality on campus." Quite remarkably, his own sense of mission gave him the confidence to allow wide-ranging debate on issues. For him, vision was something worth taking a risk for because it allows all members of the team to be aligned around a common credo, a stated set of values and articulated ideals.

His consistent leadership resulted in handsome dividends. The first stage along this arduous journey was to convince the supporting constituency that a two-year curriculum was no longer a viable educational model. Owing in large measure to Walter's fervent advocacy at the 1985 annual general meeting, delegates agreed to such a far-reaching decision, resulting in the birth of Columbia Bible College. Thus during Walter's presidency, a stumbling two-year school matured into a stable four-year, degree-granting institution.

A second major hurdle for CBC involved the political process of applying for a legal charter, allowing the College to grant baccalaureate degrees. This goal was accomplished on June 26, 1987, when the B.C. Legislative Assembly passed the "Columbia Bible College Act." In the follow-up to that, Columbia was awarded full accreditation with the Accrediting Association of Bible Colleges in October 1991.

Walter did not wilt under the often unrelenting pressure of his leadership duties. At great financial costs, aging campus facilities needed to be replaced. Indeed, a condition for accreditation mandated the construction of a new resource center. It was a joyful day for CBC when in November 1992 the new facility including a new library and faculty office complex was finally occupied. With an expanding athletic program, CBC also began planning a new gymnasium.

By the time Walter retired in 2001, several additional goals had been met. A state-of-the-art gymnasium had been added to an increasingly attractive campus. The College was debt-free. Of fundamental significance, student enrollment, which had declined to an equivalent enrollment of 150 full-time during the 1980s, grew to some 500 students, representing a diverse, interdenominational and international mix.

Walter Unger could not have laid down the burdens of his office with a greater sense of accomplishment. Small wonder that at his retirement celebration, Columbia Bible College honoured him with a president emeritus status. Reflecting on his many years with CBC, Walter advises: "We need to be careful on being too black and white on all things. We must not demonize those who disagree with us." Acknowledging inevitable controversy, Walter loves to quote Augustine: "Unity in essentials, tolerance in non-essentials and in all things love."

## TRACKING THE INNER PILGRIMAGE

Walter Unger has been a leader who left his footprint "in the areas of his passion." By common consent, he was fully engaged at every opportunity for teaching and preaching. Over the four decades of his ministry, Walter was often severely tested, as when denominational leaders felt threatened by the broad exposure to new ideas, or colleagues disagreed with some of his administrative decisions at Columbia. An African proverb says, "to stumble is not to fall but to move forward more quickly." His inner resilience never abandoned him because it established for him an enduring centre. A thoughtfully crafted mission statement committed him "to enrich the Christian community by teaching, preaching and writing," despite all personal disappointments and challenges. That commitment infused him with a continual flow of energy.

For Walter, daily journalling has been a "spiritual lifeline." In one of his "Christian Mind" entries in the *Mennonite Brethren Herald,* he allowed that more than 30 years of journalling had been "an excellent means of tracking the inner journey." At its core, journalling has been a means of critical self-examination, of setting priorities and goals, of highlighting insights from his reading, and perhaps most importantly for him, seizing on a "God-sized perspective of things."

Walter Unger loves life, taking delight in musical or dramatic performances. Golfing is something of a passion for him. He is generally up on the latest hockey or football action. Here too he is not averse to multi-tasking. He has been observed reading a book at hockey games if the need to supplement dull moments presented themselves.

Two outstanding leaders have modelled for Walter "fervent spirituality and critical thoughtfulness." The influence of A. W. Tozer was to kindle "the fires of adoration and worship." C. S. Lewis was intellectually stimulating, affirming the basics of the Christian faith with integrity. "Jack honoured truth with every fibre of his being." Such zeal also captures the essence of Walter Unger's spiritual journey.

SOURCES
The people who were interviewed, along with Walter Unger, included Myron Penner, Ron Penner, Ken Peters and Ron Voth. Other sources were

*Minutes of Columbia Bible College Annual General Meetings; Canadian Mennonite;* Peter Penner's *No Longer At Arms Length;* essays in honor of Walter Unger in *Direction,* a Mennonite Brethren forum (Spring 2001); J.A. Toews's *A History of the Mennonite Brethren Church: Pilgrims and Pioneers; Mennonite Brethren Herald;* and *When They Shall Ask: A History of the Ontario Conference of Mennonite Brethren Churches 1957-1982,* Edward Boldt, ed. A copy of this chapter with appropriate attributions is on file at the Centre for Mennonite Brethren Studies, Winnipeg.

# ACKNOWLEDGEMENTS

This collection of stories of "shapers" of the Mennonite Brethren Church in Canada would not have come about without a lot of encouragement along the way. Since I was a writer of only a portion of the biographies, I'm especially indebted to the 18 other writers who also volunteered to tell stories of the people in this book. I know how much effort it meant for many of them.

Few people know how good the archives are that we as a Conference possess in Winnipeg. The Centre for Mennonite Brethren Studies, with its holdings, and the staff there, initially Ken Reddig, later Doug Heidebrecht and his assistant Conrad Stoesz, have been an indispensable resource in bringing this volume to realization. These archivists have been especially encouraging and helpful. For some materials, the Mennonite Heritage Centre of Mennonite Church Canada and its director Alf Redekopp have also been an important resource.

One of the realities for a work such as this inevitably involves finances. This book would not have seen the light of day if it had not been for generous supporters. These include Harry and Manja Giesbrecht, Bill and Margaret Fast, Herb and Erna Buller, John Kuhl, Arthur and Laureldel Block, the Art Quiring Family of Q-Line Trucking, Jascha and Hildi Boge, Frank and Agnes DeFehr, Eileen Quiring, Kurt and Anne Wagner, George and Linda Wichert, Rudy and Kaethe Sawatzky, Ed Redekopp, Peter Durksen, Neil and Martha Rempel, Don Kornelsen (he once managed the Christian Press where we worked together as colleagues), Henry and Ruth Schmidt, Jake Suderman, John and Elma Hamm, John and Erna Friesen, and Henry and Elizabeth Esau. Their backing for this undertaking was a great encouragement.

It has been a joy too to benefit from the guidance of Yvonne Heinrichs and Marilyn Hudson at Kindred Productions, as they steered the materials of this book through its various stages, the work of Susan Huebert, who scrutinized the text with proofreader's eyes, and to hand it all over to Shelly Makus, who did the design work on it.

Finally, I am most grateful to Neoma, my wife and partner, who enjoys history with me, reads very widely, serves in the church alongside me, and has shown more than her share of patience when I was glued to a computer screen and she might have wanted other tasks from me. God bless her.

*Harold Jantz*